THE
BOOK
OF
HOPE

Jonny Benjamin
Britt Pflüger

THE
BOOK
OF
HOPE

101 Voices on
Overcoming Adversity

bluebird
books for life

First published 2021 by Bluebird
an imprint of Pan Macmillan
The Smithson, 6 Briset Street, London EC1M 5NR
EU representative: Macmillan Publishers Ireland Ltd,
Mallard Lodge, Lansdowne Village, Dublin 4
Associated companies throughout the world
www.panmacmillan.com

ISBN 978-1-5098-4637-5

1 3 5 7 9 8 6 4 2

A CIP catalogue record for this book is available from the British Library.

Typeset in Minion Pro by Palimpest Book Production Limited, Falkirk, Stirlingshire
Printed and bound by CPI Group (UK) Ltd, Croydon, CR0 4YY

MIX
Paper from
responsible sources
FSC® C116313

Visit **www.panmacmillan.com** to read more about all our books
and to buy them. You will also find features, author interviews and
news of any author events, and you can sign up for e-newsletters
so that you're always first to hear about our new releases.

Contents

KINDNESS

CONNECTION

Introduction

Five years ago, just after I had begun sharing my personal experience of mental illness, a teacher at one of the schools I visited asked me to speak privately to a fourteen-year-old student who was really struggling.

I will never forget hearing this young girl telling me she had completely given up on her life. It was heart-breaking. She explained that she had suffered with anxiety and depression for many years. She also listed the different medications and therapists she had tried. None of them had had any effect on her declining mental health.

I felt so helpless listening to this young girl express such despair. I tried to offer words of comfort and hope but none of them seemed to resonate at all.

Since that day, I have met many individuals experiencing mental health issues, along with their family members or friends, who have also told me that they have given up hope.

I understand their anguish. When I was diagnosed with schizoaffective disorder at the age of twenty and admitted to a psychiatric hospital, I too very rapidly gave up hope.

It took years to regain some sort of faith in life.

However, I eventually managed to clamber out of the deep, dark hole of hopelessness I had been in. Inevitably I have been back down in that pit a few times since then, but somehow I always manage to find my way out.

One of the ways I do this is by learning from the wisdom of other individuals who have also 'been there'. Psychologist Carl Jung called them 'wounded healers.' Even though each of us may experience mental health challenges in our own unique ways, we can still learn a lot from one another on the different ways to overcome such adversity.

This is where the idea for *The Book of Hope* was born.

I firmly believe it is never too late to find hope. I learnt this on a trip to India a few years ago, where I worked with an NGO which was trying to raise awareness and destigmatise mental illness within society. There I met a number of inspiring older 'wounded healers' who had overcome huge adversity; not just in terms of their serious mental health issues but also because of the extremely archaic mental health care they were under, which I witnessed first hand in many locations.

I have been privileged to learn from these individuals and from people all over the world (many of whom have contributed to this book) about hope, and how essential it is for anyone with a mental health diagnosis.

At this point I would like to say that hope is not necessarily a 'cure' or 'fix'. Personally, I have found that therapy, alongside medication and meditation, has helped me most along my journey. However, finding and holding on to hope has also been a necessity, especially during my bleaker periods.

My wish is that you too will find some hope within these pages.

*

I am eternally grateful to everyone who has contributed to this book. Words cannot express how inspired I am by each of these wounded healers and their stories, which have all been written with such honesty and depth. I feel unbelievably lucky to know these courageous individuals who all have such incredible strength.

I am also enormously thankful to my co-writer Britt, publisher Carole, and everyone else at Bluebird for believing in this book and making it happen.

Hope has never been more needed than in the extremely challenging year of 2020. The COVID-19 pandemic literally turned the world and all our lives upside-down. It can be so easy to succumb to that despair. I found myself back in hospital again after a relapse in September 2020. My subsequent recovery was made much harder because of the lockdown and restrictions placed upon us. But gradually I overcame this period. The most important lesson I learnt during this time was the necessity of kindness and compassion; particularly towards myself. Within this, I found hope. We have seen such kindness and compassion within our society throughout the pandemic, as well as much suffering and tragedy of course. I truly hope the former extends beyond COVID-19. I now believe that wherever there is kindness and compassion, there is always hope.

It is my dream that no other person will ever feel that they have lost all hope again. Ultimately hope is all around us, and as you will see from this book, within us too.

To start, I have listed 101 things that have helped give me hope. I encourage you to make your own list, particularly during a period of good mental health (although it is also useful compiling this list when you're not in such a good place).

As you will see from my own list below, **there is always hope**. And just as the sunshine follows the rain, even if you have temporarily lost hope, it will eventually return again.

Things that give me hope:

1. The impermanence of everything
2. Birdsong. The sound of birds singing gave me such comfort when I lived in isolation for months during the coronavirus pandemic in 2020
3. Nina Simone's anthem *Feeling Good*
4. Random acts of kindness
5. Seeing rainbows across the sky
6. Viktor Frankl's autobiography *Man's Search for Meaning*
7. Continuous advancements in science and technology
8. Stephen King's novel-turned-film *The Shawshank Redemption*
9. Our limitless imaginations
10. Butterflies. The transformation they go through in their lifespan is miraculous
11. The song *Seasons of Love* from the musical *Rent*

12. Individuals and groups tirelessly fighting for justice in this world
13. Watching live music at gigs
14. Trees. There is an oak tree close to where I grew up which is over 400 years old. Imagine all the storms it has weathered!
15. The entire voluntary sector
16. The warmth of the sun
17. Mitch Albom's memoir *Tuesdays With Morrie*
18. Any David Attenborough documentary
19. Newborn babies. According to UNICEF, there are over 350,000 born every single day
20. The vastness of our universe which we have uncovered
21. The vastness of our universe which we still have left to explore
22. Mary Oliver's poems
23. Fields full of sunflowers
24. Inspirational quotes. I have a long list of them that I'm constantly updating
25. The Eagle. These incredible birds have so much to teach us humans about life
26. The film *Amelie*, which also has plenty to teach us on the joy of living
27. Edvard Grieg's classical tune *Morning Mood*
28. Teachers
29. Brené Brown's TED talks
30. Monet's paintings
31. Libraries. The British Library is a particular treasure trove for me
32. A smile from a stranger
33. Listening to the life stories of those who survived the Holocaust
34. Florence + The Machine's track *Shake It Out*
35. The continuous changing of the seasons
36. Frank Capra's Oscar-winning film *It's a Wonderful Life*

37. Unconditional love (particularly the unconditional love dogs have for their owners)
38. Enduring love (my parents just recently celebrated their fiftieth wedding anniversary)
39. The stillness of lakes
40. Witnessing human vulnerability
41. Maya Angelou's empowering poem *Still I Rise*
42. All those working on the frontline of the emergency services and in healthcare
43. Clear blue skies
44. Simon & Garfunkel's Grammy award-winning song *Bridge Over Troubled Water*
45. Martin Luther King Jr's journey to lead the Civil Rights Movement
46. Meditation, and the return to my body and breath when I am battling with my mind
47. Forests
48. Nelson Mandela's *Long Walk to Freedom*
49. Fragrant rose gardens
50. Youth movements
51. Seeing the stars at night
52. Athletes (especially those who have overcome adversity)
53. Destiny's Childs' anthem *Survivor*
54. Waterfalls. I was lucky enough to visit Victoria Falls in Zimbabwe. I will never forget the feeling of awe I felt at its sheer magnitude
55. William Wordsworth's best-known poem *Daffodils*
56. Spending time with children and seeing life through their eyes
57. Mountain vistas
58. All the remarkable women who have fought (and continue to fight) for equality
59. Revisiting photos of happy memories
60. *Here Comes the Sun* by The Beatles
61. Street art
62. Queen Elizabeth I's Golden Age of the sixteenth century

63. Disney/Pixar's *Up*
64. Disney/Pixar's *Coco*
65. Disney/Pixar's *Inside Out*
66. The diversity of human beings on this planet
67. The Northern Lights. Seeing them is on my bucket list
68. The Galapagos Islands. Also on my bucket list!
69. *Rise* by singer-songwriter Gabrielle
70. Pinterest boards. Looking at them is my guilty pleasure!
71. Acceptance, and our capacity to forgive and let go
72. Marine life. I urge you to go scuba diving just once, to experience the magic under the sea
73. Bob Ross's *Joy of Painting* documentary series
74. Gospel choirs
75. Inspiring leaders, such as New Zealand's prime minister Jacinda Ardern
76. *'Hope' is the thing with feathers* by poet Emily Dickinson
77. Lotus flowers. This beautiful flower must grow within mud in order to bloom
78. The film *Maudie,* which charts the life of inspirational painter Maud Lewis
79. New moons
80. Farmers
81. Complete and total stillness. It is rare that I find it but when I do it is oh, so peaceful
82. Candi Staton's disco anthem *Young Hearts Run Free*
83. Reading Shakespeare's works. There is such richness in his writings and so much to learn about humanity, even centuries after he lived
84. John Nash's life story of becoming a Nobel laureate in the film *A Beautiful Mind*
85. *Gratitude*, a short film by Louie Schwartzberg
86. Puppies
87. Kittens
88. All other baby animals
89. Paulo Coelho's bestselling novel *The Alchemist*

90. Air travel. We take for granted the fact we can now fly to any part of the globe
91. The sound of waves from the sea crashing onto the shore
92. Flowers growing through the cracks in concrete
93. Sam Cooke's civil rights song *A Change is Gonna Come*
94. Personal achievements I've made which I never imagined would be possible, such as running a marathon
95. Sunrises
96. Sunsets
97. Nina Simone's *I Wish I Knew How it Would Feel to Be Free*
98. The growth of this list over time
99. Our bodies' capability to overcome disease
100. Our minds' capability to overcome illness
101. The 101 stories that you are about to read and that I have been fortunate enough to curate, together with my co-author Britt. May they bring you, dear reader, the hope that we both found in putting this book together

Jonny Benjamin

Content Warnings

This is an anthology of hope and many of the contributors talk about drawing on hope that helped them through challenging experiences in their lives. Some readers might find the content of some of these accounts more triggering, so we have added a palm symbol to the more detailed accounts to allow anyone who may find reading about sensitive content difficult the opportunity to pause.

ALWAYS HOPE

Juliette Burton
Advice To My Younger Self

I can't tell you not to go down the route you're going to go down. I can't tell you what to do. Knowing you, you wouldn't listen anyway and that's ok. I still don't listen to everyone who offers me unsolicited advice. And that's what this is – unsolicited advice.

Years ago, a helpful person suggested I avoid giving out advice or information unless someone asks for it. There's no point in offering it if the person isn't seeking it. And you're not seeking advice right now. You're the kind of person who needs to learn by observing, thinking, musing. You've got to make the mistakes you need to make – and they won't even be the 'mistakes' people tell you they are. They're lessons. And you will learn. It might take repeated mistakes before you learn some of the lessons, but life is a series of opportunities to learn, if you want to.

You'll gravitate towards people on similar paths. Draw those closest to you who have gratitude and positivity in abundance. You'll get what you focus on and it's easier to focus on the things you want if you surround yourself with people who have it.

I can't tell you one day it'll all make sense. Honestly, I'm still confused. The real secret is that all adults are. There is no magic secret to life other than to keep going, keep rediscovering that beautiful, childlike joy of being alive.

Things don't get easier; they get different. Any moment of darkness will pass. Every feeling that feels like it will go on forever will at some point end. Whether it's a happy feeling you enjoy, or a negative feeling you feel you can't withstand a moment longer. Everything shifts. I don't know when it will, and I don't know why. But I can promise you; every time you feel broken, you will come out stronger.

I'd love to tell you to fuel your body so your mind can achieve all it has the potential to.

I'd love to tell you to ignore all the outward messages telling you you're not good enough, to realise the school bullies were wrong, the adverts telling you to be thinner are wrong, the adults telling you to lose weight are wrong – their obsession is not good for your holistic wellbeing.

I'd love to tell you every day to find at least five things you like about yourself and nurture those traits. What you focus on, you'll get. If you focus on positivity, you'll get positivity. If you focus on sadness and flaws all you will feel is sadness and all you will see are imperfections.

Follow your bliss. If something makes your soul sing and want to get out of bed in the morning, follow it. Do it. Make it your reason. Sooner than I did. Do more of it. Whatever gives you lust for life and makes you want to live, do it, surround yourself with it, demand people take it seriously. If they don't, find others who will.

Above all, never give up. I know you want to. And I know you will want to right up to the day you become me, sitting here, writing this. As hard as it will feel, it will be worth it.

There will be moments, quiet moments between you and a sunset, you and another human, you and a roomful of people that will make up for all the pain and distress you've endured. For a moment you will mend. You will be exactly where you need to be. And you will feel peace. Cherish every one of those moments. They won't last, but more will come.

And when you reach the moment where you are me, sitting here, writing this to you, sitting there, reading this in your own imagination . . . think of you in another seventeen years sitting somewhere else, writing probably very similar words.

Listen. Take wisdom in.

Have a voice. Speak your truth.

Forgive.

Believe.

Get more sleep.

Spend time with your mother. She's possibly the best human you will ever meet and you must learn all you can from her while you can.

Be kind. If not to yourself then to everyone around you.

Kindness is power. It nourishes.

Kindness is beauty. The kinder you are, the more beautiful you will be.

Juliette Burton is an award-winning comedian, speaker, writer, voiceover artist and mental health campaigner. She has performed five solo shows (*When I Grow Up*, *Look At Me*, *Decision Time*, *Butterfly Effect* and *Defined*) at the Edinburgh Fringe.

Hello you.

I can't see you, but I know you're there. I hope you're ok.

So, you're reading a book about hope. Without knowing who, where or how you are, the fact that you're reading a book about hope tells me three things about you.

Thing I Know about You Because You're Reading a Book about Hope – Number One:

You need some. If you've ended up here, wherever you are, reading this, it's because you need some hope.

I hate talking about me, but if I'm going to talk a bit about you, it's only fair I tell you a bit more about me. Here are eight things that are true:

1. My name's Joe.
2. I'm thirty-one years old.
3. I can talk to somebody for hours & not say a single thing about me without them noticing.
4. I was a drug addict & I'm seven years clean.
5. I was an alcoholic & I'm four years sober.
6. I live with daily suicidal thoughts that are always there. Some days they're just louder than they were the day before.
7. I've done more good things than bad things, but I never remember the good ones because I only feel the bad ones.
8. I've got something called Emotionally Unstable Personality Disorder, also known as BPD, which is essentially a

Pound Shop bipolar; it does most of the same stuff but some of it's a bit shitter.

Ugh. There. Done.

Thing I Know about You Because You're Reading a Book about Hope – Number Two:
You are not hopeless. You might feel like you are, because if you're looking for hope it means you had some at one point but you lost it.

You might have less hope now than you've had in the past, but you're not hopeless. You're only ever hopeless when you're dead. Which you're not. Yay. Hi.

I should point out that there isn't a single thing on my list about me that you can see. They are all invisible. Things you can't see are difficult to explain to somebody who doesn't have any experience of that kind of thing, and this is made even more difficult if you know the words but don't know which order to put them in to explain what you're feeling. And even if you can, you're probably scared to tell anybody else in case they don't believe you. Arguments occur more frequently when they're about something you can't see, because if somebody can't see something, it can be denied.

Unfortunately, mental health problems fall into this category. If something is invisible and you don't understand it, you have a choice. Accept that it's definitely there, because other people who know what they're talking about are telling you it is and talking about it. So trust them, listen to them and learn from them. Or be a dick.

'Nope. Not real. Can't see it. Prove it.'

I'm not saying I don't understand that thought process, because I do. How can you believe in something you can't see and know nothing about? I get it. Mental illness is invisible, a bit like air, Nobody's having a row about air, though. I can't see air. I don't know anything about air, but I know it's real. I'm sure people have tried to explain it to me in the past, but I didn't pay attention because I don't care about air.

If I don't listen, will it affect my life or the lives of others?

No? Great. Carry on then.

I know that air's everywhere without understanding it because my whole life, I've heard people talking about it. I accept air is a thing even though I can't see it, and I'm comfortable trusting these people because they know what they're on about.

But you know what I'm not doing? Kicking off at Professor Brian Cox on Twitter, telling him that I don't believe his whiny opinions because I can't see what he's talking about so he's an attention seeker whose career is essentially a tapestry of desperate and unsubstantiated air lies. Pics or it didn't happen.

That would, obviously, fall into the 'being a dick' category.

I can't see air, but I know it's there. I can't see a relationship, but I know they're a thing. I even have some. I'm a son, a brother, an uncle, a cousin and a friend. A relationship is something independent, that lives between the two people that made it. Relationships start to corrode and collapse when they stop being cared for by both people. If they are not equal, they won't work.

Relationships are invisible, but they are still real.

Mental illness is real.

Nowadays, when I wake up in the morning the only goal I set myself is to finish that day the same way I started it, in a bed, knowing I'll see tomorrow. Even if today isn't what I needed or wanted or expected, if I can just get through today, tonight I'll have another chance at tomorrow.

Thank you for listening to me. I hope one day I get to find out more than three things about you.

Oh shit, nearly forgot.

Thing I Know about You Because You're Reading a Book about Hope – Number Three:
I know you deserve it. Just like the air, I know you can't see it, but I promise it's there. Hope.

Joe Tracini is an actor who's best known for things you probably watched hungover.

Joe began oversharing the broken bits of his brain in articles and videos in May 2018. He's also a writer, presenter and British Champion magician, who has a deep-set hatred of writing about himself in the third person.

Lemn Sissay

The best piece of advice I've had, and the one that gave me most hope, was, 'One day at a time.'

If I could talk to my younger self I would say, 'Learn to trust others because then you will learn to trust yourself. Learn to trust yourself because then you will learn to trust others.'

Life is a constant change for the better. The opportunity starts in my head. What gift will I give myself to make this interaction, this piece of advice? I will commit to it and I will press Send. I spent a lot of time working things out in my head. The head can be a very busy place. All it needs is rest. Learn to rest.

But living is about the action. What is the most honest and truthful action I can make in any given situation: one that keeps me in mind and one that is true? I commit to it. Be ok with being wrong. Stop being so committed to being right it makes you defensive. Make mistakes and learn.

Mistakes are a celebration of someone who is trying. So try in everything you do. Commit and press Send. Press Send, my friend. Press Send.

Lemn Sissay is a BAFTA-nominated award-winning writer, international poet, performer, playwright, artist and broadcaster.

He was awarded an MBE for services to literature and won a Pen Pinter Prize in 2019. He is Chancellor of the University of Manchester and an Honorary Doctor from the Universities of Huddersfield, Manchester, Kent and Brunei. He is Dr Dr Dr Dr Lemn Sissay. He was the first poet commissioned to write for the London Olympics and poet of the FA Cup.

George Hodgson

When someone asks you what you would tell your younger self, what do you say? Wish you'd gone to university, wish you'd tried harder at school, wish you hadn't had that drink at that particular time, hadn't shouted at that certain someone? All of us think 'what if?' The problem with me is, the 'what if' thinking destroys me; I will think so much about something that I could have done better or done another way, but to what end? When I was severely ill suffering from anxiety and OCD, from an unfortunate experience of taking drugs at a festival, there wasn't an hour that went by without me beating myself up about doing it. What I didn't realise at the time was that this whole experience would set me on a path of infinite opportunities. During one's darkest days it's nearly impossible to imagine yourself coming out the other side, but I can assure you there is another side and it's the brightest place you will ever see. You just cannot see it yet.

So when people ask me what I'd tell my younger self, I say 'keep going, do not do anything differently, everything is going to be ok.' There is absolutely nothing you can change about the past, but there is something you can do for your future, and it's to keep going.

Recently I was scrolling through my notes from the time I was suffering, a few years ago, and I found a quote that said:

'Yesterday's history, tomorrow is a mystery,
today is a gift and that's why it's called the present.'

Today is a gift. My gift to you is to give you the hope that everything will be ok. Take it when you feel ready.

George David Hodgson is a fashionpreneur, public speaker and mental health campaigner. In 2014 he founded the award-winning fashion brand 'Maison de Choup' following a severe episode of anxiety and OCD.

Seaneen Molloy
A Letter to my Younger Self

Dear me,

I'm not sure when you're reading this letter. When would it have been the most helpful for you to find it, tucked under your pillow, like a pound coin for a tooth? The magic that happens when you're asleep. How would you feel to wake up and find this, unfolding in front of your swimming eyes, still half in dream?

It was often hard to wake up. It was often harder to sleep. Since you could remember, you were in dread of the downstairs, the muffled monsters of night-time arguments. The mornings not any better, the alarm clock psst of your dad opening a can of beer in bed, and the day begins. These are the sounds that have echoed down the corridors of your years.

Nowhere ever really felt safe for you then. I remember it all. You couldn't even live in your own body. You starved it and purged it and hurt it. The more you hurt it, the more people noticed, and the more you hated it. The more you hated it, the more you were told, 'Stop seeking attention. Stop being a drama queen.' The more you were told it, the more you believed it.

I see you now at fifteen. You were so sad. You departed for almost a year. You wore a yellow fleece your mum bought you. She called it the fuzzy duck fleece. It clung to you for every sallow day for months on end. The effort of a bath was too great. You missed nearly all your GCSE year and had to drop two subjects. They stopped marking you as late; they were just glad on the odd days you still showed up. When you put your coat on, you didn't take it off again. You couldn't look into a mirror, you couldn't separate what was real and what wasn't, you could barely lift a hair brush.

And then one day you rose, and frenzied months followed. You kept your mum awake at night with your talking, you climbed out the window and wandered the nights. Years followed of rising and falling; kicked out of school because they thought you were too ill to continue, leaving the country, starting again, and again.

I would hope you would keep this in your pocket. You lost a lot along the way, all the starting-overs. House moves got smaller and smaller. The world did, too. From your house to the doctor's and back again. The hospital waiting room, the crisis team. The pill bottle and the water, and the long, implacable sleep of medication. I remember how you felt, like this was forever. But it wasn't.

I'm sorry to say though that you are mental. We've heard it a lot! In a lot of different ways. From a lot of different people. With a lot of different opinions on how. So, in a lot of different words: bipolar disorder, anxiety disorder. self-harm, body dysmorphic disorder, borderline personality disorder. All the disorder of being mental, coming down to one neat thing; pain. Just pain! I know, it's crap. I know you've been in a lot of pain. I know you feel bad still that you just wished for silence in the night as a child, and when the silence came, the echoes haunted you afterwards.

I know what it's like to have memories locked up in your head. I know you've acted in ways that make you want to dissolve, have been to places you can't return from, and the people you loved have gone to places that they do not come back from.

Don't follow. People are more forgiving, more open, and thankfully more forgetful than you think they are. It is not the end of the world. None of it is. None of it ever was. Your world will go on. The more it doesn't end, the more you will feel able to go on. The worst happened. It happens again and again and I promise, you're going to be ok. You don't have to keep running every time you rise and fall.

I wish you'd known that one day you'd feel sympathy, affection even, for your hated skin. That your body would do amazing things. That you'd become a mum and grow a person, and grow your heart, and fall in love. That you would rise and fall but like a bottle bobbing gently up and down over the widest sea. That things you did and said that you thought you couldn't forget, or would ever be forgotten, you did forget, and they were forgotten.

I'm sorry that there's so much grief in the years to come. You know there will be. There is for everyone. You're going to feel like it will extinguish you each time. It doesn't.

You're going to find a home. You're going to find a place and space without that itch, without always waiting for the next disaster. You're going to unpack a bag and keep it that way. You're going to be able to pick up a book again one day and read it. I remember the desolation you felt when you realised being ill and being medicated had taken that away from you. You'll be a bit slow – but you'll get there. The noise inside your brain still comes and goes and you still like it to be quiet. But lots of people like it to be quiet.

You're not going to feel ashamed anymore. You're going to tell people what happened to you. And they are mostly going to listen. What happened to you happened to me. It's happened to other people. You are not as alone as you feel you are. We were never as alone as we felt we were. In the unsleeping nights, you are going to find comfort in this. In the years to come, you're going to be able to nap again. Sometimes, strangulating panic is going to jolt you awake. But it comes and goes. That's ok.

Don't give up. Don't let the words define who you are – it is not all of you, even though it feels like it sometimes. You need to inhabit those words that you'll hear and see written down about you, explore them, unpack them. That's the way you're going to do it.

You are not going to be standing in the big clean glittery recovery kitchen, preparing wholesome foods and drinking nothing but green tea. You are never going to be slim. You are going to drink so much Coke it stains your teeth and your kitchen cupboards will be overflowing with bags and debris and all the normal things of a normal life that you never thought you would live to see.

Fold me up now and remember. Keep me safe. In the nights when the panic comes, take me out and read me again. There is enough light coming in through the window to see by; always.

Seaneen Molloy is a mental health blogger, writer and occasional BBC Ouch podcaster who lives in Belfast, Northern Ireland. She blogs at thesecretlifeofamanicdepressive.wordpress.com

Shocka

The best advice I've been given, the one that has really given me hope is, 'Most of the things you worry about never end up happening.' That is so important to remember. Our minds are full of past memories, anticipation for the future and then we have the present. I believe the present is a gift and with that, we have the answer.

Most people can't stay in the present and are lost in thoughts of the past or the future, which doesn't even exist yet. This can cause a lot of worry, so remembering that most of the things we worry about never end up happening is a blessing. It really helps reduce anxiety levels.

And it's true. If you think about your life and most of the things you worried about, they probably never happened.

If I were to talk to my younger self I would say, look inside, as all of the answers are there. Learn who you really are and get to know yourself. This world is full of distractions to stop you from spending time alone and getting to know yourself.

Apply self-love to your life daily. Truly love and respect yourself and the universe will open up in the most beautiful way.

Going through a breakdown and being sectioned seemed so serious and scary. My mum played the most important role in my recovery as she was by my side every step of the way. She was a great support system. My friends were amazing because they brought the humour out of my situation, they helped me laugh about it. Having my friends around me to help me laugh about it was a blessing.

There was a definitive moment where things changed for the better. It was whilst reading a book by a beautiful soul called Louise Hay. The book is called *You Can Heal Your Life*, and it helped me do just that. Louise taught me how to accept and love myself. I would encourage anyone who is struggling with their mental health to read that book.

I hope your journey to self-love is a fun and loving one.

Shocka was part of the grime trio Marvell, which won both Best Newcomer at the Official Mixtape Awards and Best Music Video at OMAs in 2010. Growing up on one of the most notorious estates in Tottenham, North London, Shocka has witnessed the good, the bad and the ugly, but by keeping his focus on music, has managed to stay positive, both about himself and his area.

Elizabeth Day

Hope is a small word with big resonance. Four letters which encompass so much, linked together by infinitesimal nuance, and which, when spoken in one short syllable, can mean the difference between carrying on or dropping into oblivion.

Its potency is all the more telling for its esoteric nature. Hope can come in many forms, at the most unexpected points. It can be fleeting and transient, but its impact can last a lifetime.

As difficult as it is to define, I know that the darkest moments of my life have been salvaged by hope: those glimmers of brightness that pull you through into the next moment, and then the next, until before you realise it, you're in a completely different place and marvelling at your own strength.

So for me, hope is in the tiny actions.

It is in the friend who picked me up from hospital after a scan showed that I'd lost the baby.

It is in the sonographer who performed the scan showing me photos of her ragdoll cats on her phone when I was crying and couldn't talk.

It is in my mother stripping the bedlinen every morning over Christmas one year when I had the flu and slept fitfully, sweating through nightmares.

It is in my best friend who was there through every break-up, who opened the doors of her house and filled the fridge with all my favourite food and chilled vodka tonics.

It is in the therapist who made me see that my divorce was not an admission that I was a terrible, shameful person.

It is in the poem I read on the back of a loo door when my

anxiety was spiralling, which told me that the universe is unfolding exactly as is intended.

It is even in the men who treated me badly, for teaching me that I wouldn't put up with it anymore.

It is in the shared smile in the street with a stranger.

It is in the dimpled hand proffered by a toddler who has decided to trust you.

It is in every bad decision you haven't taken and all the resilience you've built up from those you did.

It is in the beating of your heart, the tang of salt and vinegar on chips eaten by the seaside.

It is in the curve of your loved one's neck and the smell of their laundered shirts.

It is in your experience of all of these things. But it comes from within. And when you tap into hope's golden seams, you will find the most precious thing of all.

You will find that it is unbreakable.

Elizabeth Day is an award-winning author, journalist and broadcaster. Her latest book, *How to Fail: Everything I've Ever Learned from Things Going Wrong*, is part-memoir, part-manifesto and grew out of her chart-topping podcast of the same name. She has written four critically acclaimed novels and is a columnist for *You* magazine in the *Mail on Sunday*.

Radha Modgil

Hope is our ability to feel that things can get better, that we can feel better, that we should not 'give up' or stop trying to make good choices for ourselves.

Although at times we all feel that everything is lost and there is no hope, I believe that hope is not a thing separate from ourselves that we gain or lose; it is an integral part of the human make-up. Just as love is not a thing that we obtain, gain or lose but the very nature of who we are, so is hope inseparable from the human spirit.

Why do we feel hopeless sometimes? Life happens and just like a cliff hit hard by successive storms, our sense of hope can be eroded, exposing holes and cracks of vulnerability. When our mental wellbeing is impacted by life events or we are affected by a mental health condition, that sense of hope is eroded and it can be hard to see how we will ever feel better. At some point in life, we all feel like this. Hopelessness often brings with it a lack of self-care, a tendency to isolate from others and a sense of shame, all of which, sadly, can increase that sense of hopelessness. I think it is closely related to fear – fear that nothing will get better, fear of the loss of who you truly are because your inherent nature is one of hope.

Hopelessness feels so awful because it goes against our innate drive to survive and to thrive.

I often feel that hope is actually part of love; love for ourselves. Finding that love again helps us to see that we can feel better again, that we do have a purpose in life and that we do matter. When our mental health worsens it is often followed by a deterioration in our self-esteem, our ability to see the good in ourselves and in the world. This increases the feeling of isolation; it clouds our perceptions, thoughts and sense of worthiness. Love is the ultimate answer,

I believe, to many of the challenges and difficulties we see in the world, and hope is part of that love.

Hope is the series of stepping stones that lead us from the dark, shadowy side of a river to a sunnier, brighter place on the other side. It is a resource we can cultivate and use little by little. Even though at the time we can't see our progress, after a while we can turn around and see exactly how far we have come. Hope is the spark that ignites the fire that lights our way to brighter things.

Hope drives change, and change for the better, for progress in society and in the world. Think of all the inspirational leaders and individuals who have created positive change in the world. Their actions have come from challenge, often from a hopeless darkness. But they have had an unwavering sense of hope that things can get better and have taken action to make things better.

Hope is also a gift we can give those around us. We can share hope, give support and remind others who may be struggling that they will not struggle forever. Hope is a way of connecting to others just like love is, and if we develop a strong sense of hope in ourselves we light that up in all of those we interact with around us, helping it spread.

Without hope, nothing can be achieved and nothing can change. When we are hopeless we shut down opportunities for positive change to come into our life and often we start to feel worse.

When we realise hope is always part of us and it can never be lost, we can start to build it up again. It is like a muscle that we just haven't used in a while. We need to exercise it regularly to make it strong again so we can use it to help us get to where we want to be.

During some of the tough periods in my own life, when my sense of hope has been hard to find and everything feels dark and never ending, I have learned that there are reliable sources that I can draw upon to allow that chink of light in again:

- Getting the right kind of help and support – It is so important to seek professional medical or psychological support when your mental health is suffering, so you can get the right treatment and therapy. Asking for help lifts a burden off your mind and helps get you into the right place to start using other tools to build hope again. You can't do it all on your own and you shouldn't have to. There are so many wonderful mental health charities and organisations.

- Family, friends & support networks – Sometimes we need to draw on the people around us for support to help us to a place where we feel safe and can start to see that hope is possible. All of us are human and can tell you we have felt this way at some point in our lives, and we came through to the other side. That knowledge alone can be a huge comfort.

- Your 'cheerleaders' – I cannot emphasise enough the importance of other people in your life when it comes to hope. Choose your team of cheerleaders wisely and be selective about who you have around you. We all go up and down and need different levels of support at different times, but that is the beauty of human connection. It is a bit like sharing your phone charger with someone else who has a low battery. When you feel low, other people can not only remind you that there is a better day coming, but also that you matter and you are wonderful.

- Nature – Nature is a good reminder that things can get better. Looking at plants growing, birds singing, and trees blossoming reminds us that life goes on and that there is always another day, another spring, and another dawn. Being in nature allows us to reconnect with that sense of hope in life and reminds us that no dark period lasts forever.

- Music, Art, Writing, Poetry & Exercise – Creativity helps us feel hopeful again. Listening to uplifting music can help so much. So many song lyrics are based on that sense of breaking through the darkness and into the light. Getting those feelings out is helpful. Writing in whatever form, whether poetry or prose, can help you express how you are feeling, and reading hopeful stories or poems reminds you that things can improve. Exercise is brilliant for building self-esteem, improving mental health, sleep, mood and physical wellbeing, so find some form of exercise that works for you, even if it's just a walk round the block. It all helps.

- Animals & children – Being around animals and children always helps me focus on the good in life. Children's hopeful nature, inherent kindness and ability to be in the present moment reminds us that simple things bring peace. Animals, in particular, can be incredibly therapeutic for our mental wellbeing. They help put things in perspective.

- Quotes – I love a good quote and I curate a feed on my social media full of positive, inspirational quotes that remind me what is important in life. There have been many wise people throughout the ages who have also felt as you have and their words and advice can help you.

- Remembering who you are – Whatever you believe, whether you are religious, spiritual or not, we all have a set of core values that we lead our lives by. These might have been set in childhood or we may have changed them as we got older. When things get tough, it's important to try and remember what they are. You may have questions like 'What's important to me in life?' 'What do I believe in?' 'What can I bring to the world?' Remembering your purpose in life and how you can help others can be healing in itself. Sometimes seeing that we can help others can help us find our sense of hope and love for ourselves again.

- Other people's stories – I am a firm believer that we can learn something from everyone we meet. Reading stories of others who have been in a similar position or felt a similar way and learning how they found hope again can be so inspiring.

- Trying to find the positives – Life goes up, down, left and right. We go forwards and then we fall back. Life seldom goes in a straight trajectory, or where we want it to. Once we see the reality of life and accept that there may be challenging periods, we can let go of our resistance. Instead of 'fighting' against something we cannot control, and ending up battered and bruised, we can find our own power by realising there is something more effective that we can control, and that is ourselves – our thoughts, attitudes and actions. Once we find our power in ourselves, we can find hope. Whatever is thrown at us, we always have that resource.

- Finding love for yourself again – The most useful resource I have drawn upon is my love for myself. When you can tap into that place inside you that cares for who you are and who loves you, an incredible strength and hope will flow into your life. It is sometimes hard to do this, but remember there are always people – family, friends and medical professionals – around you who can help you find that love for yourself again. Caring enough about yourself to try to feel hope again is, I believe, the starting point.

Hope gives us the ability to persevere through difficult times and difficult feelings. Even if you feel you have lost it temporarily, you can find it again. Ask for help, ask for support, never give up – you are too precious for that and you have too much to give in this world.

Remember, you are not alone and you can feel better again.

Dr Radha Modgil is an NHS GP and broadcaster. She is BBC Radio 1's resident medical expert on *Life Hacks*, co-host of the *Life Hacks* podcast and presented the CBeebies series *Feeling Better* that highlighted emotional awareness and literacy for Early Years. She also works with charities like The Mix, BBC Children in Need, MIND and Barnardos.

Jada Sezer

To me, hope is a gentle bridge between what is and what could be. A bridge that if crossed will lead you from desire, to belief, to knowing. Knowing that tomorrow will be different and can be better. Hope is the understanding that things will change and that life will eventually move for you, too.

Hope doesn't have to be loud, it does not demand action. You can be still and sit in hope. Sometimes hope may ask you to step backwards before figuring out how to move forwards.

There have been times when I have misplaced my hope and times when I truly believed that I had lost all of it. When my days drifted by, in a blurry orange mess of blended sunrises and sunsets. At times my mind felt congested, filled with an oppressive fog that seemed to arrive with neither notice nor invitation. The most minuscule tasks were mammoth moments and the best idea looked like crawling back into bed because maybe then the fog would settle and softly sleep beside me. To me, even being curious in the darkest spaces is hope. You can be hopeful even whilst you dread the day. Even asking the question, 'Is this it for me?' is sometimes all that is needed for hope to appear.

There have been times when I've felt completely alone and haven't had the secure safety net of family support. Sometimes the expectations we hold do not always match the stories we are told. Let that go. Support can show up in a book, a song, a perfectly timed inappropriate joke or an expansive new question bringing light to hidden old patterns. Open yourself up. That is hope.

When I think back to my younger self, I have an overwhelming compassion for her. I'd give her the biggest hug and tell her she is strong. Strong enough to see it through and strong enough to still be standing. Even through the most crippling pain, she is capable – even if she isn't willing, yet. The biggest meltdowns will pave the way for her greatest breakthroughs. She won't always learn new lessons; sometimes she'll learn old ones again and again. Be brave and trust the process. Hope is never giving up.

Hope can be the smallest glimmer of light in the furthest corner of your mind. You're not entirely sure if its real but you hold on to it. Give your mind the space to wonder. When did you last sit in the moment between a daydream and deep desire? If I have learned one thing about hope, it's that it can show up in many different forms, it is self-renewing and self-sufficient because it is within us. We must remember to stand and fight for our right to have hope, and the right to believe that we deserve it.

There may be times when you'll turn your back on that dim little light. You might be tempted to walk out towards the darkness. But know this: hope will not judge you, it will not condemn you. It will wait for you.

No matter how dark it gets, hope is always with you.

Jada Sezer is essentially an optimist dedicated to making people feel empowered. Whilst completing her MA in Child Psychology she saw the mental health difficulties young people face and began campaigning for diversity, which led to an unexpected modelling career.

As well as hosting a podcast, *Unsubscribe*, Jada is an ambassador for the Royal Foundation charity Young Minds and an ambassador for UN WOMEN (UK).

Dave Chawner

From: Current Dave Chawner
To: Younger Dave Chawner c.2006
Subject: Letter To Your Younger Self

Dear (younger) Dave,

I'm writing to you from the future . . . but don't worry, that's not as spooky as it sounds. It's more of a *Bill & Ted's Excellent Adventure* vibe I'm going for rather than *Terminator* or *Donnie Darko*.

I've written and re-written this email about fourteen times, but I've decided I'm never going to get it perfectly right, so I'm sending it now.

I've heard things are a bit shit at the moment (how did I hear? Well, let's not forget that I'm the older you), so, I wanted to give you a little nudge in the right direction, a little helping hand.

Firstly, the fact that I'm emailing you from the future shows that things do carry on. I don't mean to give you a hard time mate, but perspective might be a word you wanna learn. Yeah, I know that things seem overwhelming and everything feels a bit intense, but stepping back from it all once in a while can be kinda useful. Don't worry, you don't get any better at it when you get older – the last time I properly 'switched off' was when Gordon Brown was in power (oh, yeah, spoiler alert, he becomes the Prime Minister . . . but let's steer clear of politics because that's just a car crash here in the future).

Things are gonna get a little stormy on the horizon. But that's ok, you can't have light without dark. Right now, 'mental health' is as interesting to you as quadratic equations. That's gonna change.

Everyone has health. Everyone has a brain. So, everyone has brain health (but we tend to call it mental health because that sounds a lot less weird!). You don't wait for any other organ of the body to begin malfunctioning before you look after it, so don't do it with your brain. After all, you don't need to be unfit before you go to the gym, and you don't wanna be ill before you start caring about looking after your wellbeing.

Mental health isn't about sob-stories, gloom and doom. It's about looking after yourself; being the best version of you. Who doesn't want that?

I can't tell you what's coming ahead (I've seen *Dr Who* and all that sci-fi crap and I know that if I begin to give you spoilers then it'll rip the time/space continuum apart and Uncle Rich will become a Dalek) but all I will say is . . . mental health is important. Don't let things get worse before you can get better.

And learn to spot the signs that things might not be great – mentally, I mean. No one's ever born with an instruction manual on how to maintain your brain, so you have to create one as you go. That doesn't mean it has to be dull, far from it, good mental health is one of the most amazing, enabling things you can ever have. So don't risk that. Keep on top of it. Keep learning and keep improving.

There, I've probably said too much already. I've gotta go now before I shout my mouth off too much and Time & Space begins crumbling like Rolf Harris's reputation.

Just, look after yourself mate. That's all I'll say. Keep in mind that you need to keep your mind in mind (that sounded really cool when I wrote it, but now I realise it's meaningless gibberish).

Take care,
Dave

(P.S. don't take maths at A-Level, you're rubbish at it!)

Dave Chawner is an author, award-winning stand-up comic, presenter and mental health campaigner. He is author of *Weight*

Expectations and has presented a series of films for BBC's *Tomorrow's World*, as well as writing for the *Guardian*, *Telegraph*, *Metro* and *Cosmopolitan*. He has performed as a stand-up comic at the Edinburgh Fringe.

Gloria Reuben

June 24, 2020

I keep needing to restart what I want to write. I'm finding it difficult to gather my thoughts during this time. Can't seem to focus lately.

The coronavirus has been a tsunami on this tender planet's population, ruining countless lives and leaving its destruction on families, careers, homes, finances and futures.

It is swift and furious in its damage. And it's not over yet.

Then just as we were in the throes of it, just one month ago was the horrific murder of George Floyd. While we were all trying to survive the first pandemic, the second pandemic that has been buried deep, festering for generations, exploded.

Once again, we all are shaken to our core. Denial no longer able to exist. Reality, in all its harsh bright and blinding light, can no longer be ignored.

I have found myself unmoored during these past three months. Every area of my life has been tossed high up in the air and I am only now, with gentleness and patience, picking up the pieces that are strewn around, and beginning to restructure and rebuild my life. While doing so, I question where my life is going. I question where the United States is going.

Anxiety, depression, sleeplessness, fear of the future, and deep-seated grief have flowed through me. Some days are better than others. But on those days when I'm not doing so well, I try my best to practice self-care so that I don't slide swiftly down that dangerous rabbit hole of hopelessness.

Mental-health issues have plagued my family since as far back as I can remember. My mother was depressed for sure. Never clinically diagnosed. But sometimes one doesn't need a doctor to tell a family that a parent is depressed. A sensitive child will know. And that sensitive child will try to 'save' mom or dad. Of course that's not possible. So sometimes that child grows up feeling depressed herself, wondering why she couldn't 'make it better'.

Depression can wreak havoc on a family, creating a chasm of confusion and mistrust that can expand dangerously if help and treatment aren't sought.

One of my siblings is bipolar. Another sibling, my little brother David, took his own life when he was twenty-one years old.

Every day since the coronavirus took over, I've thought of David. And my other brother Denis who passed. I've thought about life and death more than usual. My own mental-health challenges have been exacerbated by isolation and lack of human touch because of the coronavirus.

But here's the thing. I haven't given up. And I won't. Because where there's life there's hope. There is always hope. And there is always someone who is there to help. Always.

Sometimes it just takes someone to listen. Not to give advice. Just to stay silent and listen. Because we all need to be heard. And that kind of help is always available.

For me, what helps is journal writing, reaching out to a trusted friend, going for a brisk walk, playing the piano, spending time in nature, watching a funny movie (they're not kidding when they say laughter is the best medicine). Sometimes I just have to cry. And cry hard. For a long time. Snot running down my face and everything. No holds barred. Just get it out.

The most recent time that happened was when I went to a vigil for George Floyd. So many people of so many races were there. It was peaceful. And quiet. And beautiful. I cried so fucking hard my stomach hurt.

As I walked home I kept crying. I didn't care who saw me. (Well, it did help that I was wearing a face mask and sunglasses.) I cried and cried until I couldn't cry anymore.

I felt exhausted afterwards. Bone tired. Spent. No more tears were left.

And then ... I felt a clean, fresh newness that delicately

presented itself to me. And I allowed myself the time to just sit in that space. Everything still unknown in terms of what was going to happen (with the virus, with systemic changes in this country, with my life). But I felt the opening of my heart. The release of fear. And in its place a deep feeling of faith.

Knowing that even though I may have felt alone, the truth is I'm not. I'm not alone.

You are not alone.

Oh . . . another thing I felt was starving! I almost ate a whole pizza!

#AlwaysHope

Gloria Reuben is an accomplished actress, singer and author. She most recently portrayed Krista Gordon in the hit TV series *Mr. Robot*, released her third album, *For All We Know* in February 2020, and published her first book in November 2019, *My Brother's Keeper*, a loving tribute to her two brothers who have passed.

ACCEPTANCE

Victoria Maxwell

'Rapid cycling mixed state bipolar 1 disorder with psychotic features, mild temporal lobe epilepsy, generalized anxiety disorder and disordered eating.'

Not really something you run and put on your resume under 'achievements'.

That's the diagnosis I got after a couple of trips to 'zoobie noobie land' as I call it. That is, after two manic psychotic episodes. I was twenty-five years old and definitely did not like the mental illness labels I had been given. This started a five-year battle . . . err . . . journey of acceptance. It was a hard-won battle. It required a lot of me and a lot from others.

For years prior to this, I had been wrestling with binge eating, restrictive 'dieting', compulsive exercising and obsessing over food on what felt like a minute to minute basis. Even when I thought I had the food 'thing' licked (pardon the pun) and was going to Overeaters Anonymous (the 12-step equivalent to AA for food addiction) I was still anxious, depressed and frequently suicidal.

I was an actor at the time in Hollywood North (Vancouver, Canada), booking small but good roles opposite big name actors. I was going somewhere. I thought. What I didn't know is that I was headed for a rollercoaster ride of mania, depressions and anxiety. An amusement park ride that I never would have bought a ticket for. Scary? Yes. Fun? No.

I've always been interested in psychology, personal growth and spiritual approaches to self-improvement. As my depression and suicidal feelings increased so did my thirst for psychological and spiritual solutions. I believed that if I could just find that one thing that happened to me in childhood, that one deep-seated psychological issue and uproot it, I would feel better.

I started therapy. I did more therapy. And more therapy. It helped. But it didn't change what I hoped it would. I more or less became a really insightful depressed person.

Don't get me wrong. I think therapy (the right type of therapy) can be an amazing help. I still see a counsellor. It's one of my foundational wellness tools.

This was all before I was diagnosed. Before I had other tools to augment my therapy. At the time, counselling alone wasn't enough to help me move out of the severe depression I was in.

I remember sitting with my therapist. Lovely therapist, really. Quite effective. But I don't think she understood exactly how depressed I had become. I sat in her office on her tweedy couch, the rose-coloured walls staring at me. She was dressed in a flowing skirt and blouse that reminded me of beautiful curtains in a Bahama villa. She had these sandals too. I remember because they reminded me of something a gladiator would wear. I told her that. I didn't mean it as an insult, just an observation. We laughed. She said she thought they were sexy. They were. I also told her (for some reason) I could never see myself wearing them. That was one of the things I loved about her. We could talk fashion trends, as well as trauma.

But then she asked her 'So . . . how are you?' question that started all our sessions.

'I'm really depressed.'

'Still?' was her comeback.

That gutted me. Of course I'm still depressed, I wanted to say. That's what chronic clinical depression is! Chronic and clinical. It doesn't pass after four weeks. I had been experiencing this for at least six weeks or maybe even two months. It was unrelenting.

To be fair, I don't think I had been given my diagnosis by then, so perhaps she didn't recognize it as such. I certainly didn't.

I continued to see her. I did good work with her; made headway – to a point. But the depression and the mania that followed and the lulls in between persisted. Suicidal thoughts continued.

I started looking for spiritual solutions. Maybe if I meditated it would help. What I really thought was maybe if I meditated and got enlightened, I wouldn't feel suicidal anymore. I'd feel at peace. That's what meditation and enlightenment is supposed to offer, right?

I found a teacher in Vancouver and dove into a retreat. No preparation. No understanding of what I was really getting into. Three days of the same mantra and on the last day – POW! I felt something. I went into some kind of rip-roaring altered state. Energy ran up my spine, throughout my body. Time stopped. Colours were crisper. It felt blissful, expansive and surreal.

But I had been given no instructions on how to stay present and grounded in this extreme state of consciousness. I had never felt anything like it. Perhaps it was because of my family history of mental illness. My mom has bipolar disorder and severe anxiety. My dad was undiagnosed but fought panic attacks and depression all my life. Whether it was because I had been struggling for more years than I cared to remember with my own mood swings and biting anxiety, I don't know, but I couldn't stay with the experience and stay present at the same time.

I, or perhaps more correctly 'it', whatever 'it' was, spiralled into what the medical world called 'psychosis'; what I like to call 'non-shared reality'. I had incredibly meaningful insights and powerfully spiritual 'ah-ha's'. I saw the Oneness of Life. How we're all interconnected. But I also was definitely not connected to consensual reality and stuck in a world of my own. I thought sneakers meant the devil was near. I 'knew' Prince Charming was coming to save me.

I managed somehow to drive back home. I was living with my parents at the time. My dad, seeing the state I was in, rushed me to the hospital. That was the first of my involuntary commitments to the psych ward.

What ensued was the diagnosis above and my resolute refusal to accept it. I had had a spiritual awakening, hadn't I? I wasn't about to let the medical establishment pathologize a transformational experience.

Over the next five years, I fought psychiatrists, fired two, took medication, stopped medication, was hospitalized four more times, and ran down the street naked (in the summer, thank goodness).

Then, a turning point. During my last stay in the psych ward, I was referred to a psychiatrist. A psychiatrist who had been a beatnik in the 60s. Yes, he was that old AND that cool.

Dr. Dillon and I talked about my dilemma. How could I take medication for a mental illness I didn't believe in? When I felt like what I had been through was a spiritual awakening.

He listened, his silver hair framing his kind, wrinkled face. How was I managing? How was I feeling? My quality of life? He gently asked.

I wasn't managing. I felt awful. What quality of life? My spiritual transformation didn't seem to have helped those things. But I hung onto it, because it did shift how I saw life, how I saw myself – all for the positive. But I still struggled with razor-sharp depression, and unnerving anxiety, both of which had toppled my ability to work and function.

Dr. Dillon suggested that what I had been through *was* a spiritual experience, was an altered state that was very profound for me. But perhaps, is it possible, I could *also* be dealing with a mental illness too? One that if treated, could allow me to deepen my spirituality and improve my quality of life?

This was the first time someone, a science guy for that matter, helped me see that accepting my mental illnesses didn't minimize the meaningful mystical experiences that I held so dear. That these two apparently antithetical views weren't so antithetical after all.

From that point on, I began to be proactive in my recovery process. I agreed to take medication, saw Dr. Dillon and did psychotherapy with him. I entered a vocational rehabilitation program for people with mental health issues. I left acting behind and started an office job.

I still take medication. And yes, I still sometimes don't want to take it. But I keep on taking it. Dr. Dillon passed away a few years ago. But I now see another psychiatrist and an excellent counsellor. I make sure I get the right amount of sleep, the right amount of exercise. Running in the trails behind my house seems to do the trick.

I don't live with my parents anymore. They're happy about that.

So's my husband! I've been with Gordon, one of my best wellness supports, for over sixteen years. I don't have that office job anymore. Instead, my career has come full circle.

Through a freak conversation with another actor, I learned you can make a living as a professional speaker. In 2001 I wrote and started performing the first of three one-person stage shows about my 'escapades' with mental illness. In 2003 I was able to go full-time as a keynote mental health speaker, presenting my theatrical keynotes and workshops across Canada and around the world. I joke that I have a career I'd never have had, if I had not gone crazy in the first place! Silver linings, I guess.

My spirituality continues to play an important role in my recovery and maintaining my mental health.

I went almost two decades without a psychotic episode, or 'nonshared' reality. But in the last two years, I've had two. With the help of my husband and healthcare team, I rode them out and managed them at home. Let me clarify: there's nothing wrong with going into hospital. I've done some of my best healing there.

Recovery needs a much broader definition than just reduction in symptoms. I see recovery as the restoration of self-esteem, meaning, quality of life and moments of joy, despite struggles with the illness.

I learn something new every day about what it means to be well, what it takes to stay well. The journey is never over. But recovery is always possible. I still experience the waves, sometimes big, sometimes small, that come with bipolar disorder and anxiety. But on the whole, I surf them with a little bit more grace.

Victoria Maxwell is an award-winning mental health speaker, actor and playwright. At the age of twenty-five she was diagnosed with bipolar disorder, anxiety and psychosis and has since become a self-proclaimed Wellness Warrior and Bipolar Princess!

For her free *How to Escape Perfectionism, Anxiety & Depression* e-guide, visit: www.victoriamaxwell.com

Yvette Caster

I didn't know I'd gone mad until I was sane again. It was mania and I was seventeen. It started with a phone call – on a white landline phone because it was the 90s. I asked a boy out and he said no. I was hurt and angry, not least because we'd snogged the weekend before. I was obsessed with him, his freckles and strawberry-blonde hair. I was also stressed because of my A-level studies and all-encompassing need to be perfect at everything, not to mention the fact I was genetically predisposed to bipolar disorder.

To try to feel better after the snub I blasted out Janet Jackson's 'If' and 'This Time', but somehow the music and rage became a cacophony. This rejection was the carelessly discarded match that led to the forest fire. I was swept up and out of my mind in a hurricane of mania. My parents were out at a concert that evening. When they left I was sane, by the time they came back I was psychotic. For days, then weeks, all thoughts of sixth form were gone, my mind wiped clean of the usual worries, fears and frustrations and replaced with a set of delusions.

In some ways I felt more purpose than ever before, such was the power of the mania. I didn't sleep for long, I talked fast and wide-eyed, I wrote reams of nonsensical scrawl. I tried to convince my GP I could breathe underwater. I thought I controlled the weather. I thought the radio was speaking directly to me. Noises like the tooting of traffic outside my window took on new meaning – they were talking to me. I thought I was doing a spell to reverse Eve's curse. I picked flowers and floated them in bowls of water as part of this insane magic, placing them carefully round the house. I remember my mother thanking me for one in her room. I became a spell-caster, living up to my surname. Later I believed God had impregnated me and my child would be the second coming. My frantic mind didn't wait long before moving on to the next delusion.

During this time I stayed at home and my parents kept an eye on me. They fed me and took me to the doctor's. At one point, when I assume, my round the clock mania became too much for them, I was taken to my grandparents' house where I stayed for a while, not sleeping, convinced the few words I picked up from the raucous youths in the street outside were special; secret messages meant just for me. Eventually it all slowed down. The storm passed, the fire burnt out and I was left standing amidst the charred remains of my 'normal' teenage life.

Back home, I had the same sunshine-yellow curtains and grass-green carpet, the same blonde hair and green eyes, the *Friends* VCR box set, velvet scrunchies and inaccurate mood rings. But I was changed. Who was I now? How could I go to Oxford, be invited to parties, get a boyfriend, be a singer or indeed be anything? I believed I was broken. I couldn't see how I'd ever rebuild my life. Girls like me didn't go mad.

I slid into a deep depression, aided by my then undiagnosed bipolar disorder. I spent hours sitting, staring, mute, to the point my mother feared I'd had some sort of fit. From the age of fourteen I'd had episodes of depression, locking myself in the loo, crying incessant, incomprehensible tears. If I had known the cause it may have been better. The outpouring of unexplainable grief was worse. Now I was at the nadir of depression, a stygian ravine. With no hope of being normal again, I tried to kill myself.

Through sheer luck, I lived. Afterwards I was stoic. I resigned myself to a wasteland life, plodding along day by day in mediocrity. But I was far from ok. I suppose it was my parents who called the young people's mental health unit. Although no longer delusional, I was in a different kind of insanity. A nurse came to speak to me, and I told her about the suicide attempt. I agreed to spend time in the unit as a day patient – I didn't particularly see the point of it but I couldn't go back to school. I didn't have a life-changing experience there, but I met some other people my age who'd also been through hell. Mostly we half-heartedly completed art projects and hung around in a dilapidated common room with a muddle of donated odds and ends presumably supposed to cheer us up, from dog-eared board games to out-dated 'NOW' CDs. A highlight for me was discovering an ancient vinyl Motown record among the junk and being allowed to take it home. Hearing 'Up the Ladder to the Roof' for the first time on Dad's record player was a ray of light. But I can't say I had much hope at that time. Instead I had group chats, where I usually sat in silence, too unsure of myself and of what had happened to contribute. I had a memorable talk with the unit's leading psychiatrist, who explained my moods to me as a kind of wave or cardiogram – going through peaks and troughs more extreme than others' but with 'normal,' even moods at times too. He stressed no one was really normal. Back then, I didn't want to hear it.

The ragtag group of youths and I spent most of our time being distracted from thinking too hard about our eating disorders, OCD, depression, self-harm and ADHD. We were taught circus skills and I still can't see a Diablo or spinning plate without a shiver of horror. We helped each other in some ways we were meant to, and some we definitely weren't. During trips to a nearby corner shop I opened all the doors for a girl terrified of germs. Another with anorexia sneaked me her lunchtime crisps. In return they said I had a nice smile and didn't make me tell them anything about why I was there. We were all a bit shell-shocked I suppose. The overriding feel was that of a shit youth club. I made a couple of friends and time passed. While I didn't exactly feel myself getting better, I did start getting bored. Eventually my levels of boredom increased to the point where I just wanted to get back to sixth form for something differ-ent to do. Is boredom a cure? Either way, it seemed to work for me. I suppose my mood had started to naturally level out again too.

I went back to school a few times a week and, although the teachers had a vague idea of the truth, I told friends I'd had glandu-lar fever. At that point I was far from understanding what had happened to me and I didn't want to be defined by it. Talking's fine when you're ready, but I wasn't back then. I remember telling one

Goth I'd had a breakdown but that was more to take the piss out of her aesthetic than anything else. More time passed, lessons continued and soon I was back to sixth form full time, and back to my beloved singing lessons. It would be a while before I felt the same around friends outside the unit though. Still, I passed my A-levels, went on a World Challenge trek to Mongolia and the Great Wall of China, then went to uni. I didn't go to Oxford, which was just as well, as my first real boyfriend and best friend were waiting for me up north.

Now, twenty-odd years later, I'm still here, writing for you about hope. What can I say that doesn't imply it's an easy ride? Hope can sometimes sound like a round and shiny-faced fool. It can smack of naivety and childishness. When I was younger, hope was a big, bombastic thing meaning grand schemes, fame and fortune. I hoped for universal adoration and golden achievements so I could hold up my hands and say, 'Look, I matter, I deserve to be here.'

And, although I haven't become an international singer-songwriter as planned (yet), the intervening years have still gone ok. After uni I went into journalism, working for most of the nationals. I have won awards in both a professional capacity and for my charity work. I'm paid to travel the world then write about it. I get to read and edit some of my favourite writers. I chat about the news on national radio and share my views on TV. I've interviewed everyone from Justin Timberlake to Harold Pinter to Dame Kelly Holmes and had all kinds of experiences, from chatting to Fijian tribeswomen about feminism to sleeping dangling over a cliff. I also created and host a weekly podcast, called *Mentally Yours*, to talk about mental health. I hope it helps others feel less alone.

Looking back, it's true there were times I had no hope. During those times my family carried the torch. They had hope when I had none. They kept believing I'd get better. They took me to the unit, they drove me to appointments, they took me to alternative therapies from hypnosis to acupuncture. They brought me meals in bed when I was so depressed all I wanted to do was sleep. They had faith I would return. And, eventually, I did. After one period of deepest depression I finally went on meds and started to see the point of getting up again. My mother said the pills had given her her daughter back.

Now I believe hope is about putting one foot in front of the other, day after day. It's a shuffle, not a race. It's a decision to just keep going. It's trying to remember to congratulate yourself for getting out of bed this morning. And if that was too hard, congratulating yourself for still being here, despite how you feel. It's believing that this too shall pass. That's easier for me to say in a normal-ish mood than when I'm depressed, because it's so hard to find hope when you're in the midst of it. In the midst of it you just need to keep breathing, remember to eat and take your meds. When you emerge – which you will – you'll eventually find yourself somewhere better. You'll look at a mackerel sky and feel something again. You'll be dancing with a friend and suddenly laugh so hard you can hardly stand. You'll meet your niece or nephew for the first time and all they'll want from you isn't perfection or success or achievements or even for you to be 'normal', but to spend time with you, running races in the garden or building Lego castles.

After my first manic episode I couldn't picture a life for myself, but there was one waiting for me after all. I've made wonderful friends, had spectacular love affairs and somehow managed to buy my own place. Yes, I have bipolar disorder, but it does not have me.

Yvette Caster is a freelance journalist, podcaster, broadcaster and blogger who works for *The Times*, *Vice* and *Metro.co.uk*. Her podcast, *Mentally Yours*, was shortlisted for the 2018 Mind Media Awards.

She lives in Berkshire, and her next great ambition in life is to own a small dog.

Steve Gilbert

My mental health problems started in my late teens and by seventeen I was seeing a psychologist in the CAMHS service. At nineteen I had to leave my family home following a number of incidents with my father which made it unsafe for me to live there.

At twenty-one I was a student at the University of Birmingham, studying for my master's degree, when I experienced my first depressive episode. I had to plead with my GP for help and managed to get a limited amount of psychological support.

Then in the spring of 2008, age twenty-four, I was working as an unqualified teacher, planning to complete the Graduate Teacher Programme. Life seemed to be going well, until something shifted. Within a matter of weeks, I went from knowing what I wanted my life to look like, to entering a spiral of depression which ultimately resulted in me making plans to take my own life. It was only the actions of a very good friend that stopped me going through with my suicide attempt. I ended up under a Crisis Resolution Home Treatment Team, my first contact with Adult Secondary Mental Health Services.

It can be said that hope is the opposite of despair. *The Cambridge Dictionary* defines despair as:

'the feeling that there is no hope and that you can do nothing to improve a difficult or worrying situation'

There were many emotions that I felt at the time, but without a doubt one of the strongest was despair. It felt like the harder I tried to 'fix' what was wrong, the worse things became. Despair felt like this dark and heavy presence in my life, slowly and painfully crushing me, stripping me of any belief that things could get better. I went from being a relatively happy-go-lucky and optimistic person to a shadow of my former self. I started to believe that I had no value and was incapable of holding down any job. Work is important to me and without a sense of purpose I could see no reason to stay alive. I truly had no hope.

Fortunately for me my best friend Cathy refused to believe in my despair. At such times it is necessary to borrow hope from another. I don't know how, but she summoned the energy to have enough faith and hope for the both of us. Cathy saw a future for me that I could not see for myself. More so than medication, genuine love, care and patience from another human being can be the most powerful thing in the world. Cathy's ability to have hope on my behalf is the reason that I am alive today.

The Cambridge Dictionary defines hope as:

'to want something to happen or to be true, and usually have a good reason to think that it might.'

Let's take the first part. When I entered into my depression I wanted things to improve, I wanted to get better. But when I consider the second part of that definition, despite knowing what I wanted to happen, I had no good reason to think that it might. I could not find any evidence to support the belief that I would get better. At the time there were very few people talking openly about mental illness and I genuinely thought that I was the only person experiencing these feelings. I felt shame at my inability to 'sort myself out'.

In September of 2009 I had yet another depressive episode and made a number of attempts on my life. This was followed in 2010 by a manic episode, during which I was detained by the police, then subsequently sectioned under the Mental Health Act (MHA). I spent a total of twenty-one days in hospital, short by many standards, but long enough to understand the impact the MHA can have on a person's life. Being in hospital allowed for observation of my behaviour, resulting in a diagnosis of bipolar disorder.

In January of 2011, after two major depressive episodes, a manic episode and hospital admission, I started work with a new CPN, Jo. Jo has been instrumental in helping me learn to live with bipolar. Jo taught me that living with a serious mental illness did not mean I couldn't have a good life. I was able to build trust with Jo, an important factor in having hope. Jo reassured me at every step, including finding the right combination of meds and managing difficult periods, and we worked through it together.

I started volunteering with Time to Change (TTC) in January 2014 and this gave me a great sense of purpose. This led to probably the biggest single moment that changed my life – being appointed to the TTC 300 Voices programme. For the first time in years I felt that I was good at something, and, more importantly for my self-belief, that other people saw my value. I was being judged on my merits. My experience of mental illness stems from psychological abuse by my family. Every time a person values me and the work I do, that validation gives me hope, hope that life is worth living.

The past ten years have included regular appointments with my psychiatrist, my Community Psychiatric Nurse (CPN), courses of talking therapy, lifestyle changes and twice-daily medication, including lithium. I am still a user of mental health services, having had numerous depressive episodes over the past few years.

Nevertheless, I have worked for the past seven years as a living experience consultant using my experiences of mental illness and mental health services. In October 2017, I was appointed as a Vice-Chair for the Mental Health Act review, not only because I have a mental illness and have been detained under the act, but more importantly because of my skills and competence. I was recognised in the 2019 Queen's Birthday Honours List and appointed as an OBE for services to mental health. It is proof, if proof be needed, that people with lived experience can and do work at the highest levels in our society.

Despite my work and achievements, I still battle daily with the effects of my mental illness. I regularly experience suicidal thoughts. Some days life seems too difficult. When I am well, I have used my phone to record as many reasons as I can think of that my life is worth living, so that I can listen at times when I lose hope. Over the years I have collated messages of love and support from people, that I can refer to at times of despair. Sometimes I am unable to do this on my own, and need a friend to do this with me. It is an effective way of reminding me that I am valued, and of the respect people have for me battling my mental illness.

To each and every person who has helped and supported me over the years I say thank you. Each kind word gives me hope.

Steve Gilbert OBE is thirty-seven and a Serious Mental Illness Living Experience Consultant.

Charlotte Walker
A Life Worth Living

'You'll have bipolar disorder for the rest of your life,' said a psychiatrist I'd never met before. Gee, thanks doc. Here I am, newly admitted to an unfamiliar mental health ward, and you hit me with that. It wasn't that he was telling me something I didn't already know. It was that he made my situation sound so hopeless. After going in and out of hospital four times in three years, with other major crises just about managed at home, I was already getting short on hope. I was forty-four years old. Would I be in this state for another forty-four years?

Although I felt stuck in despair, bipolar is actually a fluctuating illness. Sometimes I'm depressed; maybe then I can't get out of bed, overcome with feelings of shame and guilt and misery, preoccupied with thoughts of death. Very often I am anxious, which makes it hard to go out and do the simplest of things. Sometimes I am elated, too; too happy, reckless, over-confident, a loudmouth, careless with money and inclined to be argumentative. But there are times in between, times when I feel like 'me', when the moods level off and the anxiety moves into the background and I can live again. This might last for a few months, or weeks, or maybe even just a few days, but it happens. Objectively, I am not in pain all the time. But when crisis hits, I can't remember the good times. I know that they happened, but they feel like a dream, and one I am convinced I will never recapture.

I take multiple medications to manage my mental health and I've also had a lot of therapy. Most recently, I was part of a therapeutic group, learning skills to help manage the overwhelming feelings of despair or anxiety. I gained lots from the course, but one of the things that really stayed with me is the concept of building a life worth living.

At times I feel like there is nothing outside of my difficult emotions, that I don't really know who I am anymore, that I don't have any defining characteristics outside of being bipolar.

This is not true.

Therapy has helped me see that I can have a fluctuating mental health condition and also have a full life. There are lots of things that I like to do, and there is scope for me to do more of them. Ok, when I'm really ill some of them have to take a back seat, but they'll still be there when my moods steady again.

I am Charlotte and I have bipolar disorder, and I take a lot of meds. Sometimes I have to go into hospital for my own safety. But I am Charlotte and I love choral singing. I am Charlotte and I like to go to yoga classes. I like dancing, even if my husband says that I am not good at it. I like playing the ukulele, even though I *know* I'm not good at that one (it's my own fault, I rarely practise). I like sending friends cards and gifts. Going to the library. Browsing antique shops. I like different forms of exercise, from aerobics through to Zumba. I like to volunteer at my local arts centre, using the skills I accrued when I was able to work. I enjoy offering the perspective of lived experience of mental illness to researchers and healthcare professionals, to help make their work more patient-centred. I could go on. In fact, when asked during group, I was able to come up with a whole forty pleasant activities that I like to do. The 'homework' for that week was to do at least one a day, and to build that into a regular practice. Sometimes when I'm really sick, I can only do one thing for one ten-minute burst, just as a distraction from the awful thoughts in my head. But ten minutes is fine. Ten minutes is great, because by that point every second is hard to live through.

I've written out these forty activities and I've got them pinned up on the notice board. Today I've managed five: taking a bath, reading, texting an old friend, walking up the hill into my tiny town, and now writing. That's pretty good going. Maybe tomorrow I'll only be able to participate in one of the forty, but the idea is to keep going, keep working at it to feel like my life has meaning and purpose. To feel like a person. At the top of the list I have written: Have fun! Enjoy yourself.

Because it's ok to enjoy yourself when you have a mental health problem. You don't have to feel awful every second of every day if you're sick or disabled. Your suffering is valid, even if it's episodic. You don't have to feel guilty if you reach a point when you can go out and about, you don't have to prove that you are unwell enough to deserve caring and sympathy. You deserve a life worth living around your condition, as best you can.

I don't really believe in the concept of recovery, not for me. Much as I could've done without hearing it at that particular point, bipolar is part of me and yes, Dr Sensitive, I will have it for the rest of my life. You don't recover from bipolar the way you recover from the flu. But I do have periods of remission, and while they may not be long enough for me to ever hold down a job again, they are breathing space, and although the crises will come again, so will the spaces in between. Right now, I'm enjoying the moment, getting out to exercise classes and singing group, putting together little gifts for friends in the midst of their own mental health crises, sharing my skills and perspective with the arts centre. I'm building what I can while I can. And that gives me hope.

I wish I had realised earlier in life that work is not everything. To have built a career and lost it to mental health problems is a hard thing to come to terms with, but it wasn't the end. In some ways, it opened up new horizons – it's surprising the number of opportunities I have come across since I left work. I wish I could go back and tell myself that eight years on I will be writing about my life for a friend's book, on my laptop on the patio, looking out at the garden, listening to the birds.

That my life will be worth living.

Charlotte Walker shares her lived experience of bipolar disorder on her blog, purplepersuasion.wordpress.com, which was the winner of a Mind Media Award; on Twitter as @BipolarBlogger; as a freelance writer; and as a service user researcher.

Eleanor Segall

I was first diagnosed with bipolar 1 disorder at the age of sixteen, after a year of depressive and manic episodes which led to me being hospitalised in the North London Priory Hospital in 2004. I had psychosis, fearing that people were trying to harm me and I didn't feel safe at home. I was admitted to the adolescent unit for four months, before recovering and being put on mood-stabilising medication to help control my fluctuating episodes. I was given one-to-one counselling, group therapy, art therapy, cooking and sport, along with the other teens on the ward. My psychiatrist was excellent, but I was still just a shy teenager whose life had been ripped apart. I had never suspected that at just sixteen my entire life was going to change.

I desperately wanted to fit in, but had been given a diagnosis that made me stand out and for a long time I struggled to accept the bipolar part of me. I didn't know what it meant for me and my future. In my teen years, I didn't talk about it publicly, only to close friends. Back in 2004 mental illness still had a huge stigma and there weren't the social media and blogs that are around now. I felt stigmatised and was frightened to admit to the world that I had had a mental breakdown.

When I came home, I became a hypervigilant teenager, making sure I didn't get drunk or take drugs, monitoring my moods and never staying out too late. Lack of sleep can cause an elevated mood state and so I made sure I looked after myself to avoid becoming hyper, argumentative and psychotic.

Jonny Benjamin and I met around this time, through our friendship group in North London. However, we didn't speak about our mental health to each other, and I definitely didn't tell him I had been diagnosed with bipolar. As Jonny has talked about extensively, he was only diagnosed with schizoaffective disorder at age twenty, although he'd had it from childhood. I often think of what could have been different if we had opened up to each other back then. I am so grateful to have him as a friend and mentor now.

What really helped my recovery was discovering that bipolar disorder seems to run in families. My wonderful dad was diagnosed at age forty, just four years before I became unwell myself. Dad also has bipolar 1, the most severe form, but unlike me he has never developed psychosis. However he has suffered with suicidal depression, mania and debilitating panic attacks that have left him, at times, unable to work. Back in the 1990s, he was never referred to a psychiatrist, just put on the wrong medicine (Valium) for over a decade. When I was twelve, Dad was diagnosed with bipolar after a terrible depressive episode (also, strangely, at the Priory North London hospital) and started on lithium treatment, which has helped to stop his intense episodes.

For years, everyone thought that I should be taking lithium as a mood stabiliser because it had helped my dad stay well, but I was fearful as the drug has certain strong physical side effects, so I stayed on other forms of medication. It was only when I experienced suicidal depression and a severe manic episode in 2014, which left me sectioned under the Mental Health Act, that I decided to see if lithium could help me. Thankfully it has, and this year I am celebrating five years out of hospital due to its ability to keep the intense mood episodes at bay.

When I was in hospital for the second time, seeing my dad well really hit home for me. Having a parent with bipolar who has been stable for over twenty years has helped my own recovery so much. Both my parents and my stepfather, who is a doctor, are so loving and caring and supportive of me. I remember one day, at my lowest ebb, saying to Dad, 'I feel alone, I feel broken, I am single with no one to love me. Will I ever get better from this debilitating depression?' My dad looked at me and said, 'Ellie, we can try different medicines and different therapies, but take it day by day. You may be lying in bed all day now, depressed and unable to stay awake for long, but things will feel better. Often in the evenings you feel happier. I am here for you, and Mum and I love you so much. Remember what the doctor said, try to get up just half an hour earlier each day.'

This is some of the best advice I have had: to take each day as it comes. Just focus on the next hour and reach for support if you need it, from people or helplines. Don't suffer in silence as you are never truly alone, even if it feels that way. Serious mental illness is not the end. You may have relapses but you can recover and you can stay well.

My dad's answer helped me stay calm. The role of my family in my recovery has been integral. My mum, who doesn't have bipolar but has a good understanding of it, has always been there as my backbone, my supporter, my driver (if I couldn't get to places due to anxiety). She coaxes me out of the house on anxious days as a form of exposure therapy. On bad days, she will help me cook or do laundry, if I am feeling overwhelmed. My dad gives the kind of support that only someone with the illness can give – from lived experience. He understands the anxious, depressed or hypomanic thought patterns. He is calm in the face of adversity and he has provided me with a home and a safe haven. I am lucky to have such supportive parents.

My sister and I have been through so much together. She was just fourteen when I was diagnosed and twenty-three when I was hospitalised the second time. As well as being caring, her training as an occupational therapist means that she knows what methods I can use to help my illness therapeutically. She also gives excellent hugs. Having her in my life has helped my recovery no end; living with a bipolar person is never easy.

Lastly, I have a supportive husband in Rob, who works in mental health. He may not understand bipolar in the way my dad intrinsically does yet, but he has let me talk to him about it and explain. His unconditional love and humour have really helped my recovery too.

If you don't have a support network around you and you can't get out in person, come and join the mental health community on Twitter. It's a community that lifts people up, celebrates each other, listens and cares. It has helped me heal and celebrate my identity. I called my blog 'Be Ur Own Light' because when I started it, I needed to be my own light. I was unemployed, struggling with severe anxiety attacks, depressed and not interacting with the world.

If I could go back, I would tell my younger self not to worry, everything is going to be ok. You will achieve your dream of being a published author with a mental health publisher. You will write for national publications about mental health and people will accept you for who you are (which may come as a surprise). You will find a medication that gives you a chance of life again and although you will develop a debilitating anxiety disorder due to the trauma you've been through, therapy, friends and family will help you heal. You will find a husband who accepts you for who you are and you will have the chance to do what you love. You will feel the sun and smell the rain again, even after suicidal depressions when you lay in bed wanting to disappear. You will travel to countries you have dreamed of and bipolar disorder won't stop you being you. You'll even write for *Glamour* magazine, your favourite!

When you're depressed, you will grow sunflowers and give them to your friends, and that will make you smile.

Eleanor Segall (Mandelstam) is an author, freelance journalist, mental health blogger, speaker and advocate, who has lived with bipolar 1 disorder since 2004. Her debut book *Bring me to Light: Embracing my Bipolar and Social Anxiety* was published in November 2019.

Eleanor started her blog 'Be Ur Own Light' (www.beurown-light.com) in 2016.

Toby Campion

In autumn 2018 I was diagnosed with Obsessive Compulsive Disorder. I'd been struggling with this and other mental health issues for the previous fourteen years but it took me that amount of time to feel able to talk about it and seek help.

The openness around mental health right now is phenomenal and things are changing in vital ways. Sometimes, though – especially when slogans around mental health seem to be used to sell products – we don't actually acknowledge how ugly mental illness can be. It can feel more like blistering green abscesses on an embarrassing body part, not something that looks good in a selfie or stuck across fast food packaging. It's unfair and foul and smells gross and can, for a whole range of reasons, feel impossible to talk about. OCD, for example, isn't just going heavy on the hand sanitiser and colour co-ordinating your desk. It's a bully in your head that humiliates you in public, it's overwhelming feelings of guilt and shame, unbearable intrusive thoughts, heart palpitations, living in a constant state of fear, believing – knowing – there is no hope of ever getting rid of the way you feel.

I've been asked if there was a moment which stood out to me as a key turning point in dealing with my mental health, a piece of advice or an interaction that helped me. In all honesty, I don't think I have one moment, or even series of moments which mark milestones in getting better. I think improving my mental health has been a gradual process, as it is for many, and one which is, at times, frustratingly non-linear. Holding close the phrase 'this too shall pass' and believing in it as much as possible has helped see me through some of my very lowest times. I also read the book *Slaughterhouse-Five* when I was younger and the Serenity Prayer framed on the wall of Billy Pilgrim's office has stayed with me. For those unfamiliar with it:

'God grant me the serenity to accept the things I cannot change
Courage to change the things I can
And wisdom to know the difference'

One thing that has helped me in accepting many things is the belief that I chose my life. Before I was born, someone with a clipboard gave me all the possible configurations of my personality, my body, my life, my soul, and I chose this one. I could have had more hair but if I had then my bum would have been flatter. I could have chosen broader shoulders and a talent for sport but then I wouldn't have had a sibling and I'd have suffered with debilitating arachnophobia. I could have picked an easier ride with my mental health but I would have been less creative or more self-centred or have been born with the head of a pigeon. This comforted me when my father died; he chose a life that ended earlier than others but which was full of humour and family connection.

I know it's to do with feeling as if I'm in control and probably if you follow this premise too far down the rabbit hole it leads to something not so helpful. But it helps me put things into some kind of perspective and remember that there are parts of me – many parts of me – that are good, parts of my life that I wouldn't change for anything. That without all these aspects of myself and my experiences, the ugly included, I wouldn't be where I am now.

An award-winning playwright and poet, Toby Campion performs his poetry across the country.

Described by BBC *Sunday Politics* as 'the voice of a generation', Toby produces the UK National University Poetry Slam & Summit and his unapologetic words and wit have inspired audiences from Glastonbury to the Royal Albert Hall.

Erica Crompton

Picture this. It's the turn of the millennium and I've just graduated with a degree in journalism from London's prestigious University of the Arts. I'm renting a nice home in a leafy part of Dulwich, I'm in a stable, long-term relationship and have just embarked on my first graduate job, assisting an editor at London's *Evening Standard*.

On paper, it couldn't sound more promising. There's just one snag. A few years ago I was diagnosed with paranoid psychosis, and it's persisting. I am suffering with a fixed belief that I am Britain's most wanted criminal. It is what's known as a delusion associated with psychosis. I believe the police are spying on me through the TV, radio and computer and feel what I can only describe as 'pure terror' because of this. It feels difficult to talk to other people, even briefly, and leaving the house is hard. My strange and paranoid thoughts are driving friends away, putting a strain on my stable relationship and making it difficult to concentrate at work.

I'm twenty-five years old. I find some escapism by watching *Spooks*, a TV programme, at the end of each day. *Spooks* is a thrilling MI5 drama, also set in London, and I draw some reassurance from seeing those familiar streets on TV – and the drama isn't all in my head when I watch.

As I struggle through each day, my relationship is breaking down. My psychiatrist is now saying that I have a mild form of schizophrenia but my boyfriend doesn't believe me. He says he's not down with my psychiatrist's 'Latin-based bull!'

So, to escape all this I enjoy *Spooks* alone each evening while my partner is out with his friends. My favourite character is called Adam Carter, a London spy, and I find myself falling for him. I can remember at one point I longed for a real spy hero in my life so much it hurt. Adam Carter wasn't real, so, I googled the cast and discovered the actor who played him, this character I adored so much, was called Rupert Penry-Jones.

The more I watched the more my heart ached. I would never meet Rupert in real life – he was always behind my TV screen. As the days passed I still dreamt of Rupert but accepted I'd never meet him.

One night after the programme had finished, as I heard the footsteps of my partner coming home, a tear fell down my cheek. 'No matter what happens in life, you'll never meet Rupert,' I told myself. My life was slowly falling apart but I just had to get on with it.

A few days later, my services were no longer needed at the *Evening Standard* and I was back to working behind the bar of the local pub. 'You're a journalist?' the locals would ask, adding: 'So what you doing working here?'

As you'll know, London property is expensive, so to pay the rent I also took on a weekend job as an usher at the Unicorn Theatre. While it was a delightful, brand-new space where children can learn through plays – a wholesome endeavour if ever there was one – I was kind of down about it. Just weeks ago I had been having drinks with a top fashion editor after work and now I was training to sell ice creams. Hardly the high-flying journalist I had hoped to be when I graduated.

To make matters worse, I was still experiencing paranoia and was convinced the other staff didn't like me. When we spoke about our previous work experience, mine was only at a dodgy right-wing newspaper, certainly not one these young people would read. So I kept my head down and myself to myself.

Once we'd finished training, we prepared for the opening night. I felt like the odd one out; everyone seemed so excited but I felt glum about being at such a prestigious event selling ice cream in an usher's uniform. Nevertheless, I told myself that we all have to do things we don't want to do.

And so came the evening. There was a gang of press outside and lots of camera bulbs flashing. I remember wishing so hard that I was a proper journalist and not just an usher. But as the celebrities started to arrive, I got swept up in the atmosphere and felt my toes burn with excitement. Cherie and Tony Blair were there as patrons and Tony Blair even asked me directly for a theatre programme, which I bust a gut finding for him, feeling it was very important.

Then I took my position with my ice cream tray and watched on as the cameras flashed at the incoming celebrities. The theatre's auditorium was heaving by now. Off in the distance, I noticed a family of three walking towards the scene.

I instantly recognised the father. It was Rupert Penry-Jones! He was coming to the opening night as he had young children interested to see the play. I was terribly star-struck! After what I had told myself before about never actually seeing him I was astounded – here he was.

It pleases me to report that Rupert is every bit as gorgeous and regal in the flesh. He wore a dark suit with a slight gunmetal sheen and he looked impeccable. But it was also lovely to see him as a doting family man, with his three children and wife all looking equally flawless.

Happiness had been fleeting lately, but that night it came back! I was delighted to be there with my ice creams (strawberry, vanilla and chocolate chip). As everyone took their seats, I took my position outside, ready to sell my goods.

Then something even more amazing happened: Rupert popped out from the theatre and asked me where the gentleman's bathroom was. He sounded just like he does on TV and he even walked to the bathroom like a spy, almost edging along the wall as he went.

That evening was a light-bulb moment for me, much like the cameras at the event. That night helped take me from a pessimist to an optimist. Today, when I think nothing good will ever happen to me, I remind myself of Rupert. 'Anything can happen' is now my new mantra.

Now I'm careful of the things I tell myself and try to stay away from negative thinking. When I'm having a bad day, or thinking this or that is impossible, I remind myself of meeting Rupert.

Of how, when life was hard, I told myself, 'No matter what happens in life, you'll never meet Rupert.' But, I did, I did meet him.

I guess the moral of the story is – never say never. Always hope.

Erica Crompton is a freelance writer living in Staffordshire with her two adopted cats, Caspar and Winter. Her first book with Professor Stephen Lawrie, *The Beginner's Guide to Sanity, a self-help book for people with psychosis* was published in January 2020. She delivers talks nationwide on living with psychosis.

Jenni Regan

The changing point for me in my mental health journey was literally the beginning of a new life. Starting a family was a huge decision to make as I had become infertile due to the crushing loss of two children. Deciding to start a family when infertile and diagnosed with a severe and enduring mental health problem added many more complications.

Like many of us with bipolar disorder, it took me years to get a diagnosis. After all, it is only when we are experiencing a depressive episode that we feel we need medical attention. I can remember having extreme highs and devastating lows from my late teen years. When down, I would paint a smile on my face to get through the day and then lock myself away so few people knew of my mood. When up, I would be the friend and party animal everyone knew and loved.

When the diagnosis finally came, it wasn't a surprise. By that stage I knew enough about the illness and about myself to realise that a lot of my moods were just not 'normal'. In fact, many of them were typical of this illness.

There was the time I had four different jobs alongside my full-time university course or worse, five different businesses, each further and further from my skills set, which all dissolved as my mood crashed. The moment I got up in the Comedy Store in London and tried to heckle the comedians. The time I spent all night awake, staring at the full moon, thinking I was having some kind of epiphany, before going into work the next day, quitting my job, dumping my boyfriend and buying a ticket to fly to South Africa. The time I bought a year's membership to a posh kickboxing gym without even visiting it, after reading an article in a paper and just knowing that it would change my life. The debt, guilt and regret that came days, weeks or months after each decision.

Still, although getting a diagnosis is useful, it can also feel a little like a death sentence. We see bipolar disorder as a lifelong condition. Suddenly your path in life is not so straight. The first big decision after diagnosis was pregnancy. I read up as much as I could about the illness. I spoke to other women who had chosen never to conceive, because of fear of 'passing it on' to a child, and also because of the risks during pregnancy. I spoke to women who had become, in their words, 'completely batshit, climbing the walls crazy' after birth.

My only way of conceiving was through IVF, which came with the warning that hormones could disrupt my mood. I was lucky to have a fantastic fertility doctor the first time round who didn't blink an eyelid when I talked about my illness. People don't realise, but you have to make a lot of legal declarations to start IVF. You have to fill in a child welfare form (and tick THE mental health problem box) and they can refuse treatment if the clinic deem you to be unsuitable.

We were lucky, and I got pregnant during our first round of IVF. The threat of illness and of losing my child petrified me, but then the most amazing thing happened: I became normal. You don't know that you are not normal until you become so. As my pregnancy progressed, I felt happy for the first time in years. Not 'high' happy and not just 'not unhappy', the result of antidepressants which have dragged me up from a low mood. But pure, clear, sparkling joy. It was as though the world felt vibrant, but not technicolour. I had unlimited patience which replaced my agitation. Doing things, seeing people, made me just feel good.

People often think having bipolar disorder means your moods are constantly changing. This is true for some but for many of us, when our condition is managed, life may have its ups and downs but there is a whole chunk that is just flat. This is the time when I can live a relatively successful life, although the danger is always lurking. Have a bad day or a fantastic day and the anxiety around this day turning into an episode sits ever present.

Pregnancy suited me and I flourished. It is interesting to think about why this happened. Firstly, I was lucky enough to win the postcode lottery of fantastic perinatal psychiatric care. Almost immediately, I was referred to a doctor for an assessment. To my amazement, we had an appointment which lasted nearly an hour where she asked about every part of my life. My records before this had been made up of hastily scribbled notes from A&E after bad episodes, from Community Treatment teams and from various GPs I had seen over the years, some brilliant, some horrific. This doctor gave me a full report, pages' worth, that has been used ever since as my full record. The doctor also put me on to the most pregnancy-friendly medication. Other GPs and medical staff were horrified that I was taking a strong anti-psychotic drug and that the dosage was increased as I grew. But it is one of the biggest and most dangerous myths that women should stop all medication as soon as they get pregnant.

They also gave me my own midwife. In London this almost never happens, but as they assigned me to the purple 'high risk' team I got to see the same lovely woman each time. I felt a certain level of stigma having that purple sticker on my files, but as with my psychiatric care they gave me regular and consistent support. Any issues were nipped in the bud before they became a problem. We also spent so much time planning – for the birth, for the weeks after the birth. Practical stuff like ensuring I was getting enough sleep by allowing my husband to do some night feeds. All the planning meant I felt like I had a safety net if things did go wrong.

Hormones can mess you up but I also discovered they can make you feel great. As well as being flooded with all kinds of messages to prepare me for motherhood, pregnancy was a time when I really looked after myself. When you don't like yourself very much, self-care may remain just a concept. Self-harm doesn't always need to be about cutting. Many of us with mental health problems will self-medicate with drink, drugs, food, bad life choices. But suddenly, for me at least, having something else relying on my body made me start treating it like a temple. My diet was planned and perfectly balanced, I was taking gentle exercise every day, practising yoga twice a week, resting and napping whenever I wanted and having early nights. All the things we know will really help our mental health but can be hard to stick to in everyday life.

I gave birth to my daughter a few days before Christmas in 2013. It was an unplanned C-section. Then, the fear set in. All my planning and self-care suddenly felt useless as my child arrived and my hormones were all over the place. I had been in hospital for a few days before the birth and had been eating crap, not sleeping very well. The fear of postnatal illness hung heavily around my neck. The birth had well and truly broken my routine and as any parent will tell you, suddenly having a real-life baby to look after without a rule book is terrifying. The first night I didn't sleep. I was running on adrenaline and petrified of this tiny little thing. After major surgery it is hard to move and my child was in a cot next to me but I couldn't lift her, so every time she cried or needed a feed I had to ring my bell and bring out one of the two night nurses who were covering a full, packed ward. As the morning finally came, I felt wired and not knackered, a huge warning sign that things were about to take a turn for the worse.

To my amazement and relief they didn't. I realised I was just a new parent and not an ill one. My specialist care continued, doctors and midwives saw me in my home. Then I had to travel by bus to my first postnatal psychiatric appointment a couple of weeks later. It felt wrong initially having my child in the waiting room (more self-stigma), although I took my daughter along to most of my psychiatric appointments until she started school. I never want her to think my mental health is something to hide or be ashamed of.

After being discharged from my wonderful psychiatrist I found out once again the effect poor access to services can have on your mental health. For me this is such a key part of keeping well, of dealing with issues before they reach crisis point. I was unwell and off work for a couple of months in 2018, no real trigger, just a result of the yearly cycle and a thought that the medication I was on was no longer working for me. I had a fantastic GP but couldn't access psychiatric care. Eventually they gave me an appointment for six months after my initial episode.

I realised I needed help before this point and so I did something I thought I would never do. I went private. I found a doctor online and two days later I was in a room for an hour baring my soul. It was exactly like being back in perinatal care, having someone who didn't rush you, who wanted to know everything. This time I was paying for it but, like my pre-natal care, it was my turning point. My doctor was available anytime. I could call, text, email, make an appointment. My comfort blanket was back. The first thing she did was change my medication. I had always been on (and complained about) the one-size-fits-all meds. My complaints about feeling like a zombie had fallen on deaf ears because they had generally kept me well. She said immediately that an active young (?!) woman like myself shouldn't be spending my days feeling like a sloth. And guess what? A change in medication has given me such an increased quality of life. We also talk about the whole person; she is not just there to hand out pills. We talk about gut health, meditation, exercise. All those things I took on board when I was pregnant which had slowly dropped off my radar.

In reality, all mental health care should be like this, not just for those who can scrimp and save to access it. Or it should be like the fantastic care I got perinatally. But it's not. Awareness-raising has been such a huge movement over the last few years which is great. I am no longer ashamed about my mental health problems, whereas fifteen years ago I wouldn't even tick the mental health box when completing an application form to do a Mind trek (which my doctor wouldn't sign unless I ticked the damn box!). I am open and tell people on a need-to-know basis. Incredibly, living in my bubble I thought the stigma battle was over but I have faced discrimination in further attempts to have another child. The first being my fertility doctor who said he would stop my (very expensive) treatment in the middle of a cycle, unless I could get a psychiatrist to write to say that my bipolar disorder would not affect me becoming a parent, despite my already having a three-year-old. The second was when we went down the route of adoption to an agency who welcomed us with open arms until I mentioned my diagnosis. I was then told that they wouldn't be progressing with our application because of my condition. No medical, not even a home visit, just a big red cross next to my name. Thankfully we have since found a social worker who took my condition as just one aspect of us as a family and we are progressing, not that we won't be turned down in the future. Awareness is brilliant but during this time care, particularly crisis care, has been getting worse. There is no point in knowing you are unwell when you can't get the help you need.

And I am well; my new medication means that instead of my mood being completely flattened to keep me from becoming manic, I now hover just above, rather than below the flat line. I have been well and free from an episode for nearly ten months now, getting through three changes in season which usually trigger a meltdown. I hope that the care I now receive along with the self-care I know I need will keep me well for longer. I hope that I will never become unwell again but that is unrealistic, and so I keep updating my personal keeping-well plan which will come into place if, and probably when, I become unwell again. I have more energy and can do the things I need to do like running and yoga more easily.

For those people who think you cannot become a parent with a severe mental health problem I would really urge you to research, plan and talk to people before deciding. I know that my daughter is at a slightly higher risk of developing a mental health problem as there is a prevalence in families. You only have to look at mine to see this in action. Five sisters, two of us with bipolar disorder, one with schizophrenia, one dead (who had definite undiagnosed mental health issues) and one who has no official diagnosis but plenty of issues.

However, I also know that mental health problems are not inevitable – for most of us our issues were triggered somewhere along the line. I am casebook: a difficult childhood with a sexual assault in my late teens, trauma after trauma. I am working hard to ensure that my daughter has the best life I can give her. We have a very calm household where we talk rather than shout. I work flexible hours so I can spend time with her. She is showered with love and affection and we do a lot of creative and physical activity. I can't protect her from the big bad world and we encourage her to do things she fears. I am doing all I can to build her resilience, her coping mechanisms, and her support network, knowing that this will stand her in good stead as she progresses through life.

This is nothing compared to what she gives me. Being unwell can make you very insular and in the past I have focused too much on what is in my head. Having a child forces you to think of someone else. I still have the actual joy and happiness I rediscovered during pregnancy, it's not as vivid but it is real and still there. And she forces me to look into the future, in a way I was never able or willing to do before. She is not a magic cure, nor is she a sticking plaster, but I remain so thankful for the fact I made that decision, even with the odds stacked against me. Becoming a mother was literally the best thing that ever happened to me.

Jenni Regan worked as a BBC broadcast journalist before moving to the charity sector. She set up the Media Engagement Service at Mind through the Time to Change Campaign, speaking nationally and internationally about the impact of the media on mental health from stigmatising headlines to unrealistic dramatic storylines.

Jenni is an expert by experience having lived with severe mental health problems for over twenty years. She is currently CEO at the charity London Arts and Health and is an expert advisor for the Wellcome Trust, sitting on their Psychosis Innovations Board, and leads the media work for the charity Action on Postpartum Psychosis.

Kathryn Grant

It's hard for me to define recovery. I cannot pinpoint a single 'Eureka!' moment or a time when I could safely say, 'It's over.' Clearly, there are milestones – reducing the dose of Olanzapine, increasing the length of time between observations, going for a walk around the hospital grounds, getting back in touch with old friends, that sort of thing. But one thing that stands out is not a particular achievement as such, but a feeling. And if I had to describe it, I would say it was the feeling of safety I got as I sat in the front passenger seat of our car, being driven home from the hospital for an extended period of leave.

The leave had been planned for a while. I knew how important everyone deemed it to be. My newborn baby and I had been in-patients at the Mother and Baby Unit for many weeks now and according to perceived wisdom it was high time we were discharged home. I had been very ill – floridly psychotic – but was responding well to treatment. At the time, the main issue I had was overwhelming anxiety and a deep sense of shame. In my opinion, that one emotion (shame) is responsible for untold suffering and certainly a great deal of mental illness.*

Anyway, back to that car journey. Going anywhere with a young baby takes some effort. The fact that I had gotten up, gotten dressed, packed a bag and gotten the baby into his car seat was quite some feat (prior to this, the most I had been expected to do was to get up and dressed and perhaps drag myself to the ward's nursery room and sit among the babies for a time). So the day was already full of accomplishments, even before we had set off. I'm not sure what was propelling me. I was still scared stiff of the baby, afraid to be his mother, happiest to let the nursing staff take charge and tell me what to do. I was even more scared of what world lay beyond the hospital grounds: an alien world full of business, jobs, responsibilities, social events, friends and families all getting on with their busy lives. Life beyond the hospital filled me with terror, and yet I had no choice but to try. I knew I owed it to my little family, to give it a go.

I got in the passenger side and sank into the seat. The baby was safely clicked into place behind me, oblivious to the journey we were embarking on. As Tom got into the driver's seat and started the car, I felt my whole body relax. Rather than become more tense as we drove out of the sprawling hospital grounds, being in that car felt so right, so safe, that I relaxed. For possibly the first time in three months, my body seemed to switch off. I breathed in the smell of the car interior and smiled to myself. The sensation of feeling safe, at ease, felt so strange that to begin with I just marvelled at its novelty. But after a few minutes, as I breathed deeply into my belly and flicked through the radio stations, I smiled at Tom. And then I turned around and smiled at our son. We were going home.

*A Note about Shame

I could probably write a whole book about shame and the damage it can inflict (although perhaps that has already been covered by the wonderful Brené Brown). Suffice to say, when we are brought up to succeed in life, to get good grades, do well at school, be a good girl, get a good job, find a good husband, do well 'for ourselves', we are creating an ever-greater distance from which to fall. That distance, between our conditioned childhood expectations and what our 'true self' actually wants to do in life, is the potential shame gap. I've learned through the experience of psychosis (which I wouldn't wish upon my worst enemy) how dangerous and hurtful these expectations can be. The shame that occurs when one's reality departs so drastically from what we were brought up to expect for ourselves causes untold fear, sadness, disappointment, embarrassment and distress. If we are lucky then we can close the gap and reduce the chance of us experiencing a catastrophic fall from grace. If we are not so lucky then perhaps a fall is inevitable. But I hope that, in future, all kids will learn from a young age that it is not just ok to 'be yourself' – it is imperative.

Kathryn Grant was an economist and management consultant when her life was turned upside-down by post-partum psychosis following the birth of her son in 2012. Now recovered, she devotes her free time to raising awareness of maternal mental illness, campaigning for improved services, and providing peer support. She is also a Mental Health First Aid instructor and a crisis volunteer for the text messenger service Shout 85258.

Ayla Lyn Jones
Be Kind to Yourself, Always

Although I was fortunate enough to be brought up in a loving family, I have always found accepting change very difficult. Change was just too challenging for my little, developing mind to be able to process. Whilst trying to adapt and adjust to new circumstances, I would experience trauma and grief.

Before I knew it, I was a twelve-year-old girl, feeling like I had no control over my life. So I clung on to the only sense of control I could find. Little did I know that what seemed initially like a safety blanket would soon become the trap of a vicious eating disorder.

These unhealthy coping mechanisms quickly spiralled until I was just existing in a world that I did not understand, and quite frankly did not want to be in. I received ongoing treatment and support, and was put on medication; however, I wasn't always compliant. Things seemed to worsen, instead of improving.

As the years went by, I became more withdrawn and detached from the outside world. I started losing myself and who I was as a person. My mental state continued to deteriorate, and by the time I was fifteen I'd experienced my first psychotic episode and been detained and sectioned under the Mental Health Act. I was in an ongoing battle with my mind by now and had completely lost touch with reality. Although I had periods of wellbeing, I never fully recovered from my symptoms. Despite being highly medicated, and trying out different medications, over the next few years I continued to experience serious episodes, never making a full recovery. After many re-admissions and referrals, I was diagnosed with schizo-affective disorder – bipolar type.

The most challenging part of it all was accepting that my *reality* wasn't really *real* at all.

But there came a point when I knew that, instead of letting the fear continue to break me, I had to break free from it. Through the highs and the lows (quite literally), I now know that no matter how tough life may get and how challenging it may be, I will never lose hope in my heart. I will never lose myself again. And whilst I'm still on this whirlwind of a journey, I am learning to listen and to put my trust into my heart and soul, instead of trusting the things my mind tells me.

The world we live in can be so fast-paced and it can be extremely difficult to process everything that's going on. However, that doesn't mean we have to move in just as fast-paced a way. Know that its ok to slow down, to take a moment, and to breathe. Even if it means you have to put things on pause for a little while, it doesn't mean it's an end. Often, it can actually be the beginning of something amazing . . . maybe something you never expected . . . or something you never imagined would be possible. What may feel like an ending, can be the start of an incredible journey.

For a very long time, the world seemed to be an overwhelming and scary place to me, one that I existed in alone. Now, coming to the end of my teenage years, I feel I am actually living my life. Even though it might not be quite as I imagined it would be, it is far greater than the life my own mind once led me to believe wasn't worth living at all.

Through the challenges came the understanding and self-awareness that have enabled me to flourish and grow. I have gained a sense of self and am finding out who I am as a person, what dreams and hopes I have, and who I hope to be. I have hope for the future, and an even greater hope and passion that I can shed some light and hope to others.

No one deserves to battle with their own minds, on top of the general stresses that day-to-day life can bring. Which is why it's so important to be gentle with yourself. In a world where, sadly, not everyone shares love and kindness, it's important to know that you deserve to receive it. So, be kind to yourself, always. It is far more important to find self-acceptance from within, than to keep searching for acceptance from others.

Born in 2001, Ayla Lyn Jones lives in a small town in South Wales. She is currently studying health and social care at college, and hopes to become a mental health nurse in the near future.

Nicola Thorp

I find that when I go through really difficult times, especially with my BPD (Borderline Personality Disorder) and depression, there is actually nothing I can do. So when I feel that there is no hope, in order to survive I sit tight and wait for it to pass, almost shutting down, just resting, not pushing myself too hard.

There is so much pressure these days to cut out the negative and concentrate on the positive, and that was actually what got me down. My philosophy is that you *should* look at the negatives because life is full of them. It's only when we acknowledge the negatives that we can also recognise the positives and build resilience. Otherwise we go through life in an 'ignorance is bliss' kind of state and then when something happens we don't know how to cope. We don't have to be this positive, happy person all the time. I used to think that feeling that way about negativity might be part of my condition, but when I spoke to 'normal' people, ie people without a mental health diagnosis, I realised that they feel like that too, it's all just part of the human condition. And that gives you hope, right?

My goal has been to reduce the amount of time that I'm affected by things. For instance, the ending of a relationship has always had a huge impact on me because of my BPD and fear of abandonment. My identity would get so wrapped up with those closest to me that when relationships ended it would feel like the end of my life. I could never understand how other people could come out of relationships feeling sad but not as though it was the end of their world. But then I figured that because I mourned so deeply, it meant that I got over it more quickly – I allowed myself to feel things as deeply as I could in order to almost quicken up the process a bit and get back to normal. It's about striking a balance between what's right for you, and what's healthy, and what you need to be able to function. Being able to do this, and having the courage to face the pain, is something I've built up over the years.

When I was admitted to hospital in 2012 I was twenty-three, and it was seven more years before I got the correct diagnosis. Initially my BPD was misdiagnosed as bipolar disorder, which meant that I was put on the wrong medication (anti-psychotics) and completely lost my sense of self. Things finally fell into place when I got the correct diagnosis. It was a massive relief – when you don't know what is wrong with you, it's difficult to treat, almost like treating a broken arm when you actually have a broken leg.

I started reading everything I could find about BPD, and it was such a revelation. This was the world I was living in! You know the film *Tarzan*? Tarzan grows up with all the gorillas and doesn't know any different, but wonders all his life why he doesn't quite fit in, until he meets Jane, and it all becomes clear. Me getting the BPD diagnosis was almost like Tarzan meeting Jane. Things finally made sense. This was why I'd been feeling the way I did and why I had these thoughts and behaviour patterns I couldn't even articulate. I just needed to be understood, and to understand myself.

I'm very fortunate that my parents are so supportive, but like many parents in the 90s, they didn't have the best understanding of mental health issues. When we were kids it was very much, 'Oh, if you're upset about something, there is always someone else worse off.' What was interesting was that going through my journey, and my illness and admissions to hospital, was a kind of education for them. They are the most empathetic and compassionate people, but this was a world they didn't understand. Now I've been able to help them when they've shown signs of depression or grief, such as when my dad lost his dad and when he struggled with his own mortality after a heart attack. We were able to talk openly about his emotions. The most amazing thing to come out of all this is the bond I have developed with my parents.

It's not lost on me that somebody like me with BPD was drawn towards acting. Luckily, I like high-pressured environments. I do a lot of live TV and radio broadcasting, and as much as it stresses me out, I thrive on it. It's like living on the edge. An adrenaline rush.

It's hard to imagine hope when you feel hopeless, but once you're at the bottom, there's only one direction you can go in. It can only get better. I find comfort in that.

Nicola Thorp is an English actress, best known for her portrayal of Nicola Rubinstein in *Coronation Street*. She regularly discusses a variety of topics on *This Morning* and writes a column for *Metro*.

Anna Williamson

Until I was diagnosed with GAD (General Anxiety Disorder) and panic disorder, I hadn't got a clue what mental health really meant, let alone what mental illness was like. At that time, a constant feeling of dread and fear followed me around each day, like a black cloud. My relationship was toxic and my job was high profile and pressured, but I was a master at plastering on a smiley face and pretending all was 'fine'. But as I found out, these things catch up with you. I just wish I had had the awareness to recognise that what I was feeling was actually perfectly understandable, and crucially, treatable. I wish I'd known how to ask for help.

In the end I had no choice as months of struggling caught up with me in a rather unflattering mental breakdown at work. When I did finally ask for help, I found that sympathy, empathy, and love were available from all corners of my life. When I finally admitted I wasn't coping and that these horrible feelings – both physical and mental – were causing me such distress, it was like a beacon of hope had appeared.

One of the best pieces of advice I have received is not to think of mental illness as being 'cured', because that simply places a pressure on oneself to be well all the time – and that is not realistic. Life can be very complicated at times, with all kinds of variables popping up at a moment's notice, threatening to throw you off balance. But just going with the flow and agreeing to tackle and navigate life as it comes gives me confidence that the rest of my life can be as happy, healthy and content as it is now. When I have a blip, which does happen, I just take a step back, use the coping strategies that I know work for me, and remind myself that brighter days will come again.

If I could talk to my younger self, I would be so much kinder to her now than I was then. I'd reassure her that life has many ups and downs, twists and turns, but they are a valuable part of our make-up. I always say that the best thing that ever happened to me was having a breakdown and being diagnosed with a mental health disorder. I understand that's a controversial thing to say, but it made me learn about myself, understand who I am, and what I do and don't need in life to make me happy. I would tell myself never to compare myself to anyone else. We are all beautifully different bespoke human beings, each with something fabulous and unique to offer the world.

I cannot stress enough how essential my family and friends were to my recovery. Trying to understand and support someone with a mental health problem is difficult for any loved one, and it is so much harder to empathise when that person is struggling with something you can't physically see, but my family were there 100 per cent. They didn't judge me, they didn't push me, they were just there with open arms, willing to listen and help. Their support was, and is, vital to me. They know me and can helpfully point out when things are threatening to unravel and I need to take a pause. Family and friends really are most important to me, and I'm truly blessed to have the very best.

I can honestly say that after months and months and months of struggling in silence, not daring to utter a word to anybody about what was going on in my head for fear of being judged or labelled crazy, the moment I stopped pretending and instead said that all-important word 'help' – everything changed for the better. They say you have to reach rock bottom to start the uphill climb, and that was certainly true for me. It wasn't much fun grappling around at the bottom, but it was essential. I had to allow myself a good rest, to acknowledge all the horrible, debilitating thoughts and feelings that were there, to start to understand what was going on for me, to learn ways to manage myself better, to get myself back on the right path . . . a path from which I have never looked back. Of course, since then there have been tough times. And there will be challenging times ahead. But knowing that when I ask for help it will come gives me all the hope I need.

Anna Williamson is a TV and radio broadcaster, author, counsellor, life coach and Master NLP practitioner. She is the dating expert on *Celebs Go Dating* and *Big Brother's Bit on the Side*, amongst other TV appearances. She is also the presenter for *National Lottery Xtra*. She is author of *Breaking Mad*, *Breaking Mum and Dad* and, most recently, *How Not To Lose It: Mental Health Sorted*, a guide to empower children and support strong emotional wellbeing.

PEACE

Zoe Sugg
Dig out the Root

Growing up I was a particularly anxious child. Always the one hold-ing back, clinging to my parents if they were there, not putting up my hand in class for fear of answering something wrong. Sleepovers were something I rarely joined in on.

Between the ages of fourteen to early twenties, my mind was ruled and riddled every single day by anxiety. Thoughts that com-pletely took over even the smallest of things I did. I would always find myself exhausted by 6pm because my mind had been racing at 100mph all day.

When manoeuvring my life as a young adult, I found these emo-tions and feelings particularly hard to navigate. You start your career, make new friends, attend meetings, move out and start your journey into 'adulthood'. This is already a seemingly tricky time to navigate, let alone when you're sitting in meetings wishing you could run outside just to feel as though you aren't suffocating any-more, or stay home instead of get ready for work because the thought of being in your job when you can't keep your anxiety under wraps is terrifying.

I first googled anxiety when I was around eighteen years old. I was fed up of having to rush home on nights out with my friends and was so confused by these feelings I couldn't explain. Nobody around me seemed to feel the same way and it felt so daunting. I was met by a few websites explaining how your body reacts phys-ically with anxiety and panic attacks and I remember mentally ticking off every single symptom yet feeling a sigh of relief that I finally knew what was happening to me. Like many, I thought just knowing I was having panic attacks would simply 'make them go away', or 'I've had a great week, so maybe they will eventually just die down or stop altogether by the time I'm X age?' The reality is not quite so simple. You can do the research, speak with others who also have anxiety and panic attacks and feel a sense of reassurance, but that doesn't mean they just dissipate.

I started speaking with a therapist weekly at the age of twenty-four and it was the best decision I ever made. Understanding the way my mind works, why I feel anxious and ways in which I can re-train my mind not to think in the way it does in certain situations is my biggest personal accomplishment.

If I could go back and speak with eighteen-year-old Zoe, I would tell her that in the future she will live a life where her thoughts aren't just anxiety-fuelled ones 80 per cent of the day. That sometimes, her mind will actually be bored and empty in situations where she thinks it never will. That she will ace that meeting and find success even though it might feel impossible. That she is not defined by anxiety and although sometimes she feels anxious, she isn't 'anxiety personified'. I'd also tell her to speak with a professional much sooner. When you've suffered with your anxious thoughts most of your life, it will take time and dedication to undo that. It might seem hard, or long and laborious at times, but now I am able to do things I never thought I'd be doing, and my mind is (mostly) quiet whilst I do them.

If you are reading this and you are having one of those moments where it just feels like the life you want to live is so far from the reality, just know that it isn't. Change can happen! The analogy that really helped me was imagining your anxiety like a weed growing freely in the ground. You can snap it off quite quickly and easily, but if you take the time to dig out the root, it will never grow back. There will always be remnants of where the weed once grew, but it will never be able to grow in the same way.

Zoe Sugg, founder of the brand Zoella, is an entrepreneur, content creator, author and a charity ambassador. Her positive, down to earth personality and engaging style of content has resulted in Zoe becoming the UK's most subscribed to female creator on YouTube. Zoe has published four *Sunday Times* best-selling books with a fifth in the works, launched multiple global brands and collaborations as well as two successful apps. Zoe has also been an ambassador for the mental health charity Mind for many years.

Oliver Kent

Towards the autumn of 2018 I experienced a crippling period of anxiety, depression and insomnia, which was made worse by the stressful job I had at the time. I realise now that the symptoms had been creeping up on me for a long time, but I hadn't noticed.

I'd always thought of myself as reasonably self-aware. I knew that I was susceptible to periods of depression, having experienced them occasionally since I was a teenager. In my final year of university, I saw a psychiatrist during a very difficult period. He taught me the value of self-care – advice which I have taken ever since. I knew the importance of exercise, eating well, not drinking too much alcohol, and arranging some therapy in the times when I needed it.

I thought I was in control of my mental health. I was wrong. Somehow I didn't notice my growing anxiety, which crept up on me gradually over a long period of time when I was too busy to take stock of it. My job was busy and I was responsible for the welfare of a lot of people. I felt that it was important to be strong, reliable and dependable. I thought that stress came as part of the package and was just something I had to get used to. To admit to feeling under strain felt like admitting to weakness and I didn't want to let my teams down. And so I unconsciously allowed my symptoms to worsen day by day, until something clicked and I was forced to confront the problem.

It turns out that anxiety is depression's noisy cousin. By this point I rarely slept more than a few hours at a time at night. When I did sleep, I suffered from nightmares and night sweats. Panic attacks were so frequent that they were almost constant and could strike at any time. I had a permanent sense of dread and a physical feeling of nausea most of the time. I often felt like I was screaming inside my own head. On one occasion a colleague asked me if it was raining outside. It wasn't – I was just so anxious that my face was covered with sweat. I used to take a spare shirt to work in case I sweated through the one I was wearing. I carried an electric fan around with me all the time, even in winter. There were some buildings and places that I found it difficult to enter or even walk past. All these things had become normal to me. It was when I had a particularly public panic attack at work that I finally realised I needed to do something. What I had written off as work stress had clearly become something bigger.

Acknowledging that I had a problem was the hardest, but most significant, step towards recovery.

I arranged to go and see my GP. I took a very deep breath and admitted what had been going on. I'm English and I'm a bloke – we don't admit our feelings easily, do we? The words 'I think I might have a problem with anxiety' were not easy to say, but I'm very glad I did.

Over several regular sessions my GP carefully helped me to see that my anxiety was severe and that I needed to take care of myself and get some treatment in order to get it under control. He advised me that if I needed to, I should take time off work to recover; advice which I tried to ignore for as long as possible. He helped me to come to terms with the fact that I was ill. It was hard to take this on board (I still find it hard to say 'ill', preferring to say 'unwell' – no idea why!). However, I came to accept his diagnosis of Generalised Anxiety Disorder and began to realise how long my condition had been building up.

Once I'd accepted that I was ill, things started very slowly to improve. I was extremely lucky, it didn't take my GP long to get me to the right combination of medication and he also found me a very good psychotherapist who I see weekly. I also keep in touch with my GP by email and see him about every six weeks, or more often if I need to.

In my recovery there are ups and downs and some weeks are better than others. No two people's experience of anxiety and recovery will be the same. But the good news is that I am getting much better. Talking about it has been, and continues to be, a surprisingly massive relief and I've been gobsmacked to discover how many people I know have struggles with their mental health. It helps to know I'm not alone.

I've had some excellent advice and support from friends, family, my therapist, my GP and my husband. I was lucky. Going through a health problem really helps you realise who your friends are. I was less lucky with my employers, who terminated my contract with no notice six weeks after I disclosed to them that I had a problem with anxiety.

I'd like to end with the three best pieces of advice I've had:

1. Be kind to yourself. It's not your fault that you're ill. You won't help your recovery if you give yourself a hard time.
2. Be patient. It will have taken a while to become ill and it can take just as long to get better. You won't recover overnight but you will get better.
3. It's ok to not be ok. It doesn't mean you're weak or a bad person. Admitting you're unwell is a sign of strength, not weakness.

If I had to choose one of these as the most important rule of all, it would be: don't give yourself a hard time. It's a hard habit to break for most of us and it takes practice, but you really can do it if you try.

Oliver Kent is a BAFTA-award winning television producer and has produced several of the UK's favourite dramas, including *Holby City*, *Casualty* and *EastEnders*. He worked for the BBC from 1998 until 2019 and was Head of Continuing Drama Series from 2016 to 2019.

Gail Porter

I'm not entirely sure when I noticed I was a bit different, anxious, self-loathing.

I got on well at school, was quite popular, but I was always worrying about something or someone. If my dad told me off at home, I would wait until I was alone, head to the freezer and grab a tub of ice cream and eat it in my room. I was a normal-sized teen, but stress would make me eat. Feeling useless, I would eat; my dad calling me piggy, I'd eat; ex-boyfriend cheating on me and calling me fat, I would eat.

Then, when I went to college, it was really easy to stop eating as I was skint. The thinner I got, the more approval I felt I got. I feel like I have lived my life looking for approval.

Anorexia kicked in. All a control issue. If I controlled my food, I could control my life. Of course that was nonsense. When I started to feel like my anorexia wasn't helping, cutting myself became a thing for me. I could hide my lack of food intake by turning up late for dinners, wearing a baggy top. or saying I had just eaten.

Cutting, I used make up or cut myself anywhere that no one would see.

My moods have always been manic. High as a kite or lock myself in a room in bed for days.

No in-between. Ever.

My life has been a series of ups and downs. working, not working. bankrupt, alopecia, homelessness.

Going from doctor to doctor. Medication after medication.

Self-medicating, rehabs, being sectioned.

Wanting to give up.

But I didn't. Obviously, as I am writing this now.

The reason I didn't kill myself was due to my daughter. If I didn't have her, I don't think I would be writing this today. I decided to take life on and be positive and make some changes. I stopped taking medication (which is not recommended, so please talk to your doctor before doing anything similar). I did it on a whim and luckily it worked for me.

When I was sleeping on people's sofas at the age of forty-five, I applied for every job going. I kept a diary. I took up running.

I got a job which wasn't ideal, but it was enough cash for me to get a rented flat. Reality series, but I couldn't seem to get anything else – a bald woman with a history of mental health issues – but I bit the bullet and did the job. I was still anxious and insecure but I survived.

I still get anxious now and insecure but I'm still surviving. I do talks across the country, helping people who are going through issues similar to those I have had. Issues we all have had. We are not on our own. Ever. You would be surprised how many people say 'Me too' when I do talks. But they were too afraid to share.

I had a documentary out in January 2020 called *Being Gail Porter* for the BBC. It was extremely hard to make as I had to cover a lot of ground about my mental health that I didn't want to confront. But I did it and the response was wonderful and it seemed to resonate with so many people.

If I can do my little bit to help, I've done a good thing.

There is always someone to talk to.

You are never alone.

And I am sending you Love and Hope.

Gail Porter is a Scottish television presenter, television personality, former model and actress. She started her television career in children's TV, before branching out into modelling and presenting mainstream TV. In the 1990s she posed nude for FHM, an image that was projected onto the Houses of Parliament.

Her memoir *Laid Bare: My Story of Love, Fame and Survival* was published by Ebury Press in 2007.

Rylan Clark-Neal
The Importance of Being You

In many ways, being on *The X Factor* meant that my first exposure to 'fame' was a tough one. At the time I used to joke that there were two people always on the front pages of the newspapers – Jimmy Savile and me.

One day we were at the judges' houses and the next we were catapulted into the limelight. And then I started receiving death threats on social media, which was incredibly worrying. Luckily, I was sharing a hotel room in Charing Cross with James Arthur by then, which helped me feel a bit safer. James and I used to smoke on the inward-facing hotel balcony, so we couldn't be seen from the street. One day I received a tweet saying, 'I can see you on your balcony.' From then on we had 24-hour security, but when the live shows started this threat was still playing on my mind. On top of that I continued to be on the front pages, and it all got too much for me. I wanted to quit the show there and then, but the producers explained that it wasn't that easy, so I stayed on.

Later that week I got my new song, and when I left the hotel there were about a hundred people waiting to get a photo. Suddenly this guy put his phone in my face to take a selfie with me and I realised he was the one who'd been sending me the threatening messages. That was when it clicked, 'It's all a fucking game.' So I started playing the game too. It was a defining moment: none of it was real, although people wouldn't admit that to your face.

I felt stronger after *The X Factor* ended. By the time I went on *Celebrity Big Brother* I'd learned to play along with it.

More recently, I left *This Morning* after a long stint to focus on my mental health. People think it's an easy job, but my days were incredibly long: getting up at 5.30am, going live on air at 10.30am, plus all the meetings and other TV commitments. I would only get about three hours' sleep. It is important to take time off when you need it. In fact, I've learned that the less available you are, the more people want you. You're not just a product.

It was Katie Price who helped me in the beginning. I realised that she had a persona, but in reality she was Katie, not Jordan. Recognising the difference between the two is important: at home I'm Ross (my real name), and I try to balance the real me with the persona.

I wish people were a little more honest. I know how lucky I am, but I've worked for it and where I am now is not where I came from. I'm also lucky to be living in a nice place with plenty of outdoor space. During the pandemic this has meant that I've been able to record my radio show from home. People take the piss that I'm always at work! But I'm fortunate to be able to take the time to stop and breathe – in fact, that's exactly what I did when I left *This Morning*.

I learned early on that fame and money don't really matter. You just have to look at what happened to my close friend Caroline Flack. I never thought she'd take her own life; I still can't believe it, to be honest. You just never know what goes on in someone's head – no matter how successful or wealthy they are.

Hopefully at the end of all this people will be nicer to each other.

Rylan Clark-Neal is an English singer, television presenter, narrator and model. After finishing in fifth place on *The X Factor*, he went on to win *Celebrity Big Brother 11*. Later that year, he presented *Big Brother's Bit on the Side*, *This Morning* and *The Xtra Factor*. He is also the host of the revived editions of *Supermarket Sweep* and *Ready Steady Cook*, as well as presenting the BBC's *You Are What You Wear*.

Dan Schawbel
My Anxious Journey

When I was growing up, no one ever talked about mental health, let alone anxiety. In elementary school, I was on the principal's bench every single day because I couldn't sit down for a second. Back then, I was regularly bullied because my anxious behaviour was seen as weakness so I was an easy target to get picked on. At home my parents would tell me that I was special and 'the best', yet I would go to school and get shoved in a locker by my classmate, placed in a closet by my teacher and made fun of by my so-called friends. I remember one night in bed, crying into my pillow, saying, 'I'll never fit in.' But instead of staying with that negative self-talk and going down a dark path towards depression, I followed up by saying, 'Maybe I don't fit in because I'm special and someday I'll do something great.' It was in this moment that I felt the sense of hope and optimism that allowed me to mentally and emotionally continue my life.

During college, my friends would always tell me to 'calm down', the same phrase that I would repeat to my mom occasionally when she was being neurotic and loud. While my relationship with anxiety at this point was mostly negative, it did start manifesting in a positive way without me realising, through my work ethic. Since college was so unbelievably expensive, I felt like I had to maximise everything, including grades, social events, organisations and internships. I even started a business doing web design for local companies. Looking back, my anxiety was driving me to work harder out of a desperate need for validation. Once I got a job, I still had this enormous urge to prove myself to combat all the bullying I grew up with. I unknowingly channeled my anxiety to keep driving myself forward and I spent my twenties feeling validated through countless achievements.

It wasn't until my thirties that I asked the scary questions, 'Who am I?' and 'Why am I like this?' These questions were unsettling because to find out the answers I had to both search deep inside myself and open up to others. What I found was that I had suffered from anxiety my entire life without knowing what it was. One day, I sat down with my mom at my parents' apartment and she confirmed my suspicions. She said that there hadn't been a thing called 'mental health' or 'anxiety' when she was younger, but she had been on pills in order to cope, and that her father had had it worse than both of us. Anxiety had caused him to work almost all the time, to the point where he would come home from work and throw up. While that wasn't the case for me, it confirmed that I had inherited my anxiety. After this discussion I went to my doctor to see if pills might work for me, like they had for my mom.

I remember walking around New York City's East Village debating whether I should take the pills or not. I ended up deciding against it, partly out of fear of the potential side effects but also out of an acceptance of who I was. That day my entire life flashed before my eyes and I could make sense of my behaviour, childhood, relationships and career. The word 'anxiety' explained my life. But I didn't want it to completely define who I was.

Being a public figure always stopped me from being open about my anxiety. That was until June 10th, 2018 when I finally had the courage to share what I was going through with the world. My friend Bill challenged me to speak openly about my problems to help remove the stigma around it. He pointed out that it wasn't authentic to post positive messages about mental health without sharing my own story. The night before I posted, I was sick to my stomach and almost didn't go through with it. My mom had always said not to tell people too much so I had grown up being very secretive and emotionally closed off.

Nevertheless, the next morning I woke up and posted a picture of me as a kid on Instagram, with a paragraph summarising how I deal with my anxiety. I explained how anxiety is both a superpower and kryptonite rolled into one – it pushes you to accomplish a lot but can also prevent you from being at peace. It's like a tug-of-war going on in your brain, where you feel like you need to do a lot, but also realise that you don't need to. After sharing, I felt liberated, as if a heavy weight had been lifted from my shoulders. I could breathe more easily. Almost immediately, I got 140 comments from people who also suffered from anxiety and who appreciated my vulnerability. From that point on, I was open to talking about my anxiety publicly. Thankfully, the stigma around mental health is starting to fade, which gave me more confidence. Today, I'm talking about mental health on big stages with large audiences using my life as a way to remove the stigma and empower people to accept who they are, and to channel their anxiety towards something good.

The two biggest things I've learned through my anxious journey are self-acceptance and vulnerability. The more you understand and own who you are, the better the decisions you'll make. And, when you open up to others about your shortcomings, you give them permission to do the same. People open up in return. You've been dealt this hand and you have to do the best you can with it, knowing that there will be struggles along the way. But, you're not alone and if other people who suffer can have a great life, so can you.

Dan Schawbel is an entrepreneur, speaker and expert on the future of work. Throughout his career he's worked with major brands including American Express, GE, Microsoft, Virgin, IBM, Coca Cola and Oracle. He is the author of three career books: *Back to Human, Promote Yourself* and *Me 2.0*. Schawbel is also the host of the *5 Questions* podcast, where he interviews world-class humans.

Matthew Kynaston

I had to find a way to fix it.

The paralysis and constant panging ebb of anxiety that would keep me sitting on benches, scrolling through my phone, or staring blankly at products in supermarket aisles for hours. Mind drowned in regret, obsessing over memories of *her*, of what I had, of what I had thrown away. Deafened by a constant, droning chatter.

I was in Melbourne, 10,500 miles from my home in the UK, living in a backpacker hostel where I worked for accommodation. I was trying to find some kind of paid work that would help change my circumstances. It was there I found Maya.

She walked into the busy hostel common room wearing worn-down trainers, a sports vest and shorts covering her small frame. She was loud. She circulated the room with her booming American accent, quizzing everyone on why they had missed out on the 'soccer'. I clocked her immediately. I noticed she had a limp, but it was clearly not severe enough to hold her back as sports and social rep. She was pumped, and everyone knew who she was.

The work-for-accommodation community at the hostel was relatively small. We all shared the same filthy dorm on the ground floor, next to the common room, so it wasn't long before we crossed paths and started talking.

'So, what's your story?' she asked.

In backpacker hostels, your story, your purpose, is very much part of the social currency. By the time I had met Maya, asking the predictable 'Where are you from?' 'Where have you been?' 'Where do you hope to go next?' had become a bit of a joke. And these were questions I no longer wanted to answer.

I didn't want Maya to know how my year had fallen apart. How

I had lost all my money, my passport and my mind aboard a deep-sea prawn-trawler. Or how the grief of sacrificing my relationship for a failed 'gap year' hung heavy on my head. How a 'friend' had recently evicted me from their sofa, my last home, and how I had then decided on, planned and subsequently failed, my suicide. I only wanted one person to ever know all of this and that was the nurse I had confided in just two days ago, before I was discharged from the psychiatric ward, and had come to this place.

Despite my efforts to skirt around the answers, playing up the best parts of my journey, deflecting questions and pulling my cheeks into a tight grin, I wasn't fooling Maya.

'Oh, you're really sad, aren't you?'

I was disarmed, gutted. Tears began to fill my eyes and I was paralysed again, unable to answer. She took my arm and led me out of the hostel to walk around and get some air.

Over the next few days, Maya went from being a stranger to the only person who really knew me. My family, back in the UK, had only the snippets of information that I would allow them about my progress. Who I had been when I left was drastically different to who I was now.

Maya accommodated my grief, at least as much of it as I was able to share. All that I told her at first was that I was 'missing my ex', 'my heart was broken', that I'd had a tough time doing some 'regional work' and that I was desperately low on money. My self-confidence and energy diminished, I wasn't getting offered any of the jobs I was interviewing for. I had started shoplifting my meals and jumping the barriers at train and tram stations. I began to imagine myself sitting down at the side of the road and begging for change.

Having someone there to listen, to understand, to report back to, was enough to keep me doing what I needed to do. Changing bed-sheets during my daily shift at the hostel was easier when I could laugh about the stains with someone at the end of the day.

A few weeks later, I was offered a decently paid job as a travel rep. But the opening was in Perth, over 2,000 miles away. This presented a dilemma for me; although my life was miserable in Melbourne, it was kind of like my home, and having been there for a month I had started to get to know people who I wasn't ready to leave, especially Maya.

'I'll go!' she said, 'Sure, I hadn't planned on going but I've got no reason to stay here.'

I had an old school friend, Hannah, who was living in Perth. She offered to put us up at least until I got on my feet. That, and Maya's support, meant that I had all I needed to make a fresh start.

We joined a cheap trip in a relocation van with several other broke backpackers. We drove for seven days, straight across the country, through the outback and the famous Nullarbor national park, the rabbit proof fence, and on into Western Australia.

Eventually we made it to Hannah's in the south of Perth. She had a spare room for me and Maya. We shared a bed and agreed that our friendship was to remain platonic. Emotionally, I felt I needed Maya and I was way too vulnerable to let sex complicate our friendship. And I still wasn't over *her*. Maya found work in a theme park, and we started our new lives.

At this point, in late 2014, there wasn't as much awareness around mental health as there is now. My new job required me to be socially active, vibrant and upbeat. I had to charm new customers into paying over-the-odds for holiday packages. When my manager noticed me being distracted or low, he would pressure me to focus, threatening me at times with my job. It worked at making me productive, but reinforced the belief that I could only be vulnerable at home.

When Maya and I were both home was the only time I could really be myself, and share the struggles of my day. I cried often, and she and Hannah both supported me as I slowly got back to my feet.

With the job going well and money coming in, I started searching for fun. The lifestyle that came with being a travel rep meant that I was drinking and smoking a lot, going to beach parties and taking drugs. I was being impulsive, staying out, hooking up with customers from the travel shop and complete strangers.

Whether it was partying more, finding new women to sleep with, taking up surfing or just drinking, I was trying all kinds of ways to erase the memory of *her*, putting time between me and the past. This had to be the only way to *fix* my mind and clear my obsession, the hope that *she* would contact me. These incessant negative witterings were still ever-present in my mind. In the rare quiet moments, when I was often hungover, I went over my failings again and again, convincing myself I had ruined my life. I still thought of *her*.

Whilst living this new life, I treated Hannah's house with contempt. Wrapped up in my own head, I didn't think to contribute or do any chores, and our room was a mess. I was treating it like a hostel. One warm evening, the collection of dirty dishes got too much for Hannah. She told me in no uncertain terms that she was fed up and that I had to leave.

I was furious and upset. Maya insisted we went on a walk to calm down.

Pacing the local neighbourhood, I couldn't see why Hannah had gotten so mad so quickly and without warning. I thought of it as her problem. I thought about packing up and leaving that night to go and stay in a hostel. As Maya and I talked it over, the anger began to fade. I started to pity myself and sorrow and grief swept over me. I looked toward the coast at the golden sunset and back at Maya, and like I had done many times in her company, I felt helpless and hopeless.

'I just can't do this, Maya. It's my head, I can't get *her* out and Hannah just doesn't understand. What is wrong with me? Why won't it just go away? Why can't I just be *normal*.'

And then Maya told me something I will never forget.

'When I was really little, my brother and sister were really good at gymnastics, they could do cartwheels, vaults and splits, all sorts of great things. They were even told they could go to the Olympics. I was also really flexible, except for anything that had to do with my hip.

'I knew that if I had not had to have my hip surgeries, I would have been the exact same. I would have been able to do gymnastics and be better at sports. I was being held back by this, I was never going to be able to do a cartwheel.

'I was really upset. As I got older I was angry, especially when I got my limp after my later surgeries.

'Then at around seventh grade, I started to accept that I was never going to be good at sports. I couldn't change it, it was physically who I was, I was always going to have a limp and I was never going to be able to do that cartwheel that I wanted to so badly.

'I knew then that I was going to have this limp forever, *but* I didn't want to feel that way forever. I just had to accept I was never going to be able to do a fucking cartwheel. I spent so many years being upset and feeling bad about myself, letting it rule me, even though it was something I had no power over.

'I couldn't work hard to fix it. There was nothing I could physically, emotionally or mentally do. It was just who I was. Who I am. There is nothing to be fixed.'

Then, she turned to me. Raised her hand to my face and tapped a finger gently on my temple.

'And that's what you have to accept. It's the same in there. You can't just *fix* whatever it is in your mind. There is no sense in feeling bad about it. You have to learn to live with it, to accept it as part of who you are.

'And look, you've travelled around South-East Asia and hitch-hiked all across Australia with a mental illness. That's impressive, that's an achievement. Who can say they've done that?'

In all the months of our friendship, I had never once asked Maya about her limp. I suddenly realised I had never really asked much about her at all. She liked to talk, and I would try to listen. But I was always preoccupied with my own struggle, obsessively trying to think my way out of my pain.

I knew then that my depression wasn't an excuse for me to continue behaving the way I was. I had been unlucky and made some bad choices, but it was as if that tap on the side of my head flicked a switch. I could suddenly see things from someone else's perspective and I realised I had a lot to be grateful for.

I had a responsibility to carry on, to find healthy ways to cope, to stop neglecting myself and the relationships I had with the important people around me.

I had to go on living. There was nothing to be fixed.

At the time of writing, Matthew Kynaston is living in south-east London and using his experiences to set up and facilitate men's mental health support groups for Mind and Campaign Against Living Miserably (CALM). He also facilitates workshops in schools with young men as part of the Great Men Project and sits on the Comic Relief Mental Health Collective.

Lucy Nichol
What If

I jolted awake like a wind-up toy finding its mojo. But it wasn't my mojo. It was anxiety's.

I thought this beast had left me many years ago. The watered-down version was just about bearable. But this dreadful, heavy haze, so familiar and yet so foreign to me, came from nowhere – kicking me in the guts like a frightened wild horse.

My vision was so sharp and my terror so real. Nighttime, day-time, it didn't matter – it was real and I couldn't hide behind a blanket of darkness or a fictional fear that I could talk myself out of. There was no excuse for this – I could see, I could feel, the light was on, the sandman gone.

Such an injustice. It felt so unfair. So many years of trying to tame it and then howdy! hola! surprise! – it's back with a spit and a snarl.

Anxiety was playing me like a victim. The return of a villainous sequel nobody was expecting to watch. But what if it wasn't playing tricks on me this time? What if this was to be the last time? What if this was really it?

An indescribably sinister disease. A spontaneous strangulation of the soul. A diagnosis of terminal doom. I had no idea what was coming for me, but I knew that it was coming for me. And although I could see everything around me, clear as day and sharp as silver, I'd no idea which direction it was going to attack me from.

If it's not disease, it's pain. If it's not pain, it's panic. But why couldn't I see that the panic was both disease and pain in its own right? If it doesn't kill me, it doesn't make it smaller. It doesn't make it fluffy. It doesn't make it nice. Facing it does not mean belittling it, after all, it simply means knowing it for what it is.

I'd faced up to things before. I've told the dog not to bite. I've peeled my aching fluey body from the damp sheets. I've told them to stop treating me this way or that way. I've stood up and said no. I know I'm not weak. Not when I know what I'm dealing with.

'What if it kills me?' I thought. What if it was something new that there was no antidote for? What if the panic never leaves me?

'What if it does?' said a new voice in my mind.

'Shut up', I said. 'What nonsense. Can't you see there's something very, very wrong?'

Yes, but why assume inevitable doom? Who knows what's next?

It was a fleeting voice, desperately trying to catch its breath, sitting deep in the mosh pit of dread. But I definitely heard it. A tiny fraction of broken light amongst the fear.

I looked all around me. This was no nightmare – I was awake all right. Wide awake. The combination of a sharp reality with a mushed-up mind is a recipe not to be messed with. But maybe I needed to mess with it?

There was that voice again.

'What if you don't die tonight? What if you sit tight through this horror and emerge unscathed?'

The clock ticked so slowly, but at least I heard it tick, again, and again, and again . . .

I could still hear it. The terror was intense, but my heart still beat. I was still breathing. It hadn't got me yet.

It seemed to take an age to pass, and the countdown of the hours and the minutes and the seconds until daylight seemed to be slowing like a jewellery box ballerina about to give up the dance.

But how could time be my enemy if life was what I so desperately wanted to cling on to? Life thrives on time. If time ran out, so would my breath. I needed time. I needed to embrace time.

So maybe this was just panic. Like last time and the time before. A powerful, despairing panic, but one that's never ended me.

What if it retreats into its hole and hibernates once more?

What if the slow ticking clock is the answer to this terror?

Tick, tick, tick. Listen softly. Concentrate willingly.

My breathing slowed, reaching out for normality. I still didn't know what would happen next. But it was better than it was a second ago.

What if it's receding?

How could I have been so fearful of it again? How could I have let it infiltrate my night? But I was still. I was calm. Listening to the purr of a cat. Able to move my still-pink feet under the comfort of the blanket. Able to close my eyes once more and dream.

What if the question became a dream? A hope?

I'd no idea what tomorrow would bring. Where once I'd hoped for simply peace, I wondered, perhaps if I could dare dream for more. Perhaps the unknown can be enticing, exciting, warming?

Who knew what beautiful birds we'd encounter on our Sunday walk, fluttering through the breeze with meal worms? Who knew what delicious silky chocolate I'd blindly pick from the box? Who knew what joke I'd laugh at, making my cheeks hurt like an assault of sour lemon?

What if? need not be my enemy. What if? could be my curiosity, my passion, my flair, my love.

We owe ourselves so much more than just peace. We deserve so much more than peace.

What if we can embrace the mystery and laugh at life's surprises?

What if we can begin to challenge the anxious nag?

What if we learn to make that new voice get louder until one day we're listening intently? Enjoying the ticking of the clock. Enjoying the now. Enjoying dreaming about what wonders the future could bring.

I fell asleep before sunrise and let myself dream. Our discoveries can be pretty amazing, if only we believe that they can be.

Lucy Nichol is a published author, blogger and freelance writer for a range of national media titles, a communications professional and a trustee for addiction recovery charity, The Road to Recovery Trust. Her first book, *A Series of Unfortunate Stereotypes* was published in 2018 and she's an active anti-stigma campaigner within the mental health community. Lucy has also lived with the highs and lows of generalised health anxiety for many years.

Natasha Devon
Finding My Inner Cheerleader

It was a huge relief when, in 2013, I was diagnosed with an anxiety disorder. I realised that my bulimia had been my terrible coping mechanism for anxiety, and why, after seeking treatment for it, I still hadn't felt 'right'. Finally, I knew who my opponent was and could begin to fight him in earnest.

I'd had a lot of therapy, a crucial part of which was learning to separate anxiety caused by genuine danger from paranoid delusions. My brain, I'd learned, was like a washing machine fuelled by nervous energy. It would send round the same obsessive, unfounded thoughts until I was convinced there must be some truth in them. They were never conspiracy-theory level. In fact, my anxieties have always been exclusively confined to very personal and specific scenarios: being convinced someone is angry or upset with me for a reason I haven't considered, or that I'm not a 'good' daughter, or that I should have brought that homeless guy back to my flat to live with me because he's going to die tonight and it'll be my fault. It was all anchored in baseless guilt.

After having CBT and counselling, I learned how to identify and silence that inner voice and tune into my logical one. I'd tell myself that people are busy and not always thinking about me, that I do a lot to make my mum and dad's life happier, that I bought the homeless man a coffee, chatted to him and showed him where the nearest shelter is on my phone and that's more than most people would do.

Of course, recovery doesn't mean never going mad. But it does mean having the ability to recognise when you're going mad and taking steps to get yourself back on track. That's why people going through the recovery process are actually the sanest people I know – they understand how their brains work. I came to realise there are actually three voices within me: the objective one obsessed with data and considering the other side of an argument (the one I whip out for TV interviews), the paranoid one intent on convincing me no one really likes me (who I squash using techniques I learned in therapy) and my inner cheerleader.

Inner Cheerleader is there to remind me to pay attention to my instincts, that it's ok to stick to my principles and to be in my corner when it feels like no one else is. Since 2016, I've started to tune into Inner Cheerleader more and more and allowed her to dictate my decisions. The amazing thing is, she's plugged me into a community of people I didn't even know existed: those who appreciate honesty and authenticity, who genuinely applaud my success and who will add their voices to the fray when I say something that is perceived to be controversial.

It feels as though I am part of an army of mental health warriors working collectively to make the world a better, fairer place and supporting each other when times are tough. It is that notion which brings me so much hope.

Natasha Devon MBE is a campaigner who tours schools, colleges and universities throughout the UK, delivering talks and conducting research on mental health, body image & gender equality. Her book *A Beginner's Guide to Being Mental: An A-Z* was published in May 2018, followed by *Yes You Can: Ace Your Exams Without Losing Your Mind* in April 2020.

TOOL KITS

Katie Piper
My Tool Kit for Survival

I can't remember a specific moment when I found the hope to over-come adversity. I think a lot of people go wrong when they wait for a precise moment where everything is suddenly ok. In reality there are many tiny moments that build up your resilience, and it's a gradual process. Getting back to where you want to be is an accu-mulation of things, such as walks, or friendships. I would say, don't look for landmark moments; it's the day-to-day things that help you heal.

The process is not like a story book, always linear. There are setbacks, but they teach you more, especially about resilience.

Maintaining hope and resilience is as much a physical thing as a mental one. It's all about balance, and this is where I rely on three main pillars: sleep, exercise and diet. These pillars need to be in sync. Sometimes I wake up in the morning feeling dreadful, and then I remember that I ate crisps the night before, or something sweet, and I realise that too much salt or sugar is having an effect on me. As does drinking too much alcohol, or not getting out of bed on time. You have to be honest with yourself. When everything is in balance it's easier to be positive. I also practise mindfulness.

One of the best therapies for me has been to connect with others, and to get advice from different places. Working with my charity, The Katie Piper Foundation, which helps adult burns survivors and those living with severe trauma scarring, helps me enormously, especially fundraising through the general public. It's amazing how many people who are not affected directly themselves donate their time or money to the charity. Their generosity and kindness rebal-ance the evil stuff – you realise that hope is not lost. In addition, you see people in the same situation as you, and realise that recovery is possible, although it's different for everyone. I like to focus on helpful comparisons rather than toxic ones.

I don't really have any words of wisdom to encourage others who may be struggling to find hope. I don't like cheesy quotes. I think that perspective is important. We're built to struggle, and we're built to last. Look at your situation and reflect on it. 'I've had a bad year.' Have you really? Has it all been bad, or was it just a few bad days? If everything was good all the time, how would we differentiate between the two?

We mustn't fear or avoid difficult times. Sometimes, we only evolve through struggles, and they help us build a tool kit for survival.

Katie Piper is an internationally bestselling author, inspirational speaker, TV presenter and charity campaigner.

Joe Wicks
I'm a Better Human Being when I Exercise

When I was growing up, my dad was a heroin addict and in and out of rehab, and although I was quite hyperactive and disobedient as a child, I made a conscious decision not to go down that path, and to prove that you don't need to be a product of your environment.

Exercise and sports have always helped me with my anger issues, and even now they change how I feel in myself. As a fitness coach, exercise is my expertise, of course, but I work with thousands of people who have experienced mental health problems, and I see the difference it makes in them, too. It's fair to say I'm passionate about it. There are huge mental health benefits to exercise, and although in the past I've talked about how it can improve your looks, my focus is now shifting to feeling good.

Exercise not only energises me, but it helps me be more kind and patient, even with my kids. Once you find the motivation to work out, the energy you have afterwards is its own reward, and spurs you on to do more.

Don't be obsessed with weight. Just go back to the basics: love your body with enough sleep, good food, and exercise. Turn the TV off an hour earlier and go to sleep – otherwise healthy eating goes out of the window. Start your morning routine with an exercise you really like. In fact, if you make your home a gym you'll be more motivated! And always remember that you'll feel better afterwards. You need to be patient and consistent – don't expect changes over-night. Just make today a success by choosing good lifestyle changes.

Use exercise as a tool. Once you push yourself harder, you'll know that you can overcome difficult situations in life, whether it's a relationship break-up, redundancy or anything else.

And while it's important not to let a 'bad' day of eating become a week of 'bad' eating, there should be no guilt or shame about food. Instead, ask yourself what is triggering your 'bad' eating habits and remember that you always come out of a workout making better decisions about food, alcohol etc. The serotonin and dopamines that are released during exercise are similar to those you experience while eating chocolate or having sex! So pick a workout that you like, and remember that a little every day is better than a lot over the course of one weekend.

In terms of food that will make you feel better, both physically and mentally, I always recommend preparing it for the week ahead, or, as I mention in my books, 'Prep like a boss!' – especially these days as we find ourselves fighting against the 'convenience society', faced as we are with advertising that pushes high-calorie food.

Now that I have two young children sleep is more important than ever to me. With the baby waking up throughout the night, I don't wake up full of energy, and I crave carbs and unhealthy foods. I've come to realise that sleep affects everything, and that better sleep leads to better mental health.

Ultimately, you have to have self-belief for this healthier lifestyle to work. Believe in what you're doing and do it for yourself, not for others: you're the one who lives in your brain and your body, not your partner, wife, husband etc. And once you lose your excuses you find success. Why procrastinate when you can do something today that will transform your life?

Joe Wicks (also known as The Body Coach), is a British fitness coach, TV presenter and author. After posting 15-second recipe videos on social media, Wicks has became one of the most followed fitness accounts on Instagram and YouTube. Since 2015 he's published bestselling books including the record-breaking *Lean In 15* series and during the coronavirus pandemic lockdown in 2020, he began *PE With Joe* on YouTube to help children stay active; this livestream was viewed by over a million users worldwide.

Dame Kelly Holmes
Dreams and Goals

In 2005, I made a choice to speak about mental health and illness after I had opened up about my own problems with depression and self-harm during my athletics career.

I was thirty-three years old, ex-military, eleven years an international athlete, when I had my first breakdown. I realised I was not invincible. Although we can all take pressure, sometimes it can get too much and we crack. I cracked!

One of the reasons I am so passionate about talking about mental health is because it normalises the subject. So many people suffer from mental health issues but feel that admitting they have a problem is a sign of weakness. They worry about how they will be perceived by others or how it could affect their career. Now, talking about mental health is finally beginning to be seen as important as conversations around physical disabilities.

Following a recent bereavement, I have also learned to separate depression from complete heartbreak. To cope with certain situations, I have to ensure that those closest to me are aware of my feelings and my need to have comfort and support through tough times. When I am struggling, I find it invaluable to surround myself with positive people. Ask for help. Don't rush, but be hopeful that you will get through it. Cry as much as you need to!

Physical fitness also plays a very important role in my mental health and wellbeing. The release of adrenaline and head space when I run or cycle is one of the best times to get perspective and expend positive energy. It can be hard to motivate yourself when you are low, but I am a big advocate of ensuring I keep myself active. That's my happy space.

Many more people are now beginning to see the health benefits of exercise. One thing I really support is parkrun – I think it's a great way to make you feel good about yourself physically and mentally. Parkrun is brilliant because anyone can take part; you can run, jog or walk. It gives you the sense of being part of a group as well as keeping you fit.

At the end of the day, we are all humans living our lives on a day-to-day basis, trying to be happy or make others happy. It is important to take some time for yourself when you start to feel overwhelmed – take time to reflect and process your thoughts. Look at where you are, how you feel and where you might need to take action.

I use 'me time': a hot bubble bath, candles and music to relax. I feel that having space where no one can disturb my inner peace is something very special.

My dreams and goals were both my drivers and my pressures. Without them I had no purpose. With them I had stress, yes, but mainly direction, achievement, hope and happiness. They are what kept me going.

Dame Kelly Holmes is a double Olympic Champion, with seven Gold, eight Silver and four Bronze medals at Olympic, World, Commonwealth and European Championships.

While at school Kelly's dreams of Olympic Gold were overshadowed by repeated physical injuries and periods of clinical depression and self-harm. These affected her up to the 2004 Olympic Games in Athens, where she won Olympic Gold in both the 800m and 1500m races, becoming the first woman ever and the first Briton in over eighty years to do so.

She was awarded a Damehood in 2005 for services to athletics.

Larry Meyler
The Mustang Metaphor

Back in September 2015 I set out on a journey, which took me not only around the world but also deeper inside myself than I'd ever been before.

At that time I was literally on my knees. Life had become way too much, a merry-go-round of depression, loss and anxiety. Inside the darkness of my head it felt like a vice was being turned tighter and tighter, a constant pressure fuelled by worry, sadness and over-thinking. I would binge drink to forget then drown in the shame and regret, beating myself up daily. It was mental torture and something had to give.

I felt the only thing left to do was to just stop and take myself out of this dead-end situation, to get off the ride and away from everything I knew. This also meant separating myself from the only positive support I had, the people closest to me, without whom it probably would've been curtains already. They understood that I had to go, to try and breathe before I sunk so deep that my life would slip away. The sandstorm of negative emotions made it hard to even see straight, it was a constant whirling chaos inside my head.

But flickering within the heavy confines of my mind there was still a little flame of hope, dancing in the distance with all its might, hoping I would see it, just waiting for me to fan it. Somehow I refused to let that get lost in all the noise. I tried with all my might to listen to it telling me I was worth it and my life was worth a shot. I turned up the volume and let that voice become louder.

Somehow I refused to give up. I refused to be beaten and have my life taken away. I decided to fight forward, not knowing where it would lead or what I was looking for, but with a determination to give my life a chance and to switch up a fucked-up mindset. I fought on, hacking away like Indiana Jones through my harsh mental jungle, trying to find a way of taking back control.

Which leads me on to one of the biggest steps in getting to grips with my own mind: changing my visualisations. Changing how I see what's actually in my head has helped me get back some control and in turn given me much more hope and strength.

There are so many metaphors and descriptions of depression and anxiety which are grim and exhausting. As I've written above, I myself used words like 'darkness' etc to describe that period of my life. But I realised that having too many negative connotations only added more sadness to what already felt like a constantly bleak situation. I know this because I live it day in day out and I believe if we keep feeding these engulfing dark visions then how can we ever see things differently?

A wise (trainee, may I add) counsellor once described what I was telling her about my past as a 'layer cake of loss', probably the first visualisation that really started to help me see my life, especially my past, in a new way. Building on from that one description, I started to change how I viewed the inside of my head, what was going on behind my eyes, the negative mental pictures which had formed over many years and plagued me since I was a little boy.

When people used to say 'just focus' it would confuse me. I'd find it hard to decipher.

What was I actually meant to be focusing on – a great abyss of shit? So I stripped it back to what I could usually see when I pictured my brain, the inside of my cranium, and I decided to add in brighter pictures and positive visualisations. This helped me envision a new way of living, a happier way, and that is when I started to discard the negative metaphors and descriptions and ramped up the fight. I envisioned waking up with a smile instead of tears.

It's like seeing your mind almost as a film set: destructive scenes can be torn down and positive ones rebuilt. I wanted to break the cycle of what my demons, those little beasts and tricksters in my head, wanted to do. I knew they would always try to steer my thoughts towards the bad, the hurt, the insecurities, the self-loathing, the self-sabotage and the past. They wanted to make me believe that

I'm not good enough and that I should just lie down and die. So I decided to take the wheel back.

This is the main visualisation I use now. I call it the Mustang Metaphor:

I see myself in a shiny yellow Mustang driving along a coastal highway. Think Malibu, with the sea glistening, the breeze blowing and the sun shining. My hands are firmly on the wheel and my foot on the accelerator. I can still see that black, engulfing cloud in the rear-view mirror, it's always there and I don't pretend it's not and yes, it does get very close, too close at times. But when I see it I know I can put my foot down and speed ahead of it.

Although the past is still there in the picture, the new bigger pictures and visualisations are a lot more powerful.

I also try to be more aware and work on my reactions to things, especially my emotions, which again plays a big part in switching up how I get through each day. This doesn't come overnight, when you've felt lost in darkness for so long or weighed down under a sea of despair – again, negative descriptions I've used in the past – then it's not easy to focus or to change those visions.

I'm now trying to clear new pathways and highways in my mind, to assess my reactions to situations, to take more moments to stop and breathe, to go easier on myself, to recognise links between my past experiences, my relationships and my behaviours and to just wake up each day and not feel exhausted before I've even got out of bed. By changing my visualisations I've given myself some gigantic tools.

I don't get it right all the time and I know that failure is part of life, for everyone. It's important to remember that starting again doesn't mean going backwards. It means starting from where you are right now and then moving forwards, building on your knowledge, fighting on.

So put your foot down and speed forward baby!

Larry Meyler, originally from Wexford in Ireland, moved to London at seventeen, leaving all he knew behind. The next twenty years he took every chance he could, like an Irish Artful Dodger!

After travelling the world, at thirty-six, he wrote his first book, *Being Brave*, which covers his personal experiences with depression, anxiety, loss, grief, heartbreak, alcohol and a difficult father-and-son relationship.

Carrie Grant
Gratitude

Gratitude is a great quality. Gratitude allows us to live in the moment, awestruck by the smallest reward, overflowing with thankfulness that this particular moment is a good moment. For a long time, for me, this place of gratitude was at the end of a long, lonely, dark road. A road that I grappled with, many a time sitting down and parking myself on the verge of it, refusing to budge until things changed and, when they didn't, somehow pulling myself up and getting back on my feet again. It was a pathway where I would often turn a corner, believing good would greet me, only to be faced with more bad news. It was in this dark and isolated space I found true grit and determination, and their sweet companion, gratitude.

You may feel at times there is no hope, that all is lost, but believe me, it is not. You may have a tear-stained face and an aching heart but these experiences are the gold that bring out the best in us if we allow them to, they test us to the core, peeling back the layers and showing us what we are truly made of.

When, at eighteen, I found myself in pain and on the loo all the time I brushed it off as a temporary issue. No visit to the GP for me, I would get through it. But I didn't just 'get through it' – it continued and to my dismay seemed to be getting worse. I visited my local GP who told me it was probably caused by job stress. This didn't sit comfortably with me so I went back a few weeks later and asked if I could have some tests. My bloods and a stool sample were taken but revealed nothing out of the ordinary.

I put up with it for another year until one day, whilst I was working in Plymouth, I found myself bleeding heavily from my bottom. My chest was hurting too. Feeling faint, I saw an emergency GP and was told I probably had a hiatus hernia (with no explanation for the other end). I was advised to take an over-the-counter indigestion medicine. Months later, in pain again, I visited another emergency GP and was given a course of tablets to boost the white cells in my immune system. Still nothing changed and my symptoms persisted.

Two years after the initial onset of illness I had learned to live with the hourly dash to the loo, with the rashes all over the trunk of my body and the ulcers in my mouth that were so bad the inside of my cheek was falling away from the gums.

It was at this point I made a routine visit to the dentist. A friend had recommended her dentist in South London so off I trotted to talk teeth.

The dentist took one look inside my mouth and said, 'Now this is interesting. Do you by any chance get diarrhoea?'

'Er, yes,' I mumbled through the dental probe in my mouth.

'Do you get skin rashes?'

'Er, yes,' I replied . . . This was spooking me out.

'How about lumps on your shins?'

I nodded, thinking my friend had clearly sent me to a psychic, not a dentist!

The dentist was also a Professor at University College Hospital. Within a couple of days, I was in the hospital and a line of students were queuing to see the inside of my mouth, all trying to guess what they were looking at.

The trough between my gums and side of my mouth was sewn back together and a few days later I went to the Gastroenterology Department to meet the consultant. I lay on my side and a massive probe was inserted into my bottom, without warning or pain relief, and samples of my bowel were taken for testing. When it was over, I lay on my side on the bed wanting to die, wanting never to have to turn over and face the doctor ever again, wanting never to have to walk past a waiting room full of people who had heard my screams. It was February 1986, I was twenty years old.

A week later I sat with the specialists who told me I had Crohn's disease, an inflammatory bowel disease that could impact any part of the digestive tract from mouth to bottom. They didn't know the cause, there was no cure and I would have it for life. To be honest, I was relieved that I finally had a name for the symptoms, an explanation of what was happening.

I spent the next three years going from hospital to hospital trying to find ways of managing my condition. I tried medication but that only made it worse. I tried every new-fangled idea, every herbal remedy, I changed my diet, I slept more, I rested more, I overhauled my lifestyle, but nothing worked. And then there was my faith. I prayed, I prayed harder, others prayed for me, they fasted for me, they gathered in groups to pray for me – still nothing changed.

In 1989, I was lying in Addenbrookes Hospital, Cambridge, weighing six stone. A whole section of my bowel had been taken away. It was a night like many others; I had been in hospital for two months and the nights were the hardest, lying in agony waiting for the next dose of meds. Counting down the minutes. I'd gone from taking one day at a time, to taking one hour at a time, to counting my life in minutes, in tiny 60-second batches of determination. I told myself that if I could manage to get through this minute I would be out of pain soon. But it wasn't just my body that was suffering. My mind had also taken a hit. My faith was at a low ebb, my inner world was fighting itself.

I'd had my life so planned out. I was determined that I would direct my adult life, I would earn my own money, live my dream, fall in love on my terms. I had it all worked out. I hadn't planned for sickness! I hadn't even considered this could happen to someone like me.

Round and round my thoughts went, desperate to find answers. I was twenty-three years old, I was made for more than this, this was not meant to be my life, why was I alone, why was this happening to me? I was meant to have a better life than this. I was meant to be out in the world, to be creating – songs, music, dance – why, why, why?

That night lying in my hospital bed was the same as all those others before. The dimmed lighting panels buzzing in the hospital ward hallway, squeaking shoes on rubber floors as staff went about their work, the hushed tones of the nurses at the nursing station, the snoring and groans from other patients.

In this dark place, counting minutes in the silence, through my despair I heard another inner voice. *Stop looking at what you have lost and look at what you have left.*

I was stunned. I hadn't thought about this before. Why had I not thought about this before? Why had I not considered grieving the loss and letting go of the past. I could not control, or change these things that were happening to me. But I was forgetting that there was one thing left that I could change – my thinking.

And then a more humorous thought hit me. If I only have one leg I will learn to hop and I will damn well become a great hopper. I tell myself I may have lost a section of my bowel, I may be in pain but I will recover and the pain will not always be this severe. I will get out of here. I will find some way to live a life that is satisfying. I will not live a half-life with half a bowel. If I sleep more hours or have to take time out to be in hospital it will just be that, time out. Time out from appreciating every moment of this glorious, wonderful life I have been given.

It was one of those important life moments that has served me well ever since. If something is taken away from you, learn to live with whatever's left. Don't suppress your grief but walk the hard road that ultimately leads you to being grateful for what you do have. There is so much potential in the 'whatever's left'. Be wowed by the small things; the sunshine, the way that day follows night, the taste, the smell, the sights, the sounds, the music, the dance, the song, the art, the seasons, the sea, the landscape, the smile on a child's face and most of all, the beauty found in the humblest of lives.

Dr Carrie Grant is a BAFTA award-winning broadcaster, vocal coach and advocate, with a thirty-five-year TV and music career. She was awarded a MOBO award in 1998 and a BASCA in 2008 for lifetime services to the music industry and has an honorary doctorate. She has both the biggest selling vocal coaching book and online course in the world. Currently a reporter for BBC's *The One Show* and co-host of Radio London's Saturday Breakfast Show, alongside her husband, David Grant MBE, she has four children (three birth, one adopted), all with special needs.

Vidyamala Burch
A Radiant Clear Sky

I was twenty-five years old. In an Intensive Care ward. In agony. Terrified.

I'd first injured my spine ten years earlier which led to two major surgeries when I was seventeen. I'd then fractured another part of my spine in a car accident when I was twenty-three. I'd 'soldiered on', but now here I was, in big trouble. I'd been hospitalised because my bladder had stopped working then found myself wheeled to Intensive Care when blood tests indicated a possible raging spinal infection.

I got myself into a complete state one long night. The fear became overwhelming, as did the pain. I felt like I'd been wheeled into some kind of living hell. People were desperately ill around me and I had never felt so alone. Just me with my wrecked, fragile body and my overwhelmed, bewildered mind.

A 'dark night of the soul' was truly upon me and I had no escape. It was the most intense time of my life (before or in the thirty-five years since) and, as it turned out, the most transformative. Sometimes light emerges from the darkest places, in the most astonishing of ways.

I'd had a medical intervention that day that required me to sit upright for twenty-four hours afterwards. This was back in 1985 when they didn't have the fancy hospital beds of today, so I was just propped up by pillows. If that sounds uncomfortable, it was. And you have to understand that I hadn't sat up for months at this point, as my spinal condition had rendered me pretty much bedridden prior to this new disaster.

So here I was: attempting to sit up, with the pain escalating dramatically. My mind became obsessed about how on earth I was going to survive like this till the morning. That was hours away. Thousands of minutes – millions of seconds – of agony stretched before me. It felt completely insurmountable.

I had a debating chamber in my mind. One team was arguing the sheer impossibility of the situation: 'I can't do it, I'll go mad' was their theme, shouted in lots of different voices as a desperate chorus. The other team was the sensible one: 'But you have to. You have no choice. You can do it'. This team spoke in much more measured tones. Sombre. Determined. Brave. But they weren't winning the debate. Not by a long shot. The other team was much louder, more shouty. More dominant. And my mind was slowly but surely slipping into despair. Unbelievable tension got tighter and tighter as if my brain was in a vice. 'I can't do it!' was winning. Hands down. And yet. The moments were passing. Morning was inching closer.

Then suddenly, out of the blue, a third voice came into the debating chamber. This voice said very clearly, with a beautiful authority: 'You don't have to get through till morning, you only have to live this moment. And this one. And this one. And this one. Endless moments of now.'

Immediately my experience changed. This voice blitzed the debate and the other teams dissolved away. Time and space collapsed. Morning suddenly seemed a ridiculous concept, meaningless in the presence of the luminous moment that had bloomed into my consciousness. I knew I could not only survive this moment. I could live it. Yes. I could do that. I was doing it! Right now. See. And again. And again. This is what it truly means to be alive.

I knew that morning would eventually arrive, but not as a place or a time. It would come along as just another moment to live, that happened to coincide with the sun rising and a new day beginning. Just another fluid, open moment in an infinite parade of timeless, spacious moments. I knew, in my bones, that the invitation and opportunity was to learn how to live into each moment as it presented itself – with my mind and heart wide open.

I write about it now with the benefit of hindsight and decades of reflection. It wasn't that clear at the time. Remember, I was a lost and bewildered young woman drowning in her dark night of the soul. But even then, I knew something completely life-changing had happened. I was a different person when the next day eventually arrived. I often say that night was the axis upon which my life has turned. I was one person beforehand, and another person since. In fact, all the many years since have been an attempt to make sense of what happened that night. The night when my inner world broke open and tension dissolved in the face of tasting what it means to live one precious moment at a time.

A few days later my condition improved and I was moved back onto a regular ward. The hospital chaplain came to see me, which was interesting as I wasn't religious – in fact I was rather cynical. But I guess the medical team wanted to help me and they knew there was precious little they could offer me, medically, in the face of my physical disability. I was going to need to learn to live with it and it's rather wonderful that they thought to send someone to offer me spiritual, rather than medical solace in my moment of need.

This beautiful elderly man gently took my hand as I lay on the bed. He invited me to remember a time and a place when I'd been happy. I took my mind to the Southern Alps of New Zealand when I'd known ecstasy as a super-fit hiker and climber before my injuries. There had been times when I had felt literally on top of the world. I remembered the sights, the smells, the sounds. The sensations of plunging into icy cold rivers on boiling hot summer days. The joy of shrieking at the top of my lungs as I splashed about and then lay in long, sun-baked grass with my whole body tingling. Oh, it had been glorious, and it all came flooding back, even though I was lying in my hospital bed with my body ravaged. The chaplain gently brought me out of the visualisation and I felt profoundly different, even though only about ten minutes had passed. This also had an enormous impact on me. My subjective experience changed dramatically due to what I had done with my mind and where I'd placed my attention. I'd never even considered my mind before this! I just lived my life, taking so many things for granted. But now the power of awareness was dawning on me, along with the tantalising intuition that it must be possible to train a human mind so it becomes an ally in the drama of life, rather than a source of so much anguish – as I'd experienced in the early stages of my dark night.

In just a few days I had experienced the agony of my mind over-whelmed by anxiety and fear; I'd experienced the miracle of allowing my life to unfold moment by moment; and now I'd tasted the almost shocking transformation in subjective experience that could arise depending on what I did with my awareness. These were indeed life-changing days.

I came home from hospital after a few weeks a changed young woman. I never went back to my career as a film editor, realising it was impossible to do with my physical limitations. I stopped push-ing against my body in aggressive denial of my reality. I began to meditate daily, alongside rehabilitating my body. It was an excruci-atingly slow process and I needed a lot of patience. But, perhaps ironically, my body being so frail meant I had a lot of time to train my mind. Months being predominantly bedbound gave me the unexpected gift of time, which I'd never have received if I'd been busy pursuing a career. Life does indeed work in mysterious ways.

Over the next few years I tried many different styles of medita-tion before eventually settling on the Buddhist path. This was mainly due to the people I met on Buddhist retreats who had been meditating for years. They had a beautiful way about them. An unselfconscious comfort in their own skin. A lightness of being. 'Yes,' I thought, 'this is how I want to be when I grow up'.

I'm now sixty. I've been meditating for thirty-five years. I can feel I am now moving into a new phase of life. Perhaps the archetype of the wise, old woman – that's something to aspire to. A longing for simplicity and less restlessness. A slowing down.

I don't know if I have lived into the qualities I so admired in others when I was young. But I do know that I've had an interesting life. No one could call it boring or conventional! I lived in a Bud-dhist retreat centre for women for five years in Shropshire and attended many intensive retreats. This is where I learned, deeply, to love and be loved. This was the gift from the kind, wise women I lived with. I was ordained as a Buddhist when I was thirty-five, which was significant as it meant having the courage of my convictions. That was good for me as I sometimes felt embarrassed about being 'weird' and I often felt a failure in my inability to lead a 'normal' life due to my disability.

But when I reflected, I could see how it was very strange to think that training the mind was weird when it is our most precious resource. It's much weirder to ignore the mind and get trammelled by the rat-race and yet, in our world, everything is so often upside down. We have so much strength within us waiting to be tapped. But it does take training. And courage.

For the last twenty years I've been running Breathworks, a mindfulness business – offering the skills that changed my life so completely to others living with pain, illness and stress. It's been very interesting to draw out key teachings from my Buddhist training and articulate them in ways that are accessible and appropriate to everyone – whether they follow a faith or not. After all, we've all got minds and every single one of us can learn to train it for the better and every single one of us suffers, perhaps unnecessarily, because our minds become our greatest tormentor.

I've been lucky beyond measure to have dear friends and companions – fellow meditators and mind warriors – walking beside me in this adventure. One of them, Sona Fricker, became my husband. Here was more love tumbling into my life alongside our shared dream of helping others.

And what of hope? I've had so many periods of unrealistic hope in my life that just led to bitter disappointment, that it's a concept I can be a little wary of. But I know from experience that lack of hope can also eat away at the soul.

I believe in *realistic* hope – capable of fulfilment, clear sighted and pragmatic.

Such hope these days is simple. Each day I hope to find the presence of mind to meet whatever arrives in life with realism and a light heart. I hope to live with a sense of flexibility and openness as the moments flow by. I hope to really inhabit my life in all its messiness, shutting nothing out through fear or doubt. I hope to live with vitality and a kind of fierce courage, no matter what happens. I hope to remember that my mind can be vast and open like a radiant clear sky. And the great thing about learning to live with a more fluid sense of life is that even if I completely blow it in this moment, there's another moment coming down the line, another chance. I hope to remember that, pick myself up when times are tough, and never forget to make the most of the fresh starts that are always arriving. Now. And now. And now . . .

Vidyamala Burch sustained spinal injuries as a young woman which required multiple surgeries and left her with partial paraplegia and severe chronic pain. After experiencing the transformative powers of mindfulness and meditation to manage her pain, she founded Breathworks in 2001, to help others cope with pain and suffering. Breathworks has grown into a flourishing international organisation with 500+ accredited teachers in over thirty-five countries. Vidyamala has written three books: *Living Well with Pain and Illness*, *Mindfulness for Health* and *Mindfulness for Women*.

Danny Sculthorpe

At the age of fifteen I was diagnosed with type 1 diabetes and put on a lot of weight. I lost the weight when I got a job at a sheet metal shop in Manchester, but a vicious circle had already begun.

I began my rugby career as an academy player at Leeds, and in 2001, at the age of twenty-two, I was signed by Wigan Warriors. There were no other diabetics in professional rugby and I felt like the odd one out. However, even though I had captained England twice, the real downward spiral started after I signed with Bradford in 2010. I endured three months of injury hell pre-season, culminating in a prolapsed disc during a weights session. After back surgery for the disc I was sent home, but two weeks later started to suffer unbearable pain in the bottom of my back. I ended up back in hospital for three months, having been diagnosed with sepsis and two types of MRSA.

My back injury was excruciating, but the withdrawal from the various drugs I was given to help the pain was almost as bad. Back at home, although I could just about get off the couch, I couldn't even make it to the bathroom. This was when I started to feel suicidal. I had lost my job, my career and the family house because Bradford had basically ripped up my contract. I felt like I was a burden to my wife and kids. Nevertheless, I kept my depression to myself. It was a typical bloke thing – you just have to be strong when you're 6ft 4in and weigh 17 stone, right?

At my lowest point I found myself in a car park in Wigan with a bottle of gin and a box of pills, but when I thought of my wife and kids, I couldn't go through with it.

The turning point was when I finally pulled off the mask and started talking to my wife and friends about my suicidal thoughts.

It was like a massive weight had been lifted. Yes, medication has played a role in my recovery too, but *talking* was what saved my life.

Exercise has also been vital for me in terms of beating my depression. Getting into boxing, in particular, has helped me massively. And I'm careful around alcohol as it is a depressant. You end up spending a fortune but the problem is still there.

These days I work for the charity State of Mind and when I give talks, especially with members of the construction industry, I have two messages for people:

1. Talk to people. If you see a difference in someone, ask them how they are. You may save a life.
2. You don't have to be on a sports field to be part of a team.

Danny Sculthorpe is an English former professional rugby league footballer. He last played as a prop for the Widnes Vikings. He has also played for the Rochdale Hornets, Wigan Warriors, Castleford Tigers, Wakefield Trinity Wildcats and the Huddersfield Giants.

Life brings myriad experiences and sadly suffering is one of those. When life deals us a tough hand, we might find ourselves struggling to keep our heads above water. But we have a terrible tendency to add insult to injury. Our ability to critique our own life performance usually has a ferocity rarely seen in even the most pressurising sports coach, the most demanding teacher or the most punitive tiger mother. We are truly our own worst enemy. We needle, undermine, ridicule and pour scorn on ourselves and do so all the more when times are hard.

I was once with a group of psychologists who all shared what they said to themselves when times were tough. There was a shocking preponderance of harsh and demeaning self-talk, reminiscent of much of what our clients bring to us in therapy to work on.

So, my plea is to go gently on yourself. I am not a fan of constant, mindless affirmation, and think that an ability to reflect on what could have gone better is the best way to learn and develop. It feels important that I can notice moments when I could have parented better, or remembered something that was important for a friend that was struggling, or communicated an idea more clearly at work. These things are important to me and my sense of who I am, and I hold these values close to my heart. If I can think about whether there's anything I could have done better, I stand a chance of learning and improving the stuff that matters to me. However, in order for that reflection to have value, I need to have hope that change is possible, and believe that I can keep learning. I need not to come down on myself like a ton of bricks.

This is sometimes called self-compassion. Compassion for ourselves can be seen as an essential part of being able to give compassion to others, and receive compassion in return. I have worked with many staff across the health service who are extraordinarily compassionate to the people they work with, but struggle to extend the same compassion to themselves. It seems that being kind to ourselves is the hardest thing to engage with. In cognitive behavioural therapy, we often encourage clients to imagine what they might say to a friend voicing a similar thought or belief – it is rare that our response to people we love would ever be so harsh. The challenge is often in shifting from knowing there is a logical inconsistency, to actually feeling differently. One of the powerful things about Jonny Benjamin's story, as told in his first book, *The Stranger on the Bridge*, which opens with Neil Laybourn stopping him from taking his own life, is the way that Neil's kindness to him on the bridge gave him hope – perhaps through a sense that he deserved to be believed in. It was as if Neil held the hope for Jonny when he couldn't do so for himself. So summoning people to mind who have been kind to us, or believed in us, can be a helpful way of accessing some self-compassion and some hope when it is otherwise thin on the ground.

You especially need to go gently on yourself when you are low on sleep. People having a tough time don't tend to sleep well, whether it's struggling to fall asleep, waking up with your mind whirring away, waking with nightmares, or waking way too early in the morning and finding it impossible to fall back to sleep again. When my kids were small and never quite became the dream sleepers I'd prayed they would be, I noticed how rapidly my world view deteriorated with no sleep. I would become overly focused on everything that was wrong, was unable to problem solve and had some of the worst rows I've ever had with my partner. I've spotted it at times of poor sleep since – a complete loss of perspective and a sense I was epically failing at life. The double whammy of sleep deprivation is that the more you worry about getting a good night's sleep, the harder it is to come by; who hasn't lain awake with the thought, 'I must get to sleep'? – the thought least conducive to relaxation possible.

What I've shared with people I've worked with, and tried to put into practice myself, is that these times are a signal to take it easy.

Prioritise sleep, and if sleep won't come, focus on as much self-care and rest as possible. It is a time for minimising big, meaning-of-life reflections, and not making significant decisions or drawing conclusions about anything.

There are a range of other physical factors that impact on mood. These include, for some women, being pre-menstrual or menopausal, for some people withdrawing from antidepressants or any drug known to have withdrawal effects and, from my years working in eating disorder services, being on a reduced calorie intake.

The emotion that most often accompanies a lack of compassion for ourselves is shame. We experience shame for feeling what we feel, whether it's anger, envy, sadness or exhaustion. We are often masterful in our ability to pile shame on top of whatever other feelings we might be experiencing.

As a newly fledged clinical psychologist in the mid-90s, one of the most stressful parts of my job was assessing suicide risk. We would ask people about it as part of the assessment process and there was always a moment of passing relief when someone said they had kids. The protective factor – 'I could never do that to my kids' – always felt fairly cast iron. This is why two suicides by fathers in my local community felt so shocking and baffling when they happened. I initially couldn't make sense of the circumstances in which leaving your children fatherless would make sense. And then shame came into view and it started to feel a little clearer. If you feel that your struggles are so shameful, so toxic even, to those around you, then removing yourself from the situation can feel like an act of self-sacrifice. Of course, the ending of a life will involve multiple elements, but I'd like to highlight the potency of shame. The campaign message 'It's ok not to be ok' responds to this, trying to validate the legitimacy and normality of struggle.

Men, in particular, can experience an overlay of shame and critical thoughts ('I shouldn't be feeling this way, I'm weak' etc) that sometimes counteracts the potential benefits of sharing their feelings. Shame can often be violent and destructive, at best forcing us into hiding, at worst causing intensely self-destructive urges.

So what can we do about this? Andy Bradley, Director of

Frameworks4Change and compassion facilitator, has tried to befriend this powerful and destructive part of himself by writing his own letter to Shame:

'Tolerance, forgiveness and patience are helping me to be with you – my shame – to include you in my awareness, to approach you gently and even on occasions to smile, as I realise that you are part of me but that you are just one of the many little I's that make up my big I.'

Like Jonny's, Andy's journey has not been a smooth one, and I find his approach inspiring.

Sharing our pain with another, whether in person, over the phone or virtually, is one of the most powerful ways of ensuring that shame does not win through. To do this we need to find ways of expressing how we are feeling.

As a mother of three boys, 'Put it into words' has long been my mantra. Whether that's expressing rage instead of belting someone, or finding words for sadness or despair, I have been an endless verbalising nag. There are so few role models for men talking about their difficulties, and so many factors that actively mitigate against it, that we need to do all we can to encourage each other to try to overcome the barriers. Jonny has been an extraordinary role model for being open about his ongoing struggles. I admire his honesty in sharing that his journey has been a bumpy one, and his courage in resisting the pressure to be seduced by the happy ending narrative and pretend to be permanently well.

Putting our suffering into words can be hard when we've struggled for a long time, when we're lacking in close friends or when we feel we've worn out those we have. We may have tried to open up and been met with confusion, fear or rejection. Being on the receiving end of the pain of others is not easy, and we tend to avoid what we cannot solve and what makes us feel uncomfortable. Trying to discern those people who might be better at listening and supporting us is an important part of holding hope.

Being willing to keep trying at something even when it doesn't go well (such as finding someone who can be there for us when we're distressed) is sometimes framed as resilience. I am wary about this concept as too often it is used as a stick, either for beating others with, or playing into our own highly developed capacity for self-flagellation. I recently chaired the Compassionate Mental Health gathering – a series of events that address the way we think about mental health – and I noticed a young nurse leaving a session in distress. I approached her and she shared her challenging journey through life (including violence and family estrangement). As a student nurse in mental health services she felt she had let people down persistently. As she wept tears of frustration and grief, she repeatedly apologised for not being more resilient. So many times I have spoken to NHS staff who have poured their heart, soul, and considerable unpaid overtime into services that are damaged by endless organisational challenges, and when they have momentarily snapped by becoming emotional or unwell, have been told that they need to work on their resilience. We cannot continuously get up over and over again in the face of continual challenge. Sometimes we need to lie down, take a break and cut ourselves some slack.

Seeking help for our suffering is often channelled in the direction of psychological therapy. As Joint Head of a large psychological therapies service, I am of course an advocate of the power of psychological therapy to transform lives. However, I sometimes worry that this expert model risks distorting our response to distress and trauma. It can make people without specialist training feel they are out of their depth, and that they may do more harm than good if they say the wrong thing when they respond to distress in others. It can make us feel that we need an expert to diagnose and treat our difficulties which can heighten our sense of impotence.

I once worked with someone for a long period of time. She had struggled with mental health problems for many years and the sessions were challenging. However, our work finished and her distress was markedly improved. She no longer needed input from mental health services and had resolved many of the difficulties she'd had for years. What had made the difference? She acquired a dog. The range of ways this impacted on her life were in my view far more potent than anything we had done within the therapy.

There are so many ways to navigate distress that I would

encourage you to be alert to the vast range of possibilities that life offers up for change and new experiences. Although it can be unpredictable, it's safe to say that the more we have the courage to open up to others and to share our vulnerability, the more likely we are to make the connections that might help us to find a way through. I've seen opportunities come through chance meetings, volunteering or new work experiences, new relationships or friendships, even bereavements.

I am not writing off therapy. Even when therapy has not worked for you the range of models, and more importantly, the range of people delivering it, mean that one unsuccessful attempt doesn't mean you should dismiss it. Different things will be helpful at different times in your journey, so just because it wasn't helpful once, doesn't mean it might not be again.

However, don't neglect the power that connecting with another human being, or a group or community of people can bring. It's worth spreading your support net wide, considering the online community (with care, of course), Samaritans and support groups. It generally feels better when you say it out loud. It enables you to reality check your thoughts and feelings, to shine a light on them and test them out, rather than keeping them hidden in the echo chamber of your mind. Above all, it gives you the chance to connect with others and to realise you are not alone. It can be a lightning conductor to hope, but we can never find it if we hide ourselves and our feelings away. There are so many more aspects of finding hope I could have explored, and before I finish I'd refer readers to Johan Hari's extraordinary book *Lost Connections*, which explores how the way we live our lives can make us vulnerable to experiencing distress.

But finally, please go gently on yourself, and when you're ready, try to be open to new experiences and to connect with others.

Benna Waites is a Consultant Clinical Psychologist, ABCi Associate and Joint Head of Psychology, Counselling and Arts Therapy for Aneurin Bevan University Health Board.

COMPASSION

Ben West

It was a miserable, dark Sunday in January of 2018. I had just had a shower and was listening to music on my bed. A-levels were on the horizon and I hadn't done the work that was due the next morning for maths. Unfortunately, these would soon prove to be rather trivial adversities. I was part way through Rudimental's 'Not Giving In' when a piercing and purely terrifying scream radiated from my brother's room. In true fight-or-flight fashion I threw my headphones off and ran upstairs, expecting someone to have hurt themselves accidentally. There are few moments in life where we truly lose control of the reins and the whole world stops spinning. Unfortunately, this was one of those moments. I opened the door to discover my fifteen-year-old brother, Sam, had killed himself.

The autopilot kicked in and I started CPR which went on for around twenty minutes. Then I completely lost control. From then on, I was a passenger. Once the paramedics had left I went upstairs to my parents' bedroom where Sam had been moved to, and picked up the syringe caps and other bits that had been left behind. I also moved a rug over the enormous blood stain that was on the carpet from where the air ambulance doctors had performed surgery. All I could think of was how horrific it would be if my parents came home to see that.

It still feels surreal even now, almost as though I'm remembering someone else's evening. The days following the incident were as horrific as you can imagine. I didn't have an appetite, I was shaking, I had a sense of terror surrounding closed doors for which I was prescribed medication. But after what must have been several days my friends took me out for lunch and that's when the autopilot started to disengage and I began to slowly start taking back some control.

I'd love to be able to write 'and from then on I recovered'. We could leave it there and all go home. Unfortunately recovery from something like this is never straightforward. I needed a way of expressing how I was feeling, something I could link to Sam. I tried counselling but I didn't like that. Whenever I met up with friends I wanted to have a good time and not burden them with the shit that was going on behind the scenes, although to their credit they did actively ask about it when the moment was right. I think that's the big problem: there's never a right time to talk about this stuff. I just wanted to inject as much normality into life as possible.

It was at this point that I had the idea to start campaigning. This gave me a way to try and turn what had happened into something positive. My close friends jumped on the idea and, cutting a very long story short, in September we walked 200km to raise awareness for teenage mental health, which unexpectedly attracted a huge amount of nationwide attention. As a family we went on to set up The Sam West Foundation, which works to support projects that are proven to help young people suffering with their mental health. Within days we'd received tens of thousands of pounds in donations. And suddenly I had an outlet to express how I was feeling, which also had a link to Sam.

For a long time I thought this story was always going to be sad. I thought that I'd forever look back and feel upset. I am pleased to announce, however, that this is not the case. Sure, when I look back I miss Sam, and sometimes that can really get to me. But most of the time looking back brings an enormous amount of pride for what we have achieved in Sam's name. It brings the knowledge that because of how we reacted, we have already helped other people, which is a truly incredible feeling.

There's an amazing quote from Michael Irvin: 'Look up, get up and don't ever give up.' I'll take this quote to my grave because it's how I've tried to live since Sam's death. Shit happens in our lives sometimes and it's important to know that it's absolutely ok and totally natural to not feel ok, but it's equally important to know that if something's happened and you're feeling low you need to get up and do something, whether that's doing something for yourself or doing something for someone else.

Sam will always be sorely missed, but what gives me hope is that when I close my eyes at night and drift off to sleep, Sam's somewhere, wherever that might be, and I know he's proud of us.

After the tragic loss of his brother to suicide, Ben became a dedicated mental health advocate, setting up PROJECT WalkToTalk, an initiative that organises national walks to raise awareness for mental health and give young people a safe space to talk openly. Ben has since led a petition attempting to make mental health first aid a compulsory part of teacher training.

Lotte Stringer

My brother Hector took his own life in 2011.

We set up our charity, Hector's House, initially as a signposting website. It has evolved organically from there and we now provide a crisis line, educational talks on living well, focused holistic prevention, Rapid Transformational Therapy, as well as raising awareness by sharing our story. We believe that suicide is preventable.

Why do we do this? As Hec's sister I don't want any other family to go through what we have been through. We want to help by providing services at all points of a mental health journey. We believe we can help keep that person safe, alive, and living the best life they possibly can.

After suffering with the loss and trauma, and living with the aftermath of suicide, I believe that my lifestyle must reflect on what we've learnt.

I advocate movement, eating well, getting sunlight, sleeping well, watering yourself (like a well-kept house plant), keeping your gut healthy, talking therapy, and most importantly, being honest about how you are feeling to yourself. It may sound a little holistic for some, but truly practising what I advocate has helped me to overcome PTSD (Post-Traumatic Stress Disorder). My desire to want to live well, to recover, to believe without question that this is available to me, was my turning point. I had to know and believe I was strong enough to live better, without PTSD.

I manage my mind daily – giving it a work-out through meditation, much like I exercise my body at the gym. It becomes a way of life, a lifestyle of hope, giving me the energy, understanding and intuition to help others. This wouldn't be the method used at crisis point, but for me to live well, to stop myself getting to crisis point, this method is very successful.

My advice if you are going or have been through something traumatic is to treat yourself as though you have been! Be very gentle with yourself, your feelings, your mind and body. A mental trauma is still as stressful as a physical one, no matter what form it takes. Baby steps lead to strides, small steps to recovery. You will get back to feeling more like you again, a stronger, more honest you.

My advice to someone struggling? Keep going, no matter how hard it feels. It will feel better. Everything takes time, give how you are feeling time to work through. Hold on to anything that gives you hope.

Learn to meditate, quieten that inner self-critic.

Learn to express feelings: 'The feeling that cannot find expression in tears will cause other organs to weep.' (Marissa Peer) So true!

High-five yourself! Be proud of you, turn your inner critic into your very own cheerleader!

And please, please, please reach out to family, friends, us, anyone. We all want to help. Take that first step.

We hear you. You matter. You are important.

And never, ever use Dr Google!

Lotte Stringer is CEO of Hector's House. Lotte's story is a message of hope, aiming to give individuals tools to build and retain resilience through her #EATMOVELOVE movement.

A trainer, dancer, and dog lover, she has a keen interest in exercise, diet and nutrition. Lotte is also a Rapid Transformational Therapist and has worked at an assistance dog charity.

Dick Moore
Faith, Hope and Love . . .

It was a soft autumnal Monday in mid-September. I was working in the school's staff room when a colleague poked his head around the door to tell me that I was wanted in the school office. As I got up from my chair, he told me that there was a police car parked outside. My world tilted. A lovely policewoman and policeman were waiting in the office as my wife and I arrived almost simultaneously. They told us gently and with compassion that Barney, the third of our four sons, had been found in a hotel room in Reading and that he appeared to have taken his own life.

My first thought was that I would not be able to cope with such news and that I would follow Barney's example and escape from the agony that had suddenly become our world. There was no hope that this pain would go away.

We walked the few hundred yards from the school office back to our house. The sun was setting, there was a faint breeze carrying the laughter of children. We didn't say much. As we walked through our door, I remember thinking, 'What now? What does one do half an hour after learning of the death of a son? Make a cup of tea? Take the dog for a walk? Pick up the telephone?' That evening remains a blur, but a remarkably ordinary blur. No hysterics, no surge of anger or guilt or denial – just an awareness that life had changed for ever.

We spent the ten days between Barney's death and his funeral surrounded by family in another son's small house near Fording-bridge – where Barney's funeral was to be held. We walked, we talked, we ate, we drank wine. We planned the funeral service. He had left on his iPad twelve pieces of music for use at his funeral, pieces that he had collected in the two days before his death. We listened to the music and cried. And cried. And we still do.

The funeral itself gave me the first glimpse of hope. Hope that something positive might rise from the horror of Barney's suicide. Friends and family – young and old – colleagues of ours, colleagues and friends of Barney's, his former teachers . . . the depth of compassion, of humility and of empathy was palpable.

And amidst the tears, amidst the confusion and the searing grief, something special began to germinate. A realisation that we weren't alone. That people cared. That people wanted to help and were deeply frustrated that they could not do so. Or so they thought. For it is people who create hope; it is people who give us the strength to carry on.

Barney's suicide brought empathetic melodrama from my sisters, rock-like wisdom and certainty from my father, assurance from my closest friends that they would always be there, that they would not forget. And love, masses of love from everyone.

The day of Barney's funeral, two of my closest friends announced that we would all be going out for a curry that evening – my family and their families. It was a ridiculous suggestion and I declined their offer. But those friends are nothing if not insistent and the evening found us all in a Fordingbridge curry house. Despite my misgivings it was a remarkable evening. There were tears – lots of tears – but there was also laughter – much laughter. For me, the laughter blended with the tears and made them more bearable. They obviously changed nothing but, somehow, the laughter gave me hope, hope that the future might not, after all, be entirely dark.

We all deal with grief in different ways. My wife and I are very different in the way we process and react to our emotions, so we have grieved in our different ways. Neither is right or wrong, they are just different. And, nearly eight years after that awful September evening, we have used our different personalities to explore paths into the future which suit us. We share one objective: to use Barney's death to offer some hope to those for whom hope might be in short supply. Barack Obama suggested that 'If you go out and make some good things happen, you will fill the world with hope, you will fill yourself with hope.'

I don't enjoy any religious faith. I don't believe that Barney is in a better place. He's dead. But something has changed. I sometimes look up – towards heaven, I suppose – and say quietly, 'If you are up there, God, I suppose that this might be what you get up to: taking tragedy and creating the silveriest of linings. Taking darkness and introducing light.'

I certainly feel a sense of spirituality which had been largely absent before Barney's death. I feel a sense of acceptance and of calm, despite a continuing lack of certainty. I understand Martin Luther King's belief that 'Only when it is dark enough can you see the stars.'

St Paul told the Corinthians, 'And now these three remain: faith, hope and love. But the greatest of these is love.'

I'm not sure that he was right. Love has certainly been the key to surviving Barney's suicide. The love of friends, the love of family, the feeling that we are not alone, that people understand, that they cared deeply about Barney and they continue to care about us. But I think that the greatest contribution that love has made is to give us hope. For whilst there is hope there is a future.

Dick Moore has been an English teacher, rugby coach, and school housemaster, the latter for almost twenty-three years. Circumstances led to a passion for adolescent emotional wellbeing and he is now a qualified instructor for Youth Mental Health First Aid. Dick is closely involved with the Charlie Waller Memorial Trust, has appeared on BBC radio and TV, and in 2015 gave a TEDx talk.

Poorna Bell

It is one of the greatest ironies, that a person bereaved by suicide, someone who knows first-hand the life-altering, devastating effect of such a death, is 65 per cent more at risk of taking their own life.

It's an irony because suicide is mistakenly thought of as a selfish death – that the person didn't care about the effect this would have on everyone around them. When in actual fact, it's a death that arises from a place of such unbearable mental distress and pain that escaping one's very existence seems like the only solution.

When someone you love dies by suicide, especially when that person was as close to you as a partner or a child, their pain passes on to you. You then finally know the true meaning of the word unbearable, because that's what this type of grief feels like.

It assaults your mental health to the point that you can't see when you won't feel like this. But it passes, and I know, because when my husband Rob took his own life in 2015, I felt like that. Life was unbearable every second of the day for at least the first ten months. And four years on, I no longer feel like that.

When he died, I went from someone who'd never had any mental health problems, to someone who now knew what depression felt like. I knew how truly awful it felt to have your emotions locked behind a door that you couldn't access, no matter how hard you banged against it. And I also knew that there were many times when I just didn't want to exist. I wouldn't say I was suicidal, but I knew that my reality was so painful, anything seemed like a better alternative.

I was very lucky to have a strong support network. They absorbed a lot of the anger that just poured out of me in those first year. They never said 'too much' or 'enough'.

But I also needed to hear from the people like me. The ones closest to the person they'd lost, which tends to be a parent or a spouse. Because this didn't just feel sad, or painful. It felt like a huge part of me had been cut away suddenly, and there I was, in the home we shared together, not knowing how or where to begin.

When I started interacting with people on social media and writing more about grief and suicide, messages of hope came through. 'Hold on,' they said. 'It will pass. It will get easier. I promise.'

I knew the words but I didn't understand them. Everything was so raw and they didn't feel like they applied to me. But I fashioned these words into anchors, and I tied myself to them on the days when I felt indifferent about being alive.

And I learned the final thing, about my grief. That friends and family can shape and create a space for you to feel loved, even when you feel destroyed. That strangers can offer you such kindness that it will make your day spin on an axis from dark to light. But ultimately, you are the person who determines how you rise from all of this.

That means choosing to live. It means not just existing but choosing what gives me joy. Saying no to things you can't stomach. Noticing the tiniest moments when you feel better, and alive.

I remember the first time when I did feel an emotion that wasn't endless sadness. It didn't last long – maybe five minutes at the most? And I remember marvelling at it – like a giant soap bubble that was just turning and glistening in the light. It seemed so strange and new in that blasted landscape of grief.

And even though it passed, I thought: *I have to remember this.* Because this is proof that my emotions aren't fixed, and that things can change in a positive way. Over time, the pain lessened, and it became less vocal.

There are still some days when I struggle. When I miss Rob so much it feels like the edge of my grief will never dull. But now I have amassed so many things that give me a reason to be here, but more than that: give me joy.

But I don't think I would've gotten here if someone else hadn't given me a message of hope when I needed it most. And so to anyone who really needs to hear it, however you get there, and whatever the journey, the one thing I can guarantee you is that it gets easier, and it will pass. Hold on.

Poorna Bell is an award-winning journalist and author, working as UK Executive Editor and Global Lifestyle Head for HuffPost.

She is an experienced public speaker, with experience ranging from doing keynotes to moderating events for FTSE 100 companies to running seminars for corporations. She is also an accomplished television and radio broadcaster.

Kevin Hines
Number 26, Golden Gate Bridge

A circular, black-and-white analogue clock adorned the off-white wall. Groggy, my eyes strained then refocused. It was 4am. My father and I had been in the filthy, sock-smelling emergency room overnight, and now we were in limbo, waiting for a cheap, wood-framed, uncomfortable bed to come free. It was a solemn San Francisco morning: 1 May, 2004. I was twenty-three years young.

It wasn't our first time in this predicament, my father and I waiting anxiously in a white-walled room on the third floor of the locked-down unit within the St Francis Hospital Psychiatric Ward. We had been here before, three times in fact. So often that in a moment of levity I referred to it as my exotic hotel stay. Time and again, I had to live in places like these – to equalise, to heal, and to regain a semblance of sanity. You did not misread it: I was on my third psychiatric hospital stay. I would see the inside of a place like this four more times over the course of the next seven years. Why? Well, the answer is not as simple as 'I lost my mind' or 'I just went nuts.' No, those self-berating descriptions are vague and quite frankly offensive to someone who has suffered mentally like I have, and like I do. The answer is much more complex.

Number 26. I am number 26 of the 39 people who attempted to take their lives by jumping off the Golden Gate Bridge and survived.

Most have never regained full mobility. I have been blessed enough to regain all mobility and maintain my physical fitness. Others have stayed in silence, keeping their stories to themselves. Many have simply gone on with their lives, eventually passing on of natural causes. Some have opened up, begun speaking about their experiences, sharing with the public what they can about the perils of suicidal ideation, great suffering and pain. These stories of triumph over adversity are not just important for readers, and followers of the mental health movement (an absolute civil rights movement of our time), but imperative for so many people's continued survival. In the drab, smelly hospital, focusing – not only on the health of my brain and body, but also on my metaphorical heart, the searching of my soul – became key.

The idea of achieving total physical, mental, emotional, and spiritual health is what got me through from one day to the next. Morphing from the self-loathing, self-critical creature I had become was not easy. But eventually I came to the realisation that it was not only possible, but even plausible. It began to seem like the most likely outcome. I only reached this positive outlook with a tremendous amount of therapeutic dedication and an unhindered drive. The kind of drive that needed to be drawn upon minute by taxing minute in order for me to survive and thrive.

I built on the solid support of a group of personal protectors who would guide me in times of episodic crisis. This was a group of loved ones, family and friends who opted in to my 'Let's Keep Kevin Alive' plan.

With the help of a *Time* magazine article on fighting bipolar disorder, depression, and all the other symptoms of my disease, I formed a mental health plan. Something concrete to keep me alive when all I could do was ponder, and plan my death by suicide. This 10-Point-Plan has kept me on an even keel, even during the worst of times.

1. Therapy (the kind that works for you)
2. Sleep (7-8 hours nightly)
3. Education (about your diagnosis or personal struggle)
4. Exercise (3x+ weekly)
5. Meditation (daily)
6. Medication (same time every day, with 100 per cent accuracy)
7. Refrain from drugs and alcohol (completely)
8. Proper nutrition (anti-inflammatory foods)

9. Coping mechanisms (what works for you)
10. The Mental Health Emergency Plan (opt in family and friends to your plan)

This is how I strive to live body, mind and brain-well.

Kevin Hines is a suicide survivor and suicide prevention speaker, who gained nationwide fame for surviving an attempt on his own life by jumping from the Golden Gate Bridge in San Francisco, California. His story gained wide coverage and he has since become an activist promoting suicide prevention. Hines has appeared many times on TV and at schools and campuses world-wide, sharing his story, Triumph Over Adversity.

Carl Burkitt

If you asked me what gives me hope, the wannabe poet in me would love to say:

The sound of morning birds serenading the world outside
    my bedroom window
The feel of my wife's breath on my neck
The sight of my nieces and nephew playing and creating
    new planets
The persistence of leaves growing again and again each year
My dad's bearhug arms
My mum's 'how are you?' texts
My love of writing
Photos from our wedding day
The existence of crisps

And while it's true that all of those things do help to some degree, I think the biggest thing that gives me hope is the fact that I'm not dead.

As a thirty-four-year-old male in England, I am statistically the biggest threat to my life. And that knowledge rolls around my head every day. I'm not exaggerating.

A week before Christmas 2011, my uncle Jim took his own life. It was the single most difficult and confusing thing my family has experienced. I was living in Southampton at the time, working in a marketing job that I didn't particularly enjoy. I was away from my family and, unfortunately, was not in a place where I felt I could talk to anyone about how his death affected me. Not because I had no one around me – I had lots of friends – but because I didn't understand it, and society, while we're getting better, is often too scared to talk about such subjects.

But I wanted to do something. So, like any scared little man, I decided to run, and raise money for the mental health charity, Mind. My instinct was to put my body on the line and not engage with the issue mentally.

However, a part of the fundraising process saw me write about Jim. I found the writing therapeutic, useful and, strangely, fun. And eventually my silly little brain realised that charities have marketing teams too. It *literally* never crossed my mind before then that I could use my powers for good! So, long story short, I embarked on an eighteen-month struggle of rejections before travelling to London to bag myself a job at a mental health charity.

It was here that I finally started looking at my own experiences of mental health problems. At university I went through a tricky break-up and saw a counsellor, but I'd shrugged that off as just me being tired, stressed, a sensitive person. It was a blip. But surrounding myself with open, understanding, empathetic people at the mental health charity helped me come to terms with something I'd always tried to hide: I eventually owned up to having a history of depression, a history of self-harm and a history of not being kind to myself.

You see, for me depression does not just bring a deep, seemingly irremovable sadness painted across the surface of everything I enjoy and love. It also brings with it rage. A rage pointed directly at me. And my actions. My failings. My thoughts. My feelings. My response to others. And on and on and on until it culminates in me physically hurting myself.

Until very recently I didn't tell anyone about my self-harm for the usual, sad reason many people don't: shame. I was ashamed to be someone who hurt themselves. I was ashamed for being 'weak' and 'useless' and 'an attention seeker'. I felt I just needed to keep it to myself, stop being silly, ignore it and eventually it would go away.

But it didn't go away. I'd been self-harming since my mid-teens while pretending everything was fine. And then in my late-twenties it became progressively more frequent, until, from the age of thirty, it was an everyday occurrence.

Just over three years ago I woke up in immense physical pain. The night before I'd been at a party and got talking to someone. As can often happen under the influence of alcohol, the conversation took a bizarre path which led to miscommunication. I went home feeling terrible about myself and how I had allowed that person to make me react in such a negative way. My self-esteem spiralled downwards and I hurt myself more than I ever had before.

Feeling the pain in the morning, I knew something had to change. That week I told my therapist and my wife the full extent of my self-harming, and it was then that my journey really began.

It's not easy telling other people that you self-harm, but telling the right people can be amazing. I'll never take those people for granted. What they did was not only listen, they helped me see that I had the power to stop. They helped me see I was not weak, or useless, for self-harming; I was not attention seeking. They helped me see that it had become my way of dealing with difficult emotions which over time had turned into an addiction, of sorts. It was a habit that I was not just suddenly going to drop overnight – it had become my coping mechanism. They helped me see that by accepting all of that, I could discover new coping mechanisms.

A big part of me developing my new coping mechanisms was to start spotting the signs of when the urge is on its way (eg being furious at myself for making a basic human mistake, which brings with it hot and itchy skin, tense muscles, aching hands, claustrophobia and a kind of overwhelming blurred vision, etc).

Once I spot those feelings, I now talk to myself with compassion and understanding, just as I would to anyone else going through a tough time. I go for a walk. I hold my wife's hand and tell her what I'm feeling. I read the little cards I've made that I keep in my wallet that remind me I'm human and it's normal to experience these feelings. I write. I play my favourite music. I run on the spot. I tell myself it will pass (because it always does). And then I forgive myself.

I make it sound easy. It's not. It's a constant struggle and I can't guarantee I won't self-harm again. I can guarantee, though, that I most certainly don't want to do it again but if I *do*, I will remember to be forgiving, understanding and accepting of myself, and then crack on with my new coping mechanisms.

So, what gives me hope?

Being able to write what you've just read. Knowing that I've overcome years of hiding my thoughts to become more honest and open about my feelings. Knowing that I've managed to kick a self-harm habit I've had over half my life. Knowing that if I do it again, I can kick it again. Knowing that no matter how often, and how aggressively, I tell myself I am not resilient, the cold, hard facts suggest otherwise.

I get hope from the blood still pumping through my veins. I get hope from being kind to myself. I get hope from knowing that if I continue to be kind to myself, I might die an old man, rather than the way statistics suggest. I get hope from finally realising that I deserve that.

And of course, I get hope from the existence of crisps.

Carl Burkitt is a writer from sunny Swindon, living in smoggy London. By day Carl is a mental health campaigner and market-eer, by night he enjoys reading, writing and performing poetry online or behind a microphone. You can find Carl's work at carltellstales.com.

Courage

Aaron Gillies

I wanted to die.

Not an ideal way to start a story of hope is it? But I found my hope in honesty, in being truthful, no matter how shitty that truth is. And you can't get better without dealing with the shitty parts.

I wanted to die and that's all I knew. The person I wanted to be was already dead and in my opinion the person that now existed in my place didn't need to be here anymore. These were the conclusions I had come to by myself, without consulting friends, family or professionals. It was just my own brain telling me that I was worthless. Depression is great at isolating you, and when you're isolated there is no opportunity for another opinion: it's just you against your brain, and your brain can be an absolute dick at times.

I stood in front of the bathroom mirror staring at whoever was reflected at me. I didn't recognise him: the bags under his eyes, the grey skin, the unkempt hair. This wasn't someone I knew, but I knew it was someone that I hated. I wanted to see that man disappear. I wanted that version of me to go away and not bother another human being again. I wanted to die, but at no point did I want to kill myself. At no point did any of this feel real or like it would have any consequences. That moment felt like forever. I started to cry. Then I looked at that man – that stranger – and slowly, viciously, whispered 'fuck you.' It was in that moment that I realised I didn't want to die; I just wanted that version of me to die. The version I hated. The version I didn't understand.

I'd been drinking and I opened an empty Word document and emptied my soul onto the keyboard. Every dark thought, every horrifying emotion, all of the worst of me in one rambling, poorly spelt rant. I uploaded it to the internet. I posted it. I passed out.

I woke up as the empty bottles from the pub next door were emptied into the bin with an explosion of glass and regret. With the taste of stale cigarettes and cheap rum in my mouth, I staggered from my bed and collapsed into my desk chair and opened Twitter. 99+ notifications. I'd never had that many notifications before. Why would I? I started reading and then started crying.

'I was there. I now have a husband and two children. It gets better.'

'That was me, this has been me, I'm still here. I'll be here if you need to talk.'

'My partner went through this last year, it was tough but they made it through. You will too.'

'If you need help, I'm always here, DM me and I'll send you my number.'

'I don't know you, but I love you and am glad you wrote this.'

'Don't listen to that side of your brain, talk to someone you love, be honest.'

'I tried to end it. I cannot tell you how glad I am that I am still here.'

The messages went on and on. All positive. All beautiful. All from people I didn't know, people I had never met, people who didn't need to write to me, who weren't getting anything out of it, who just wanted to reach out. People who understood.

I am always one to say how much I hate people. But when I say that, I mean the people on public transport who eat with their mouth open, or who ignore queue etiquette when ordering drinks, or who have the keyboard clicks on loud on their phones. People in general are actually pretty good. People care. They will listen. They will offer advice. They will do things that are selfless and they will help. People save people.

It was after this incident that I was diagnosed with depression, and the moment that it had a name I knew I wanted to fight it. It was a thing now – not a feeling. An Actual Thing. 'Know your enemy' is an extremely good phrase which I only knew about then thanks to the band Rage Against The Machine. I wanted to know my enemy. If you got a death threat in the post, you'd want to know who sent it to you and this was no different. I researched him, this assassin within myself, I read as much as I could about him. It turns out that he'd attacked other people before. People I loved, people I admired, people I would never expect. I wasn't the only one going through this. After years of feeling alone, I finally knew that a lot of people had been fighting the same bastard. And knowing I wasn't the only person fighting this gave me hope for the first time in years.

I kept reading and learning and gathering stories. I wanted to know my enemy before planning my attack. I found forums where other people spoke about it openly, I found poems, songs, novels, movies . . . they were hard to find but they were there. I immersed myself in a world of survivors, hoping I could join their gang. I'd never wanted to be a member of anything more than that. I sat in pubs with friends and talked openly about how I wasn't ok. Each one wanted to help as much as they could. I told my family, they told me they loved me. I had felt alone for so long and in just a few days I discovered an army waiting to fight for me.

Be honest. That was the first thing I learned when I started talking openly about my mental health. Be true, to yourself and others. None of this is your fault, it's your brain being a dickhead. You're not being selfish, you are trying the absolute best you can in the situation you're in. You're not a burden, you are loved, and love is all the good bits and all the bad bits and love is dealing with both. Together. Talk, if you can talk. Write it down, if you want to. Be honest with yourself. Remember you're not alone in this. It can feel like you're suffering by yourself but we are all suffering, there's just different amounts of it. Being honest saved me. Talking about it saved me. People saved me.

You're not alone. You are valid. You are worth it. Be stubborn. Be here.

Have hope.

Aaron Gillies is author of *How To Survive The End Of The World (When It's In Your Own Head)* and, in his own words, 'Twitter idiot who can be found under the name TechnicallyRon.' Aaron is also an ambassador for the suicide prevention charity CALM, with whom he hosts a podcast called *Conversations Against Living Miserably*.

Henry Johnstone

Hope:

'A feeling of expectation and desire for a particular thing to happen, also a feeling of trust.' (Google)

Hope can find its way into every fabric of our lives and, perhaps most poignantly, it will find its way into the lives of those who need it the most, because hope is deeply understood by those who experience its darker side: Hopelessness.

I've written this so that someone else who is experiencing hopelessness might read it and know that all is not lost. No matter how dimly the light inside you flickers, there is hope; there is always hope. Even in the midst of hopelessness you are one step closer to coming out of the other side.

I've had mental-health issues for as long I can remember.

From the first de-personalisation episode at age eleven, through to emergent bipolar, OCD, ADHD, dyspraxia and dyslexia. Although the last two are not strictly under the same banner, they both added to the pot of what I used to think made me cursed. I found it hard to learn and to remember, and episodes of de-personalisation left me shaking and terrified that I was a stranger in my own head and my memories belonged to someone else. I felt frozen in the absence of self.

Now I believe these obstacles to be a blessing, a way to help build communities and an understanding on a profound level of the suffering others experience.

I want to share with you a memory from the dark days. It was the moment that in hindsight seems so utterly unlikely to have been the trigger for a shift, but the more I have shared it, the more I realise it was.

In 2004 things were bad. As they say in AA, I was 'in the madness'. My mind was shredded, my body not far behind. Addiction, spurring me on and compounding undiagnosed mental illness, had me in a choke hold.

After years of stealing, lying, hurting and damaging my family, I felt so agonisingly guilty and ashamed that I left home determined to suffer, because I needed to suffer. I felt wrong; my moods swung violently from sweetness and regret to blind rage and anger through to the pits of nothingness and profound meaninglessness, an absence of self. OCD meant I couldn't perform simple tasks without repeating them for hours or biting my skin and tongue in long periods of self-harm that left me unable to speak. I was violent, I was angry, and I wanted to die in the most painful way possible.

The only time things made sense was when I was high, or drunk, or coming out of a self-harm episode. When I suffered it all made sense. So that's what I did: I made myself suffer, and I welcomed every episode as further evidence that I deserved to feel this way.

I didn't know then what I know now. I wasn't a bad child, I wasn't a fuck-up. What I was, was in pain and I needed something to believe in. First, I needed to admit that I needed help, but I was deeply ashamed of my behaviour and I just couldn't reach out. Not then.

We had endless arguments, and my parents were at a loss as how to help me. Nothing they did made a difference, no approach worked. They watched as their son became someone else. The little boy who had dabbed his mother's head with a flannel whilst she was sick, the little boy who picked flowers for people because he wanted to show love. The little boy whose imagination was wild, bright and beautifully naive. The little boy who said he'd never grow old of hugs and always wanted to show love. That little boy had all but disappeared. In all honesty, I tried to murder that little boy with darkness. He was love, I was not.

It was winter in Manchester, and early morning. I had been woken up and moved on by police officers for sleeping behind a bus stop. I liked bus stops; there was a light directed away from the rear glass so whoever was there wouldn't be able to see me. I hated being seen, I hated the thought that anyone would see me. Not only physically see me but see what I tried to blot out with drugs and drink. A child who was ashamed, lost and scared and a child who despite all the shit they had done and the pain they had created still missed his mum and wanted nothing more than to ask for forgiveness and a hug.

I guess that possibility was too painful for me to embrace; I didn't deserve it, so I just put myself in positions that I felt would push me further into self-destruction. I could do that. I was very good at that.

I remember it being cold, and experiencing some kind of loose pride that as I had slept the frost had settled over me. If it caused me damage then it was good for me. I'd been living on the streets for a month . . . ? Maybe longer. I'd found some kind of warped solace there, I was invisible. I could be left alone with my addiction and no one had to know what I'd done to be there.

I didn't set a course to where I ended up that day, it just happened. Through the walk there, I had sobered up and with no more booze in my system, that part of me that I had tried for months to shut out came flickering back to life. I hated it so much, it had everything that I tried so hard to avoid having. Feelings. Feelings were bad. Feeling meant love, and love was not a feeling I could bear to feel. Love was connection and connection meant hope, and hope meant some life that was different from this one. That was too far to go; that was impossible. Maybe I'd walked here on purpose, I don't know, but I found myself at my parents' house. It was dark. My mother and father were, I presumed, asleep. I still have dreams of that house. They had a new door – I had kicked the other through after a frenzied drive to steal money. But I wasn't here to destroy anything, not tonight.

I wish I could tell you more about my feelings in that moment or why I ended up an emaciated boy, crawling through a tiny basement window, glass sticking into my skin.

I don't know why I chose to, but I lay on the cold concrete floor, shivering and seeing my breath fog. I lay down and pulled my knees to my chest and I cried. Deep primal sobbing. My body shook and

I let it. I cried to my mum, I cried to the feeling of her hugging me, the smell of her clothes, the perfume that in boarding school years past I had sprayed on a cloth to smell when homesickness struck. I was crying not to damage or suffer, I was crying to heal.

I hoped somewhere deep inside those three floors above me, as she lay awake probably wracked with worry, my mother felt something. A connection.

I don't remember how long I stayed there curled up on the floor. As the sun started to rise, I crawled out of the same window and left.

Something changed after that moment. I'm not going to lie and tell you that everything came together in the days that followed, because it didn't. I was still a child, and I was still lost but I had begun the shift toward a better life. By crying I had begun to face what I had long feared and pushed myself into darkness to avoid.

It was hope, and hope is difficult to contend with if we feel we are undeserving or we are so lost that there seems no way out other than a way which is infused with more suffering. Hope means that we are worth more than what we feel now, hope means that on some level we can accept that we are able to change and that it's going to be ok. I want you to know that I fought against hope so violently and destructively, I tried to murder all the hope that flickered inside me. I never thought that my life would change, much less so that I would be the one to change it.

My hope came from admitting all the feelings of pain I had harboured and kept locked away. Soon after this I began to reach out and build a network of people who understood me. I managed to build a bridge with my mother and in time I told her that I needed help, that I couldn't do this on my own. I went to rehab and got clean, I saw a therapist who helped me understand my emotions and work on the guilt and shame. I learnt how to manage the de-personalisation. I allowed myself to experience depression, I learnt ways in which to manage my ADHD and OCD. The dyspraxia still makes me very clumsy and my dyslexia still makes numbers unintelligible. But life is doable now where before it was not.

Our journeys mean we have to pass through periods of agonising hopelessness and this part of the journey remains one of the most painful in human existence. Hopelessness cannot exist without it transforming into hope, and it is there for you. It has always been there for you and it always will be. You are going to be ok, you are not alone, we are here for you.

Henry Johnstone is a life coach, speaker, podcast host, and metalwork artist.

At fourteen he was sectioned as a threat to his own life and placed in secure hospital accommodation. After a diagnosis of acute bipolar illness, he was sectioned twice more and led a fiercely troubled life, becoming both an alcoholic and a drug user, experiencing homelessness and self-harm.

Now aged forty, he has been clean for ten years, has a degree, is a qualified and accredited coach, and is about to get married.

Laurie Dahl

When I first became unwell in 1992 mental health issues were not as openly discussed as they are now. Mental health problems were something that happened to someone else. Rumours abounded around my Polytechnic about a lad who had withdrawn his whole student grant (this was some time ago) and handed it to strangers passing the cashpoint, in what was obviously a mental health crisis. At that time, I was not aware of a now well-known fact: one in four of us will experience mental health problems in our lifetime. The ubiquity of mental health in the public consciousness – so welcome now – was decades away.

Years later, I can look at the events that led me to becoming unwell and see how my 'stress bucket' was dangerously overflowing. I was undergoing, in order of importance: the end of the relationship with my first serious girlfriend (which was perhaps due to the depression shrouding me); my family fracturing, with my adopted sister admitted to a young people's psychiatric unit the very same day I was admitted to hospital; the pressure of running a football fanzine as a small business from a bedroom in a shared house; my grandfather dying from cancer, and my dad being vulnerable and distraught as a consequence; leaving Polytechnic with a disappointing but deservedly poor degree; and the pressure of starting life in south London with immediate family at the other end of the country.

My bucket was overflowing, and then some. I'd been aware I wasn't right and had booked a GP appointment, but I wasn't aware I was depressed. Why wouldn't I be upset at the loss of my first love? The GP was old-school and not particularly psychologically minded. His advice, as I described the problems that were overwhelming me, was to write a list, arrange them alphabetically and prioritise them.

Not long after, I experienced the trauma of travelling across the country in a psychotic state. I almost jumped into a river in Warrington to escape the imagined Freemasons, was arrested and assaulted by the police, locked in a police cell for 18 hours floridly psychotic, then admitted to a hospital in Stafford. Following my GP's advice, I arranged my belongings on the hospital bed in alphabetical order, wracked with indecision as to whether to place the orange as F for fruit, or O for orange.

When my life was at its most chaotic and I was hitching across the country, getting into scrapes, it had felt as exciting, or frightening, as a film. Now I was psychotic I believed it actually was all a film. I had no understanding I was in a hospital, although the nurses, Jay and Stephanie, told me I was. I formed a close bond with these nurses and told them I was 'not a number, but a free man'. (As a result they went, one weekend, to Portmeirion, where the TV programme *The Prisoner* was filmed.)

I began to realise that this was no minor experience. People talked about me having 'a nervous breakdown' but my mum told me it was more serious than that: it was 'a mental breakdown'. Who had a notion of psychosis back then? There was just madness and sanity. My mum's 'glass half empty' nature meant she pounced on me, when during my recovery I said once, 'I can see the light at the end of the tunnel.' 'No,' she said, 'you're on an underground train, and you might come into the light at the stations once in a while, but you're mired in darkness 90 per cent of the time.'

Bizarrely, those profoundly negative words were the advice that most sticks in my mind. That, and the nurses saying, 'It's like breaking a leg – and can take just as long to recover' and 'Schizophrenia is like alcoholism, even if you're sober, you're always an alcoholic.' There was no getting away from this new self, the seriousness of my condition, But even in this gloomy, almost desperate time, a resolution to do whatever it took to recover was germinating. If this was fight or flight, I was going to fight. I would do whatever I was advised to do. In this way, accepting the seriousness of my situation was something that really helped me. It gave me a sense of the implications: would I be a revolving-door patient? Was this the pattern of relapse? These, the side effects from medication? Would my life be reduced to the desperation of delusion and despair? Would I ever love again? Work? Have a career? A family? It's terrifying to face the prospect of all one's hopes and aspirations being dashed.

What gave me hope was my friends sticking by me, the unstinting support of my parents, and ultimately meeting my partner. Incrementally, I also got to answer a lot of those questions. There was no moment of epiphany. Each time I passed a landmark in keeping well it slotted into my foundations, holding me up and giving me something to build on. If I'd remained well for one year, why not another? Keep doing what you're doing. Each time I survived an emotionally challenging situation without relapsing I built up a little more hope. I also had a notion from my aunt, a psychiatrist in the US, that medication had an ongoing healing effect, which encouraged me to stick with it, although I'd become fatter and slept too much.

After spells on the wards I spent years at a Day Hospital where there was 'mental health education': relaxation, country dancing, creative writing and endless defeats at the pool table. My nurse was a bluff Yorkshireman, loving his rugby, with an eye for the ladies that I'd been taught at Poly was 'the male gaze'. Yet Gary Tubman was perhaps the most important influence on my life. We worked together, building me up from rock bottom, via his angry insistence that I bring in the stockpile of old meds I was intending to overdose on, and endless silent one-to-ones. Gary and the Day Hospital gave me firm foundations on which I could rebuild my life.

When I became unwell in the middle of my three years at Day Hospital it was friends and family that saved me. That, and the care of a precious nurse, Beverley Hume, who became a lifelong friend. She would visit me on her days off, bringing her daughter in on passing visits. Years later I become godfather to this daughter. If she cared this much about me, if Gary did, maybe I was a worthwhile person after all? Thoughts of suicide were challenged by how upset they and my family would be. My protective factors were shielding me. My best friend, Barney Robson, also visited me almost every day. When I said, 'I'm sorry, I haven't got anything to say' he was happy to sit with me in silence.

Blind Pete, another young man I believed was Jesus of Nazareth; Simon, who sprinted full pelt down the whole length of the central corridor; Paul Tobias who kept up a commentary of when the fallopian tubes were opening and closing, went about their own recoveries in this weird, somehow wonderful ward. Throughout, I had the support of friends and family. Others found it impossible to visit me in such a place, could not cope with my psychotic episodes and couldn't sustain visits. So many peers at Day Hospital had precious little companionship. My friendships, new and old, were what gave me the strength to come through this and I owe them, and my family everything.

After three years the daunting, dreaded discharge date came. And then I met Emma, who would become my wife. Somehow my 'I'm mad, me' chat-up line didn't repel her. With her support and by staying on the medication (I always rapidly became unwell when stopping) I have remained mentally well for the past twenty-seven years, now over half my life. And I was able, with the advice of Gary, to start a career in mental health nursing, working in the same hospital where I'd been a patient.

Springfield Hospital and its staff not only saved my life but have given me a career as an RMN. I am informed by my own experiences, striving to give the nursing care that helped me when I needed it most. This has culminated in my combining a career as a university lecturer at Kingston University with working as a 'bank' nurse one day at weekends. I try to help the people who are where I once was: at their lowest.

I recognise my recovery journey will not work for everyone and am never unaware of how remarkably lucky I have been. As I endeavour to replicate the levels of care that so transformed my life, I always remind myself that, as John Bradford said in the sixteenth century, 'There but for the grace of God go I.'

Laurie Dahl is an RMN and Senior Lecturer in Mental Health at Kingston and St George's University. He lives in south London with his wife and two daughters.

Erin Turner

What makes us human? Why do some of us fight for survival amidst the most agonisingly difficult life situations, whereas others choose to end our lives, seemingly with much to live for? And is there any way to predict which camp we are likely to fall into? What part does hope play in our will to live and how can we learn to influence it in ourselves and those we care for?

As a psychiatrist these are questions I ponder. Studying, reading and research can never teach us as much as our patients, whose life stories can be fascinating and disturbing in equal measure. I work with young people who have been diagnosed with psychosis and schizophrenia, usually at a time of their lives when they are entering adulthood. A time often full of hope – of finding a lifetime partner, gaining a place at university, getting a job. It is therefore under-standable why the period of recovery after a psychotic episode is often hampered by depression, precipitated by the realisation that life has taken a very different and somewhat rocky path. This, along with the period before they receive treatment, is considered the most 'risky' time for a young person with psychosis.

Society has placed a huge burden on mental health professionals to determine which of our patients are 'a high suicide risk'. Assessing and acting on high risk of suicide is essential as the consequence of 'getting it wrong' is devastating for family, friends and (although often unconsidered) their psychiatrist and mental health team. Yet it is remarkably difficult to accurately predict which individual is likely to take their life.

The more I practise psychiatry, the more I am convinced that it is face-to-face compassionate care that makes the most difference to individuals. Giving hope to the hopeless is one of the most important, human, life-enhancing things we can do as doctors. Perhaps to better understand the significance of hope we must first understand despair. To be human is to have hope. To be human is also to know despair.

I have felt despair many times in my life. I have been close to death following peritonitis and sepsis. I have lost a close friend to cancer. Yet the most difficult time of my life followed an early morning phone call to inform me of the sudden death of one of my patients. At the time I was a relatively new consultant filled with an energy and desire to do my very best for my patients. So when I heard that Simran, a young man with a particularly severe form of schizophrenia, had died, I was devastated. I was wracked with guilt and self-blame, convincing myself that I hadn't done enough to save him; that his death was somehow my fault. This over-exaggerated sense of responsibility led me down a path of self-doubt and shame. The pain I felt for Simran's family ate away at me, anxiety and sleep disorder followed. My turmoil reached tipping point once I became aware that his family blamed me for his death. Hypervigilance ensured I was unable to relax, and each time my work phone rang I panicked, as memories of that early morning phone call were retriggered. No one, other than my husband, family and close friends. knew how bad I felt.

The anxiety I experienced heightened as the date of the Coroner's Court approached. Doctors who are involved in an untimely patient death have a duty to give evidence at Coroner's Court. Its purpose is to determine the cause of death, not to point fingers of blame, yet most doctors I know feel very much that they are under scrutiny and it is hard not to approach 'giving evidence' without a sense of being 'on trial' oneself.

The Coroner's Court and internal investigation exonerated me from blame. Yet I still had to learn how to stop blaming myself. Reflecting on this time I think I lost perspective. I also lost hope in myself and my ability to ever again enjoy my job. I gave serious thought to resigning.

Suicide among doctors is higher than average. Female doctors are four to five times more likely to end their lives than their male counterparts. Doctor suicides are often linked to a patient complaint. Society expects doctors to be emotionally resilient, yet forgets sometimes that we too are human and feel pain and loss as keenly as everyone else. And when you add the shame and guilt that often accompanies an unexpected patient death or a complaint, you can begin to understand the high suicide rate.

So, how did I regain hope in myself and my ability as a psychiatrist? Well, when it boils down to it, I think hope is just believing that things aren't going to stay as seemingly hopeless as they are at this moment. That if you just keep surviving, take a breath in and out and repeat, and try to keep 'living' life (go to work, pick up the kids from school, make dinner) there will come a time when life feels a bit less bleak. There will come a time when you actually start enjoying life again without feeling guilty. If I had booked to see my GP, she may have suggested, quite sensibly, that I take time off work. But actually I feel that work for me was therapeutic. While I was with my patients I could focus on something other than the turmoil I was experiencing. And by going through the daily motions of 'living', gradually I began to feel like my old self again. One day I noticed that I wasn't feeling anxious when my phone rang and that I wasn't having to repeatedly check up on my sick patients during weekends off.

What has that experience taught me? Principally it has helped me identify with the despair I see in many of my patients and to understand better how powerfully trauma affects our psyche and our confidence. It has helped me better understand the importance of self compassion, which is easier said than done when you blame yourself, but essential all the same. And it has helped me realise that it is the simplest of words that we can give to patients to help them regain hope: 'You're not always going to feel like this. You are going to get through. You are not alone – I will help you'. As I reflect upon the survival conundrum as set out in the opening paragraph, the perennial human struggle between hope and despair, I strongly suspect that such timely and meaningful expressions of hope are never wasted words. Imparting hope is profound and may just be enough to save a life. I believe this implicitly.

And what would I tell my younger self, or better still, my son who is just setting out on his career in medicine? I would say that being a doctor is an amazing privilege. However, with that privilege comes huge responsibility and you will make mistakes. When you do, particularly if you feel unsupported by the organisation in which you work, confide in someone you trust. Try hard not to blame yourself or suffer in silence. And if you can laugh a little, accept you are not perfect, and find good colleagues to work with, then you will be stronger for it.

No matter how bleak the situation, dawn always follows night.

Dr Erin Turner is a Consultant Psychiatrist at the Solihull Early Intervention in Psychosis Team. Erin and her work were featured in the BBC documentary *David Harewood: Psychosis and Me*.

Abbie Mitchell

My greatest moment of hope came from a conversation I had with a psychiatrist when I was nineteen, lying in my in-patient hospital bed. The doctor was doing his usual rounds, seeing how each patient was doing, when one day our conversation suddenly got stripped back to the very basics.

'Who are you, Abbie?'

'What do you mean, who am I?'

'Who are you?'

'What like, what do I do for a job?'

'No, tell me who YOU are.'

The psychiatrist was referring to me as a person. Someone made up of character traits and experiences. He wanted to know more about my personality, what made me tick. Not just my diagnosis and my trauma, but me as an individual. The question perplexed me for a while, firstly because no one had ever asked me anything like that before and secondly because . . . well, I wasn't sure. This conversation somehow paused the distress that I was experiencing in my head, and allowed me to think about who I was, separate from all the distress. It made me feel human again, not just a clinical problem. Being very unwell, I had succumbed powerlessly to my debilitating depression and anxiety. Before I had been admitted, with intrusive thoughts of self-harm, I had begun to lose hope.

A little back story. When I was fourteen I lost my shadow, my right arm, my dear, beautiful, glistening-eyed, wide-smiled, mum. Even writing that just made my heart skip a beat. I lost her in a way I could not understand, as a not-so-blissfully ignorant fourteen-year-old attending secondary school with no PSHE or mental health education. I lost her to the darkness that is suicide.

The years that followed were a turmoil of emotional distress and grief intertwined with the usual highs and lows of being a teenager. Before this I was Abbie; happy go lucky, apple-of-mum's eye Abbie. Abbie who did well at school. Abbie who wrote creatively and drew. Abbie, not without her own mental health struggles such as disordered eating, but Abbie who was unaware that this was a problem and who was plodding through her teenage years. When Mum passed (ouch again), I suffered deeply.

After the initial weeks of shock and disbelief, I tried to resume 'normal' life. I went back to school, to my friends who were equally in shock, who didn't know what to say although they were still there for me. They struggled as I began to 'play out', experimenting with alcohol and taking risky behaviour a little too far. They were worried but didn't know what to do. They could not protect me, that was not their role. I began to put myself in dangerous situations because deep down, I was quite happy to risk my no longer 'perfect life', because I might get to be next to my favourite person, who was no longer here with me. I wanted to be with Mum.

I went from therapist to therapist (never having it explained properly, in young person's terms, what the different types of therapy were, or what the word therapy actually meant) but my mental health struggles were always still there. The thought that perhaps being reunited with my mum would finally bring me peace became stronger and stronger. But somehow I finally reached out to my family and at nineteen went in for hospital treatment. After one week inside, I had the conversation that took me out of my sadness and reconnected 'me' to myself. The conversation that brought me hope.

My time was well spent in hospital, with lots of rest, an escape from the outside factors that were over-stimulating my brain, a chance to think about who I wanted to be, to learn about different types of therapy and medication. And hope. Hope can come back when it has been lost. It can come from the most unusual places where you would never expect to find it, but it is there. Hope will be a hero, it will give you a chance when you think there is nothing left. It's something I wish my dear mum had found.

Hope.

Abbie Mitchell is a Project Manager at a youth charity and a mental health & suicide awareness advocate. She blogs about her own experiences of grief and recovery at sunflowerandme.word-press.com/blog. She has also made a series of YouTube videos, *Suicide Taboo and Life without You*, with her best friend, who lost her brother to suicide ten years after she lost her mum.

David Wiseman

PTSD is something that you feel, sense even, as if a physical being is there with you. Following you. It can be terrifying. It's there when you're tired, when you're trying to fall asleep, when it's noisy, when it's crowded, when you're washing your face and can't open your eyes because of the soap . . . in short, when you're vulnerable.

I served as an infantryman in both Iraq and Afghanistan. I loved being a soldier, it was what I was born to be. Taking a small team of British soldiers out in the countryside of the Helmand Province, embedding within Afghan forces and engaging in warfighting was exciting and seemed natural to me at the time.

Then on 3 November 2009, we received a frantic call over the radio.

'Send help. British casualties. We are at the police station.'

Within seven minutes I was on the scene with seven other soldiers, and what we experienced that day defined who I was as a soldier. It also shook me to the core.

When we arrived at the police station, a few British soldiers were on the roof, firing their weapons to the north and waving at us to enter the compound. Without wishing to rush in, I quickly manoeuvred my team so the building had an outer cordon, an additional layer of security. Then I grabbed my medic and ran into the compound, a two-storey concrete building encircled by an eight-foot wall.

Just by the entrance a British soldier lay covered in blood. He had received five gunshot wounds to his legs. One round had gone through both his forearms, that he'd held in front of his face, and a single round had entered his face through his eye socket. God only knows how he was still alive.

After applying tourniquets to his legs and leaving my medic to continue treatment, I moved further through the compound. Round the corner of the building I was struck by a truly horrendous scene. Five men lay dead or dying, three atop each other and two more spaced along the wall of the building. Each man had been strafed by multiple rounds and the carnage this had wrought was almost beyond belief. A bullet wound is not like you see in the movies – a neat hole with a trickle of blood – rather it breaks bones, contorts flesh and creates a hole the size of a tennis ball as it exits the body. Each man had between five and ten such wounds across their bodies.

As we treated the dying, it was clear that a very seriously wounded British soldier was lying beneath two of his dead comrades and it was up to us to get him free. Moving the dead men and trying to pull him out is without doubt the most traumatising thing I have ever experienced. It is the action that caused the most damage to my own long-term health.

There were other men on the roof that needed our help. But I still had no idea what had caused this devastation and so, utterly alone, I entered the building and cleared darkened room after darkened room, making sure each one was empty, fearing all the time that enemy insurgents were hiding in each one. Making my way to the roof, and speaking to the only two British soldiers there who had not been seriously injured, it was clear that this had been an inside job and two rogue Afghan National Policemen were responsible for the murder and serious injury that had taken place. The perpetrators had fled but this was the moment the local Taliban commander chose to launch his attack on the building with a trickle of gunfire and a series of strikes, in an attempt to exploit our weakened state.

Eventually we were reinforced, we got our wounded away and we respectfully dealt with our dead comrades. Despite our best efforts, five men died that day and a further nine were seriously wounded, many with multiple gunshot wounds that resulted in life-changing injuries.

I have often heard comparisons between the trauma

experienced by soldiers and that experienced by civilians involved in sexual assaults, or terrible accidents. I think it is wrong to compare anyone's experiences, one is no worse or more serious than another. But in order for them to be treated well, there is one important difference to be understood. I can only speak for myself, but I know it's also true of many other veterans: our traumatic experiences are wrapped up in a great sense of pride. We often encountered our trauma whilst enacting our raison d'être, making it even more difficult for us to process the fact that it is the violence for which we have been trained and which we execute with honour, that causes us so much heartache. All this provides our therapists with complex tasks to unpick when it comes to what is good and what is bad.

All I know is that on that day in November, if my team and I hadn't reacted in the way we did, and to such a standard, many more British soldiers would not have come home to their families. So, given the choice, I would return to that day and go through it all again.

In those two months at the back end of 2009, my small team of nine British soldiers dealt with twenty-five casualties throughout Nad E'Ali district: Brits, Afghan soldiers, policemen and civilians. including women and children. And on 15 November 2009, just twelve days after the attack at the police station, I became the twenty-sixth to be treated.

I was part of a patrol aiming to engage with and defeat the enemy at close quarters. During the fire fight that ensued, I received a gunshot wound to the chest. The round entered just below my collar bone, bounced off my ribs and then rattled halfway down my torso before coming to rest in my right lung, where it remains to this day.

My right lung collapsed immediately and the hole in my chest created a 'sucking chest wound', named after the sound it makes when you breathe in – ominous, since it shows that air is entering your chest cavity. On top of this, the round had nicked my axial artery, which meant that my chest was not only filling with air, but also with blood, resulting in a pneumo-haemo-thorax; essentially, my good lung was now running out of room for it to open and unless I was cut open and drained quickly, I would suffocate.

I stopped breathing a few times on the ground but as my medic shook me in desperation, he must have swilled the blood around just enough to allow my good lung room to open, thus buying me a few more minutes.

Eventually two helicopters circled above. One suppressed the enemy positions with sustained machine gun fire whilst the other landed and picked me up. The US medic in the back leaned in. I remember his heavy smell and his impressive bandit 'tash as he held me close and yelled in my face above the sound of the rotors, just before he plunged a scalpel into my side. Without anaesthesia he stabbed, then cut through skin and sinew before shoving a tube through my ruined rib cage, allowing the blood to drain onto the floor of the Blackhawk and allowing me to take my first full breath in what had felt like an age.

So, that is what broke me for a while.

At first, I didn't know I was broken. Despite being incredibly emotional nearly all the time, I just wanted to get back to work and tried to hide everything from my colleagues. The physical and emotional pain lived out of sight – or so I thought.

My wife knew, obviously. You can't hide anything from the one you love. But it wasn't until a work colleague and friend took me to one side that I started to realise that I needed help.

People do not understand PTSD. They think it means that you are jumpy and overly aggressive; at constant risk of flashing back and reliving what you went through.

PTSD is more than that.

Living with PTSD means having to have a busy mind because a relaxed mind will automatically fill with things you don't want to think about. It means being tired all the time because that amount of thinking takes energy.

The moments when you can't have control over what you think fill you with dread and make what should be the most relaxing times of the day into the worst times – waking up and going to sleep. You know that the first thing you will think about in the morning and the last thing you will think about at night is that incident, that face, that pain . . .

It means that you either must be so exhausted that you fall asleep quickly, or you dull your thoughts with alcohol or you go through a series of mental exercises to stay thinking as you drop off.

But PTSD is a wicked and mischievous creature. These exercises only work for so long and soon you'll feel the PTSD laughing at you as you start on your coping strategies. Someone you don't want to see will be sitting in your 'safe place' and once again, sleep alludes you.

Living with PTSD means that even when you're not actively thinking about it, it's playing somewhere in a loop in the back of your mind. You find yourself in a conversation with a stranger who all of a sudden starts looking at you strangely, because the conversation has lurched into stories of horror and you didn't even know you'd started telling them.

It's living in fear and embarrassment. It's having to explain that you need to sleep with the light on because when you wake from dreams you need to immediately see where you are, to see something mundane and in the present in order to ground yourself. The consequence of not doing so will be immediate panic, screaming, your eyes streaming as they frantically see horrible things in the corners, your feet scrabbling at the bedclothes in a vain attempt to run from the terror that grips you.

It means numbness and isolation as no one can really know what this means. It means depression and the constant need to find dopamine to feed the brain with pockets of empty joy. Empty joy that can be found in instant gratification. And even though you know deep down this behaviour will be self-destructive, you follow yourself willingly to new lows.

It means screaming in a toddler's face, a sheer white face that doesn't understand why his daddy is so terrified when he creeps up on him.

It means the brain overloading and lacking the ability to cope with too much information or stress. Resulting in, best, a short temper, quick to anger with teeth clenched and fists gripped. At worst, your brain giving up for a period and just throwing itself into neutral. The world keeps moving but you are not part of it, just an observer. Your mind is full of cotton wool as the flashing lights, the screaming kids or the intense meeting just carries on going. Arms and legs are heavy and suddenly overwhelming fatigue means you can barely keep your eyes open.

The mind loves to make sense of the world and in order for it to do this, it needs to file things away properly. For experiences to become memories, the mind needs a point of reference so that it goes in the correct 'brain file'.

This is what people call processing.

But my processing got stuck. I had no point of reference. My mind couldn't make sense of what it had experienced and so the experiences didn't convert into proper memories. So my brain had to keep them close to the surface, it had to keep replaying them over and over in an attempt to make sense of them, before filing them properly.

This resulted in all sorts of issues, including intrusive thoughts, nightmares, high emotion, fatigue, hyper-arousal, hyper-vigilance. And one of the strangest sensations was the feeling that I was being followed. Followed by one of the soldiers that I had watched die.

My reason for telling you this was because it scared the hell out of me. But it almost had to reach crisis point before I told anyone else because I thought I was completely losing my mind. The mind does strange things when it experiences trauma and keeping these things to yourself is not the right way to deal with it.

I could explain all the other things, but the feeling of being haunted was not something I had ever expected or could under-stand. That is until I considered it from a position of processing.

When I experienced the bloody aftermath of more than a dozen people being shot at nearly point-blank range, followed by creeping through a darkened building searching the shadows for people who might wish to kill me, perhaps the only thing my mind could relate it to was a horror movie. My mind was trying to find a toe-hold in previous experiences and this was the only one it could find.

But it took me years to come to this conclusion. And in the

meantime, whenever I was driving alone at night, whenever I turned the light off, whenever I covered my face in soap in the shower . . . he was there with me. Don't get me wrong, this wasn't psychosis. I never actually thought someone was there with me, but there is a big difference between the thinking part of your brain telling you that everything is fine, versus the feeling part of your brain screaming that a dead person is sitting in the back of the car, propped up in the corner of your bedroom or lying on the stairs looking into the bathroom.

It filled me with terror multiple times a day, reinforced by the fact that these images weren't based on a scary story or TV show, but were lived experiences that my brain craved to bring to the surface, experiences that were in full HD along with the sensations of smell, sound and touch.

My therapist once told me that she couldn't stop this person following me around. However, she could get me to a point where I would no longer be so terrified by his presence. In fact she was wrong . . . she actually did a bit of both.

I was in therapy for years, centred around talking therapy, CBT (Cognitive Behavioural Therapy) and a lot of EMDR (Eye Movement Desensitisation and Reprocessing Therapy). EMDR was incredibly difficult, to be honest. Sometimes the images that came to the fore during these sessions mutated and changed over time. That memory of me pulling the wounded solider from underneath his comrades altered to him either pulling me in with him or him leaping out and attacking me. Again, my brain was trying to process the experience and turn it into a memory by playing around with it, corrupting what had actually happened to see if the new version would fit into a file. But I got stuck with these versions, they wouldn't shift and after God only knows how many sessions, it was decided that I had progressed as far as I could go with the treatment.

Nevertheless I had come a long way. The three things that made a huge impact on my recovery during this time were swimming, giving up alcohol and meditation.

Physical activity has long been linked to good mental health and for me, the immersive nature of swimming resulted in pool time being the only time my brain could be completely empty. All I could think about was my breathing, my form and counting my lengths. After a hard swim, my body would be charged with positive endorphins and I would buzz for an hour or so afterwards, and was also more likely to sleep that night.

Drink clouds the brain and slows everything down. It reduces your inhibitions and lowers your defences with regards to emotional regulation. It was incredibly positive for my mental health to completely abstain for a number of years whilst I got better.

And, finally, meditation.

After treatment finished, I still lived with this person following me around. Terrifying me, filling me with horror and making me dread time on my own. I had downloaded 'Headspace' and used it religiously to learn how to meditate and find some peace in my own head, but living with intrusive thoughts makes meditation difficult and often my mind would take me back to that moment of pulling this dying soldier free, bloody, with terrible wounds all over his body and face.

One evening I was sitting on a train, commuting back from London after a busy and stressful day. In an attempt to restore myself and find balance, I tuned into a piece of guided meditation. I started to focus on my breathing but soon, as so often happened, my mind was taken over by intrusive thoughts and I was back at the police station. Two dead men lying atop another dying man and I was reaching into all this to pull him free. The video in my mind mutated and corrupted, and followed the path of him trying to pull me in with him and after I resisted, he came out and attacked me, biting and scratching at my neck and face . . . but instead of recoiling, instead of fighting back, this time it was different. I remembered what my therapist had told me and combined this with my learnings about meditation; the images you see in your mind may be powerful but they are just images – don't fight them, just observe your thoughts.

I chose not to fight my thoughts.

I chose not to fight this soldier.

Instead, in my mind, the memory mutated once again and instead of me screaming and punching, I embraced him. He carried on struggling and trying to bite, but I held on, hugging him close and telling him it'll be ok. And soon, he calmed, and held me back. We held each other.

That was two years ago.

He has not haunted me since.

David Wiseman joined the British Army in 2006 and was commissioned from Sandhurst into the Yorkshire Regiment. He is the author of *Helmand to the Himalayas*.

Richard Cosgrove

'I'm going to kill myself.'

If I was crying, I couldn't tell.

'I'm going to kill myself.'

This was my mantra as I hugged myself, head bowed, eyes crunched shut, standing under a scalding hot shower that felt cold. The words came unbidden, constantly, always when I was alone.

'I'm going to kill myself.'

Every day, when I was alone and nothing occupied my mind, when I couldn't ignore the disembodied, crushing pain of depression, the thought would come.

This wasn't a stranger's thought, something from outside myself, or a stray memory. It was a truth I was stating, as certain as my saying, 'I'm eating fish finger sandwiches' while eating fish finger sandwiches. Me telling myself what I would do.

I don't know when that thought first appeared. It seemed it was always there. And I can't say when another first appeared – quiet, confident, and determined words: 'No. I will not.'

I was first diagnosed with clinical depression in 2014. But all through my life I've consistently had what's euphemistically described as 'low mood'. In one of my few childhood memories I'm sat, curled up, in my school playground, wanting to sink into the ground. I was eight or nine years old. Despite this, I did not seek treatment until I was in my thirties. Today, I know this unwillingness was due to my own fears about mental illness – internalisation of society's stigma – and my own inability to ask for help.

I've had at least three mental health crises in my life.

The first was when I was about nineteen. I referred to this as a nervous breakdown, but it was not diagnosed. The second was diagnosed as clinical depression and anxiety disorder in 2014, but began much earlier. And the latest began in 2017 and ended as 2019 began. In each case, my recovery took long months.

My memories during these crises are vague and undefined. While I can recall some life events, the emotions and pain I felt are hidden. Looking back is like trying to remember a nightmare: I relive the terror, but I can't remember what caused it.

During my last two crises, I had an advantage I lacked when I was nineteen: Twitter.

Twitter allows users to publish 140-character messages about what they are doing or thinking to the internet. But I think it's the Twitter hashtag that enables its users to form and find communities. It's became an online space where people who can't talk about their lives openly due to prejudice – including people of colour, political activists, LGBT+ people, and those with physical disabilities and mental illnesses – can speak out and connect to others like them.

Before I began using Twitter, I thought depression wasn't a real illness. I grew up in an English village, in a conservative upper-middle-class family, learning about the world from the *Daily Mail*. My family sniggered at mental illness and ignored its presence among us. They taught me that people didn't get depressed – they felt sorry for themselves. So at nineteen, as my mind was fracturing, I found myself thinking, 'There's nothing wrong with me. So what's wrong with me?'

Then, in 2008, I joined Twitter. And I read stories from people saying their day-to-day life was crushing them, that they struggled to get through it. They described how I had felt for much of my life. But it was years before I realised they were describing their symptoms of depression. And it was a far longer time before I accepted I had those symptoms as well.

In 2010, I was made redundant and thrown into the world of freelancing, something I was not prepared for. I struggled to find steady work. Soon afterwards, my relationship with my best friend lay in ruins. I couldn't face waking up. I couldn't socialise. I couldn't focus. I couldn't think clearly. I was always angry. I was always sick. I wanted to speak to people. I couldn't speak to anyone. I was choking. My skull was being crushed. One afternoon I realised I was getting worse – not by the week or even day, but by the hour and by the minute. I realised I was in danger.

Then I remembered what people on Twitter who endured depression had kept saying: get help.

Terrified, struggling to speak, I called my doctor's practice.

'I need to make an emergency appointment, please.'

'What is the reason?'

'I need help. I'm spiralling and I don't think I can stop. I'm scared I'll hurt myself.'

I remember I was crying. And I remember the receptionist's calm, clear and urgent voice.

'I'll have a doctor call you back as soon as I can. Can you wait?'

'Yes. Thank you.'

She made me promise to call an ambulance if I got worse and hung up.

In the late afternoon, one of the practice's doctors called me. We talked about what was happening to me.

'I'll write you a prescription today. Collect it and start it. And I'm booking you in for an emergency appointment tomorrow. Is that ok?'

I couldn't say 'yes' at first. I was crying too hard. But this time from relief. Now I knew there was help. I knew I was going to be all right.

The prospect of taking antidepressants scared me. All I'd heard about them was that they could be addictive, even make people violent or suicidal. But my doctor talked me through their effects and the myths around them. They warned me the pills would take at least a fortnight to take effect. I didn't care about that: someone was helping to arrest my fall.

Within two weeks, the pills were working. I felt calmer and I was able to focus on my new job as a high school teaching assistant. For a time at least. After some ups and downs and a change of medication my mood became stable, and at times I was even able to feel happy.

My doctor also prescribed me a course of cognitive behavioural therapy (CBT). The therapy taught me to recognise the 'wrong thinking' that is a feature of depression and to challenge those thoughts. Today, I use CBT every day to challenge negative thinking and move my focus out to my senses, rather than let it intrude inwards, to my darkness, when my mood falls.

While I was in a crisis, the friends I'd found on Twitter supported and advised me. I learned I could turn to them for help. And, much later, I learned that in turn I could offer them help and advice when they needed it.

In 2017, my life collapsed again, partly due to the financial fallout of my previous crisis. Debts that had mounted up while I was unemployed were crushing me. Depression took advantage of my vulnerable mood and attacked again. But this time it was different. This time, I knew what was happening. This time, I knew I could help myself.

When I noticed my mood had fallen, I began monitoring myself using the standardised 'mood self-assessment quiz' which is used by mental health professionals to evaluate levels of depression and anxiety in patients. I kept a record of the results, charting my scores on a graph. When I saw my scores were trending down sharply, I called my doctor again and I went back on medication.

This bout drove me into a deeper depression than before. But I knew how to recognise what was happening now and how to fight back, though for quite a while it was a fight just not to get worse.

That changed one day, in the shower, as I was trying not to scream.

'I am going to kill myself,' I thought.

I don't know when I first said 'no', but that was the time I knew I would survive and beat my depression.

It took almost a year, but the suicidal thoughts stopped. Saying they are gone would be a lie. Instead, they quietened in frequency and volume, and are now just an occasional annoyance, easily swatted away. A mosquito. Today, my thoughts are different.

'I'll fight. I'll fix my problems. I'm worth something. I'll survive. I love my cat and my friends. And they love me.'

Now, today, as I write this, I know that if I spiral down into depression again, no matter how far I fall, I'll be able to find medical help. I'll have friends who'll support me, and I'll be able to recover.

'I am going to kill myself.'

'No. I'll survive.'

Richard Cosgrove is a freelance sub-editor, copy editor and writer. In 2020, at the age of forty-four, he was diagnosed as having Attention Deficit Hyperactivity Disorder (ADHD). Richard uses social media to speak out about mental health issues. He can be found on Twitter at @rcosgrove.

Jazz Thornton

If you told the girl once sitting in a psychiatric unit that one day she would be travelling the world as a mental health advocate, she would have never believed you. I battled with mental ill health for nine years, and the first time I tried to take my own life I was only twelve. I always felt different growing up – I couldn't maintain friendships, I struggled to engage in everyday life and I always had this little voice at the back of my head telling me that I wasn't good enough.

To give you context, I come from a background that is depressingly common, being born into a broken household. When I was three years old I was sexually abused by three different men and from that moment the script of my life shifted. My Child Protection files say that I went from being 'happy and bubbly' to 'dull and lacking emotion'. It's no wonder that for the next seventeen years I struggled with my mental health. I carried the belief that I was a burden, that I didn't deserve to be here – I genuinely thought that the world would be better without me. I lost count of the number of times I woke up in hospital following a mental illness-related episode, or watched them close the door in the psych ward, sitting with the sinking feeling that I was trapped there. And yet, while I believed that this was my reality, that this would continue to be my reality for the rest of my life, it wasn't.

I remember the exact moment that things started to change for me. I had just tried to take my life – for the very last time, as it happened – and a woman, Esther, who I have known for ten years, came and sat with me. I remember just sitting there crying as she looked at me and asked, 'Jazz, why are you crying?' I replied, 'I am just so tired of fighting.' And what she said next not only changed my life, but became the message I carry to this day:

'Jazz, what do you think the definition of fighting is? I'm not sure you have been fighting. I think you have only been surviving, and it is only when you learn how to fight that the change you are longing to see is going to happen.'

I sat there stunned – I thought I had been fighting this whole time. But when I looked up the definitions of surviving and of fighting, this is what I found:

The definition of surviving is 'To continue to live or exist in hardship, manage to keep going in difficult circumstances.' Having a survival instinct is important, it is what keeps us going when times are tough. Sometimes the only thing we can do in that moment is survive, and that is ok. But if we stay in survival mode for too long, it can lead to us accepting our situation / feelings / behaviours as our normality.

The definition of fighting is: 'To engage in a battle or war, fight to overcome and destroy an adversary.' Pretty different to surviving, huh?

In the fight back for my life I had to learn how to engage in this battle, how to stop simply surviving and start fighting. It was a long and hard journey. It meant learning how to fight; it meant making decision after decision to ask for help instead of running away. But eventually, I did fight through. I pulled through the other side and began to change the script of my life. And ultimately, the very thing that nearly took me out, my mental illness, turned into one of the greatest strengths. It turned into a story that gives people hope – a story that has been heard in governments and in schools, in businesses and in communities. A story that I get to stand up and share every single day.

When you are in the middle of your darkest hour it can feel impossible and incredibly hopeless. If you told the girl once crying in a white-walled hospital room that she would one day be happy, that she would walk into every day with a smile on her face, she would have laughed. But no situation is too big or too dark to be turned around. You are not a lost cause, you are not too far gone. Don't give up. You never know where the next chapter of your life will lead you.

Jazz Thornton is an international mental health advocate who co-founded Voices of Hope. Jazz uses her experience of mental illness to advocate for change around the world, speaking at conferences, events and schools. She directed the award-winning series *Jessica's Tree*, as well as viral video *Dear Suicidal Me*. Recently, she released her bestselling book *Stop Surviving, Start Fighting*, and her story is also being told through the new feature film *The Girl on The Bridge* (2020).

Gian Power

At first glance my life probably looked perfect. Graduating from university and embarking upon my city career, it certainly felt that way. Back then, mental wellbeing wasn't something I had to take seriously. Until May 2015, when everything came crashing down and my life changed forever.

On 7 May, my father left for business overseas and never returned. He was murdered. My world was turned upside down.

At twenty-three, I found myself leading an international murder investigation and fighting in court for justice. This continues today. When I returned to work after three months, I felt completely over-whelmed – working long hours, doing intense accounting exams and looking after my family whilst managing my father's case through the night. My head was constantly raging with emotions, from sadness to anger, confusion and panic.

My father's body was eventually found by the Indian authorities and flown back to Heathrow so we could say our goodbyes. The results of the DNA test I had demanded came back on the same day as the funeral – to reveal this wasn't actually my father's body. This second blow felt almost as powerful as the first.

These tough life lessons about uncontrollable situations and self-ish human greed pushed me to the brink. I realised I needed to look after myself and take the concept of self-care seriously. More than anything, I needed a glimmer of hope to keep me going.

In the most difficult of times it can be hard to see the light amongst the darkness, to see the positives in the negativity that takes over – but try. Finding the positives, no matter how small, can get you through the worst of times and help you to keep going.

One particular moment happened whilst I was working at

PricewaterhouseCoopers in 2015. I was struggling to make ends meet, having lost everything my family owned, and I felt overwhelmed by despair. A leader at the firm took me for a walk, listened to me and said something that gave me a glimmer of hope: 'You may not have your dad today, but think of one day when you will create your own family, have your own children and can share all of the wonderful memories with them.'

To many this may sound obvious, but it hadn't crossed my mind. I hadn't thought about the future because I was so stuck in the past. I realised then that I had a choice: I could choose to create a new life for myself full of happiness and purpose, and focus on what brings me joy.

In addition, at times when I felt situations were out of my control, I realised that there was one thing that I could control – I still can and so can you – and that's how I respond to a situation. Nobody can take that away from us. I can decide whether I will become angry, calm, happy or sad and I can tune into my emotions, move around them. It was an incredibly powerful realisation.

Every day I tell myself to LIVE. Embrace life every single day because we are so lucky to be here and have so many opportunities around us. 'Remember life and then your life becomes a better one', are words from a song by Lukas Graham, whose music has helped me through some difficult times. Song lyrics become so much more pertinent when you've lost someone.

Then there's the importance of self-belief. 'Believe you can, and you will, believe you can't, and you probably won't' was a quote given to me on my final day of school, aged sixteen. We have to love ourselves, be kind to ourselves and have a positive mentality. Reward yourself, take time for you. Even the smallest negative self-talk can take all of this away. Don't be afraid to love yourself.

My sister Emma is my best friend and as my sibling is the only person who can relate to the emotions I have gone through; she's been a rock through the most difficult of times. The same goes for my mum who is the strongest lady I know. Friends have also been monumental in my recovery, they are like my family. I've learned that it's no longer how long I have known someone that matters, it's the strength of the relationship. There's such value in having loyal people around who truly care about you. It's not about the number of friends but the right friends, people who don't judge you but accept you for who you are and actively listen when you need it.

Shortly after I lost my father, my grandfather passed away and I took time out to reflect on the loss of two generations of role models who had taught me so much. It wasn't easy. I took a day off and sat in Hyde Park alone, every emotion possible coming to the surface. Realising I had too many negative people around me at that time, I decided to write each of them a letter to get words from my head on to paper. I then distanced myself from these people and anyone else who didn't have my best interests at heart – it was the best thing I have ever done. I encourage everyone to think about who they're around most. Do they lift you up and bring out the best version of you?

From that moment on I resolved to surround myself with positivity, happiness and gratitude. I am now grateful for everything in my life and fill every day with positive thoughts.

Gian Power set up his first business aged thirteen and later worked at Deutsche Bank and PricewaterhouseCoopers.

In 2015 aged twenty-three, Gian's life changed forever when he found out his father had been murdered. This experience sparked his passion for prioritising wellbeing and inclusion in the workplace. Gian is the founder of TLC Lions and The Unwind Experience.

He now hosts his own round tables in the House of Lords, stressing the importance of inclusion and wellbeing in the workplace.

Rebecca Elliott

None of us can see around the corner, let alone into our own futures. Perhaps that's a good thing? Who really wants to know, with total certainty, what's in store for them? Sure, there might be good things ahead, but just around the corner there may well be heartache and terrifying challenges.

Imagine me, back in my early twenties, believing I had my whole able-bodied life ahead of me. Little did I know that my body had other plans; I had a fault in my DNA that would create a calamity of physical disability as I grew older. Ehlers Danlos Syndrome is a genetic condition affecting my body's collagen production: the ligaments holding my skeleton together are far too elastic and this makes my skin stretchy and my joints ridiculously loose and bendy. As a child, I frightened my school friends with contortions of my weird, rubbery fingers and I was also born without a hip socket and that needed surgical correction before I was able to walk properly.

Up until I was thirty-three, I managed my condition very well. I was a motorbike-riding wills and probate lawyer, a working mum with no physical disability, except a slight limp. But once the arthritis set in to my wonky skeleton, becoming disabled was an inevitable process of degeneration. I went from walking around the park with my son, to watching others do the same with an envy I pitied myself for experiencing. I tried for the longest time to remain the capable Becky I'd always been. But I had to stop riding my motorbike when I could no longer climb onto it and though I tried to keep walking and working, these attempts became smaller and more futile, the distances ever shorter, the targets often abandoned altogether as unachievable. Finally, I lost the ability to walk more than a few steps, unable to overcome the sciatic and arthritic pain by sheer mental will. That's when I stopped being 'Becky' and became 'Disabled Becky.'

I gave up working in 2008. We lost our home because I could no longer pay for it. We lost our next rented home because despite paying rent to a rogue landlord, *he* didn't pay *his* mortgage and we were evicted. All this took place in the midst of epidurals for my spine and facet joint injections so painful that I cried out in the operating theatre.

I spent my days reclining in my chair or lying on my bed all day every day, I transferred between those two places. My muscles became fatigued from the strain of holding me up, unlike the average person, whose strong ligaments keep their skeleton together without much effort. I would describe the steady background pain of a chronic pain syndrome like Ehlers Danlos as being like having flu, permanently. Lying on (or in) my bed eased the widespread pain that became unbearable after sitting up for a while. I had a bedspread which covered my bed during the day, and for me, it delineated a division between the day and night. I wasn't actually *in* bed the whole time. I was *on* the bed, but not *in* it! It was a small but important distinction in managing the challenges of such an intense narrowing of my life.

The mind-body connection is strong and as my physical health declined, my mental health worsened commensurately. Depression became like an old friend, resurging in intermittent waves, almost as crippling as my crumbling bones. Anxiety about how we would manage in the future without my secure income left me with acute panic episodes where I couldn't speak for hours at a time.

I have never been very good at not thinking about the things that hurt me and when someone says, 'Just stop thinking about it,' or 'Don't worry about it,' inevitably my brain turns to *exactly* the thing I'm supposed to forget. It's a natural reaction; tell anyone not to think about a pink elephant and suddenly they imagine that pink elephant in all her glory. So it's not always possible to distract myself from my dark thoughts; when I'm locked beneath the black veil of a severe depressive episode, I have absolutely no motivation to do any of the activities that might occupy my brain long enough to distract me from it. And I know that pain gains strength when I give it my undivided attention, so it is incredibly important to turn my focus away from it wherever I can.

After giving birth to my youngest son via a very traumatic emergency caesarean, I was diagnosed with postnatal depression. After I left hospital, a specialist psychiatrist visited me at home. She was the first doctor to suggest that – for me, at least – distraction was likely to provide a very good coping technique for my anxiety and depression. And she was right. Although back then I hadn't fine-tuned my distraction skills, I benefited greatly from her advice, as well as the antidepressants she prescribed.

Since then, I've seen that distraction *can* pull me from the darkest places and it has become a valuable implement in my mental health toolbox. I've learned to use tricks to lure my brain away from my pain intensity levels. A cuddle from my husband lasting more than twenty seconds will cause my brain to release the neuropeptide oxytocin, a natural painkiller produced by my body which reduces sensitivity to pain. Those hugs make me feel brave and remind me of the reasons I push onwards, even on the worst days. Each evening, if my concentration levels are good enough, I'll lose myself in a good book. If not, I'll turn to my Kindle and plug my imagination into a box set, allowing the drama to carry me away to a different world, one where my pain is irrelevant.

One of my favourite films is *Rocky*. I love his battle. I love that Rocky wins his fight, though not in a straightforward way. He doesn't defeat his opponent to win the boxing title but he *does* win, on his own terms. He sets his own target and he goes for it. He pours all his efforts into running up and down those steps and going the distance with his boxing opponent, even if he can't actually win the title. My world is very similar. Every day, when I open my eyes, I'm at the foot of those Philadelphia steps.

Back in the early years of my physical decline, I was told by a Pain Management Consultant, that I needed to 'find acceptance'. I wondered exactly what he meant. Did it mean accepting my limitations or accepting that I would have a lifetime of pain? One rather jolly orthopaedic spinal specialist assured me that my degenerative back pain would improve in my sixties, as by then my bones would naturally fuse through the ageing process. I was only thirty-three at the time! Did I really have to wait thirty more years for some relief? Was that the acceptance I was supposed to try to find?

The word 'acceptance' has intrigued me ever since and although I can't pinpoint exactly when it happened, I do know that I have now finally come to accept my condition. It only took a decade to get here.

Acceptance meant accepting that Ehlers Danlos Syndrome would always be part of my world and that pain would always be a consequent part of that. But while I accept pain as my constant companion, always in hovering in the background looking for a way to join in the conversation, I don't have to let it limit my activities. I have become more flexible and willing to adapt the type of activities I could do, even with my disability, in order to stay part of the world at large.

I'm determined to continue running up those metaphorical steps – just like Rocky – and though I'll sometimes get knocked down, I'll keep going. I will use what I've learned about how to manage my pain, anxiety and depression. I'll keep taking the medications and never be ashamed of that because, for me and so many others, they help make doing the impossible, bearable.

Another form of distraction has been my love of books, through which I indulge and express myself, despite the considerable limitations of my physical world. I love reading and my home is filled with tall bookcases, packed two rows deep. And I've always loved writing.

Now I get to escape into worlds of my own creation for a certain amount of time each day. My body relies on a wheelchair but my brain does not and with the new technology available, it's possible to achieve a great deal from your own bed! Google voice-to-text means I can dictate from my pillow, in order to bring my stories to the page. And this is how I make space in my world for my good friend, hope. She is more than just a companion. She is a true friend.

As long as pain levels remain in a fragile equilibrium with hope, it is possible to imagine the wildest dreams worthy of pursuit.

Hope kickstarts my days and whilst I try to avoid unrealistic notions of what might come to pass, there has to be a magic of sorts in order for hope to work. Mundane hope doesn't cut it; it has neither charm nor sparkle and it won't entice me from my bed over the hurdles of pain to put my feet to the floor and get dressed for the day ahead. I need to dream big dreams in order to face down huge challenges and sustain hope.

I may never actually achieve my ambitions, but that won't strip me of hope. I will have a wonderful journey along the way, albeit a different one to that which I imagined as an able-bodied, invincible young girl. If anxiety, depression and pain persist and stay by my side, I will not believe that makes me weak, or unworthy. And I will try not to feel like a failure just because I may never be *cured* of my mental health conditions or physical disability. I simply choose to aim for feeling *better* and fire that hopeful arrow off into the distance, chasing it down one gentle day at a time.

Born in the Midlands, Rebecca Elliott spent most of her working life as a Wills and Probate Legal Executive and also worked in the Probation Service. Most recently, she ran a pub, where she cooked brilliant pork pies on *Britain's Best Dish* on ITV. Rebecca is a Mum of two boys, Sam and Joe, and wife to Paul. She is disabled, with Ehlers Danlos Syndrome, and passionate about improving the lives of others with mental/physical illness or disability.

Japheth Obare

It all started in 1995, three years into my agribusiness. I can still remember it clearly. After completing high school, two of my friends and I decided to set up a business in organic farming, as there were few jobs around and our parents had little money to send us to college. This was work we enjoyed as it gave us an income and enabled us to appreciate nature. We used a few chemicals to deal with tough diseases, like blight, so when I fell ill, I assumed that it was due to inhaling these chemicals.

I went to the local district hospital and had some tests but nothing much was done. Around this time, my father was seconded to head the Kenya Scouts Association and moved to the capital, Nairobi. By then I had started hallucinating but my father insisted I join him in Nairobi, as he had found me a college place at the Railway Training Institute. So I travelled to Nairobi, despite my poor condition. Unfortunately I got worse and was taken to Mbagathi Hospital in Nairobi, where they told me I had cerebral malaria. At the time this was a common diagnosis for mental illnesses in Kenya, due to the lack of mental-health professionals. Thankfully I recovered and seemed to be getting on with my life. But I left college after a year, realising production engineering was not my forte. Then I tried computer programming, which I liked, but didn't think would result in a job, so I quit that too. My father was very disappointed in me and stopped supporting me. I was left on my own.

I grew up in a very large family, with nine brothers and four sisters. We lived a humble life in Siaya and went barefoot to school in Siaya township. My father wanted us to have a good education and invested in us heavily, despite his small salary. His dream was that one of his children would go to university. However, he struggled with alcohol and spent little time with us. I was quite wild growing up and was always in trouble both at home and in school. I loved birds so I kept some pigeons that I would sell from time to time to earn some money. I paid little attention to school work and was academically average most of the time.

My adolescent and teen years were difficult but improved after I became a Christian at twenty and embraced the teachings of the Bible. I ended up joining Youth With A Mission but my illness returned while I was undergoing Bible training in Madison, Wisconsin and in 2002 in Chicago I was diagnosed with psychotic disorder.

From that time on, my judgement was impaired due to hallucinations. In 2005 I was diagnosed with paranoid schizophrenia, this time in San Francisco, California. Instead of embracing my diagnosis, I went to war with it and sank into a state of denial. I strongly felt I had been misdiagnosed as I wasn't hearing any voices at that time. So I went ahead and enrolled at San Francisco City College for accounting classes. I took medication for a while but then stopped and continued to struggle mentally, although I decided not to share this with anyone, including my friends and family. Towards my graduation, things became serious and I then started hearing voices. I completely lost touch with reality and knew my life was in grave danger.

I made the decision to return to Kenya as it was an environment I was familiar with. So in 2008, I returned to Kenya, still keeping everything secret. Friends and family failed to understand me and resorted to cooking up stories that were quite hurtful. I had my own demons to deal with and spent most of the time in my own world of madness. Coming from a strong Christian background, I believed that I was under demonic attack and engaged the voices spiritually during the whole time, thinking that prayer would resolve the issue. I was working so at least I had a steady income, even as I lived in hell.

When the voices started, they threw me off balance in a big way.

They were very loud. It was almost like having headphones on at full volume. This went on for seven years, during which life was full of terror for me. I was quite paranoid during this time and would suffer from bouts of panic attacks. Then I read an article about Peter Bullimore in the *New Scientist*, and how he used therapy to tame the voices. I decided to try it and after a while, the voices did reduce in loudness. After some time, they went quiet altogether for short periods of time. That was the turning point for me. Nowadays, I can go for six months without hearing any voices and during these periods, I am usually mostly ok even though I still struggle with a bit of depression. I hope this inspires others who might be reading and encourages them to give it a try. It may work for them as well.

In 2015, my elder brother died and I lost it. I became psychotic and ended up in Tanzania. This was when I realised my war against my diagnosis was an exercise in futility and I decided to embrace it. I came clean with my family and friends. They saw a psychiatrist who made the same diagnosis as I had been given in San Francisco. I did recover but was struggling with bouts of depression so bad that I started planning to take my own life.

Since then my family has come to terms with my illness and understand it more. They have been very supportive and have chipped in for things like medication and general support. My friends – the ones who are left – are also quite supportive.

At my lowest ebb I said to myself, this illness has robbed me of everything, including opportunities, dignity and my sanity. However, I knew I was not alone in this predicament and felt the need to organise my peers so that we would be able to help ourselves. I knew nobody else would do it for us, given the stigma associated with mental illness.

So I went ahead and started the Schizophrenia Society of Kenya back in 2016. Now I can see that focus, discipline, hard work, and consistency are the keys to success. That finding one thing you are good at and sticking to it passionately eventually leads to a means of earning a living.

One thing that gave me the strength to carry on despite all the challenges was Lupita Nyong'o's statement that 'All dreams are valid, no matter where you come from.' I was also inspired by a scripture that says 'Do not despise small beginnings'. These words give me hope.

Japheth Obare was born in April 1975. He is currently the chairperson of the Schizophrenia Society of Kenya and has twenty-five years of lived experience.

The Right Words

Aaron Balick

The Four Words that Changed My Life

In order to train as a psychotherapist, you have to be in psychotherapy yourself. It's a peculiar thing, learning theory on the one hand, while being a patient on the other. One mistake lots of trainee therapists make is that they try to use their own personal therapy as just another learning experience, instead of using it to be a patient. They listen and observe the therapeutic process so they can understand how it all works, rather than immersing themselves in the therapeutic experience.

At my initial induction to psychotherapy training, when we were told that we would need to find a therapist for ourselves, a wise trainer said, 'Be as sick as you can possibly be in your own personal therapy.'

'What do you mean?' I thought to myself. 'I'm not sick.'

Looking back, perhaps a better phrase would have been 'Be as unwell as you can be,' or 'Be as vulnerable as you can be,' or even, 'Be as crazy, hurt, aggrieved, anxious, fucked-up, emotionally messy, teary, and snotty as you can be in therapy.' She was trying to tell us not to use therapy as students, but as patients – patients who need therapy. More than this, we should not try to show our therapist how thoughtful, introspective, or sane we were. This is a big temptation. After all, we are training in psychotherapy and we want, at least unconsciously, to show our therapist that we're very sane and very thoughtful and will be a good therapist.

My trainer, however, knew better. She knew that unless you really own up to your crazy side, unless you really accept where you are unwell, fucked-up, unresolved, or, to use her words, 'sick', you'll never be a great therapist. She said that we could learn all the theory in the world, but if we were unconscious of our own psychological or emotional blind spots, we couldn't be of assistance to our clients going forward. Being a good therapist isn't about being entirely mentally healthy, it's about knowing and accepting yourself as completely as you can – your sane bits and your insane bits. Psychotherapists are no more sane than anyone else (in fact there's a pretty good argument to say that we are generally less so). Even after lots of therapy we continue to carry our wounds around – we just hope that we carry them more gently and consciously.

Well, I know this now. But I didn't know it then. I didn't listen. I didn't understand, and I fell right into the trap she had warned us about. You see, I argued to myself that I didn't *need* therapy. I was just fine, thank you very much. Further, I'd read all about Freud in my MA, so I'd already psychoanalysed myself. Because I didn't need therapy, and I already knew Freud, I would simply use therapy as the opportunity to see how it all worked in practice – as less of a client and more of an intern on work experience. I thought I'd shadow my therapist to learn the trade. After all, I was not 'sick'.

Fortunately, I had a therapist who got the measure of me. She was not going to let me get away with being a client on 'work experience'. She was not going to be charmed by my knowledge of Freud, or the eloquent way in which I expressed myself and my feelings. No, she was going to be my *psychotherapist*, not my mentor. And I found that hard. While she was warm and welcoming, she was also firm and boundaried. She didn't let me get away with the same stuff that other people did. For example, I'm quite good at diffusing tense moments with humour – it's a well-developed defence of mine. She didn't buy it – she didn't laugh! She held me to account. She required that I be honest, both with myself and with her. While I wanted her to see how smart, thoughtful, and introspective I was, she didn't want me to escape my own pain, vulnerability, and unfinished business. When I waxed lyrical about how my parents' relationship informed my current one, based on well-known psychotherapeutic principles, she didn't buy it. What would it be like for me to drop the wise-guy act and really be present and authentic in my therapy?

Let's just say that it took some time to break down my bravado to the point where I could actually come into her office and feel vulnerable; to go in there and tell her how I felt all fucked-up, confused, not good enough, anxious, etc. When I began to really, honestly open up and share my inner life with her, I began to see all the unwell parts of myself that I'd previously been hiding away. Putting into words what had previously been in my head was revealing. For example, I found I was unreasonably anxious most of the time about my health – I was a true hypochondriac. Once I realised how anxious I really was, she was able to show me that this anxiety *wasn't really about my health at all* but about something deeper and more fundamental – we just needed to find out what it was. Over time the pieces started to come together. My father died when I was fifteen after a long and at times quite horrifying battle with cancer. During this same period, the AIDS epidemic was in full swing, and I wasn't even close to coming to terms with my sexuality. When I did finally come out as gay at eighteen, everybody was terrified of sex – and every sneeze, pimple, or rash felt like it was the beginning of the end.

It became clear to me just how insecure everyday life could be. Parents could get sick and die, and there was nothing anyone could do about it. I found myself with a sexuality that I didn't want and couldn't change, in a context where that sexuality often resulted in death. Like most people, I just got on with it. At twenty-five I thought I felt fine and signed up for my therapy training with the idea that I would soon be able to perform therapy on people like a cardiac surgeon works on hearts – as an observer, working scientifically and objectively with a set of learned skills. What a surprise it was to find that though there are indeed techniques to be learned, the greatest skill of a psychotherapist lies in the personal capacity to sit with fear, grief, anxiety, terror, grace, silence, and the unknown, with total presence and equanimity. If you can't learn to do that with yourself first, you won't be so hot at doing it with someone else.

In the few years after starting therapy I gave up being a good student and became a good patient; I allowed myself to be as sick as I actually was. Still, I remained a trainee and continued to be curious about the process. I still very much wanted to make sense of everything, find a reason for every symptom and pretty much think myself better through a forensic analysis of my struggles – as if I were a psychoanalytic Sherlock Holmes. My therapist was patient with me, sometimes humouring me and talking theory, and other times taking a different approach. Whatever it was, *it was very serious.* I kept a diary of my sessions, ruminated on what was said, scrutinised my reactions. It was still something I wanted to do well. I mean is there anything more fascinating than discovering the intricacies of one's inner mind?

One day in therapy we came upon a very tender and vulnerable part of myself, and I found it very hard to share with her what I wanted to say. I was filled with fear and anxiety. When we looked deeper into what was happening, she pointed out that I was full of fear and anxiety about a feeling I didn't want, or feel able, to experience. This made sense to me, but my fear grew stronger because now it seemed that she wanted me to have that feeling there and then, with her, and I didn't think I was ready. The fear grew into a kind of panic as I worried that the feelings were going to come out on their own accord, and there was nothing I could do about it. When she saw this fear in my eyes she said to me, without a hint of alarm or concern: 'They're just feelings, Aaron.'

I felt as if the rug had been pulled from under me. While the *content* of what she said was surprising enough, the tone of dismissiveness in which she said these words was the real shocker. This woman, this psychotherapist who had been treating my feelings with such gravity for so many years, suddenly seemed to dismiss them in the same noncommittal way that someone might passingly brush away a bit of lint from a lapel, saying, 'It's just a bit of lint.'

There I was after three or four years in psychotherapy *taking every thought and every feeling so seriously* and then this? After all, feelings are the bread and butter of therapeutic work, right? If therapists got paid by the expression 'How did that make you feel?' instead of by the hour, we'd all be fabulously wealthy. I sat in my chair dumbfounded. What do you mean, 'They're just feelings, Aaron?'

In this state of total incomprehension, something interesting happened. I felt a release, a lightness, a liberation – as if a heavy weight had been lifted from my shoulders. While the moment before had felt so foreboding, so full of anxiety and dread, now I felt light as a feather. 'Oh,' I thought, 'maybe they *are* just feelings.' Though the effect of this intervention was immediate, it took much longer for the wisdom of this short phrase to really sink in.

I began to understand. You have feelings (or they have you) and then they go away. Simples. Then there are different feelings, other feelings that replace the feelings that were there before. But these too are just more feelings: and they are also nothing to be afraid of, they are not going to kill you. Sure, they can be unpleasant and even painful – but so what? Then it's just an unpleasant or painful feeling that will also go away. The permission to see feelings as 'just feelings' was so liberating, it was permission to not have to be scared of them, not to have to take them so fucking seriously! They are just things that come and go.

This logic of 'just feelings' continues to vex me to this very day. On the one hand I am a psychotherapist who takes feelings very seriously. I work with them, try to understand them, honour them, and give them the required space we need to work them through. On the other hand, I recognise that they are 'just feelings'. That doesn't mean I stop taking them seriously, it's just that I realise that when we take them *too seriously* they become something that we think we can't handle, that we need to avoid or overcome. The paradox that I learned from this is that while understanding your feelings is indeed very important, learning to accept and tolerate your feelings – *all of them* – may be even more important.

Take anxiety, for example. Most people are anxious about feeling anxious. That's the most popular way to be anxious. Why? Because we believe that we can't handle the anxiety: that it will tear us to pieces. If we weren't scared of anxiety, what power could it hold over us? If you could say to yourself, 'It's just anxiety', wouldn't that take the edge off? It certainly makes it seem less terrifying.

But, you might argue, you don't want to diminish feelings do you? I mean, what about grief? Isn't that an important and serious feeling? It's the same answer. Grief, however terrible it is to experience, is also just a feeling. It's a feeling that will come when you experience loss. Trying to avoid it, because you're scared of how it will make you feel, will only make things worse. So instead you let the feeling be. 'This is me,' you can say to yourself, 'experiencing grief.' Does it hurt? Yes. Will it kill you? No. Will it pass? Yes. Is it serious and important? Yes. Is it also just a feeling? Yes.

Our problems in mental life are not that we have feelings that are painful, but that we often believe we cannot tolerate them, and therefore we avoid them. By making them less scary, by understanding that however powerful they might be, they are 'just feelings' can be enormously liberating. Even a psychotherapist like me, who spends every working day of his life taking feelings seriously – I also know that feelings are 'just feelings'. And when feelings get on top of me, and sometimes they still do, I remind myself, 'They're just feelings, Aaron.' It makes all the difference. I would suggest you try it yourself. Go ahead. Next time you're on edge because there's a feeling brewing that's just about to emerge, or you find yourself overcome by feelings that overwhelm you, remind yourself gently, 'They're just feelings, <insert name here>.'

Aaron Balick PhD is a psychotherapist, cultural theorist and author applying ideas from depth psychology to culture and technology. He is an honorary senior lecturer at the Department for Psychosocial and Psychoanalytic Studies at the University of Essex (UK). His books include *The Psychodynamics of Social Networking*, the illustrated children's self-help book *Keep Your Cool: How to Deal with Life's Worries and Stress* and *The Little Book of Calm*.

Aaron is the director of Stillpoint Spaces, an international psychology, co-working, therapy and events hub. He is based in London.

Rachel Kelly

It was my mother who gave me my first glimpse of hope, just over twenty years ago, when I was lying in bed, suicidal, with severe depression. I had come home after a brief spell in a psychiatric hospital where, ironically, I'd felt even worse. The feeling that I would never recover, that my life was utterly pointless, and that I could no longer stand feeling so unwell, was overwhelming. I kept screaming that I wanted to die.

As my mother stroked my hand, she started reciting a phrase from the Bible that reminded me of my childhood: 'My grace is sufficient for thee; my strength is made perfect in weakness.'

It would have been impossible for me to learn anything new at that desperate time, but I could remember these words from my youth without much effort. It was a different mantra, more positive than my previous chant that I wanted to die.

'My grace is sufficient for thee; my strength is made perfect in weakness,' my mother repeated.

I clung to those few paradoxical words. Words were what I knew, what I had always relied on: loving poetry when I was growing up, writing essays at school and university and churning out copy at work. And aside from the sonorous beauty of the language, I was soothed by the idea that God's grace would be enough for me and that when I was weak, then I was strong.

That moment, and that insight, proved the first hopeful point in a story that had begun a few months earlier, one May evening in 1997, when depression struck me seemingly out of the blue. I was working as a journalist at *The Times* newspaper and was a mother of two, married to Sebastian, a junior banker.

One night I was taking our two small sons – a six-month-old

baby and a toddler – upstairs for bathtime. I laid them on their towels, kissing their rounded tummies in our normal routine when my heart started racing.

That night I was gripped by insomnia. I thought I was having a heart attack, my heart was beating so wildly. I paced the house all night, checking and re-checking the children. When I lay in bed unable to sleep, my worries went round and round, the anxiety worsening like a skater who carves ever deeper patterns on a frozen lake.

I was worried about trying to work, trying to be a good mother, trying to be a good wife. I became more and more overwhelmed with worries. I was bursting with an active sense of dread that disaster was about to strike. Something terrible was going to happen and I couldn't do anything to stop it. It felt like I was on a plane that was going to crash. In the space of three days, I went from being mildly anxious to being unable to move, in an agonising foetal curl on the floor, suicidal with fear.

It proved to be the start of my first major depressive episode, born of overwhelm and anxiety. I was ill for six months. I was treated with antidepressants and sleeping pills and got back to work, hoping the issue would go away.

My luck held, but then I had a second breakdown several years later. That time, the trigger was something as seemingly insignificant as holding a Christmas get-together. Our house was packed with family, friends and neighbours for our annual Christmas drinks. I had been trying to be the consummate hostess, twirling strangers together as if I was choreographing an elaborate dance.

My mistake was to briefly pause for breath in the kitchen amid the dirty glasses and empty trays. At that moment I knew the battle was over. All the physical symptoms I knew from the first episode were back: the racing heart, the sense of dread, worries piling on worries.

Once again my fears solidified into agonising physical symptoms. Once again, all I could do was lie in bed and scream. I was screaming because of the pain. I was screaming that I wanted to die. Every bit of me was in acute, dynamic, physical agony. It was as if I was crashing, hurtling at high speed. That time I was ill for the best part of two years.

Days merged into nights. There was no getting up and no going to bed, no mealtimes, no dawn or dusk. All signposts of daily life had gone. The only respite was to knock myself out with sedatives. My mother would consult the doctor and give me his prescribed dose of tranquillisers, which made me dizzy and nauseous but momentarily lulled the demons. At night I would take both the tranquilliser and a sleeping pill. I devoured the pills, longing for oblivion, crunching them as if for nourishment.

Very slowly my anxiety began to subside, but the recovery was bumpy. It was as if I were climbing out of my tunnel up onto a mountain with multiple false peaks. I would get to the top, only to slip back down the other side.

Through this acute period, I kept finding that words and poetry gave me hope, a process that had begun by my mother sharing her mantra about my strength being made perfect in weakness. Poetry had long been an unusual ally of mine. Throughout my twenties and early thirties, whenever a friend needed comfort, I would send them a poem that had helped me, and friends would return the favour. Some joked that I ran a sort of poetry pharmacy, prescribing words instead of pills. Now, in sickness, I was the one in need of poetic consolation, and friends as well as my mum were a rich source.

Some mothers and daughters are bound by a shared love of baking; my mother and I had always been united by poetry. I was a child again, lying in bed as she read to me. It turned out that all these years she had been keeping a book of snippets of poetry, prayer and anecdotes that had particularly struck her, entitled 'consolations'.

I drank up the collection as if it were ice-cool water offered to a parched traveller. I wasn't well enough to listen to, let alone read, anything longer than a few verses and even that could exhaust me. I didn't have the attention span to read an entire novel. So poetry's brevity was a blessing. So too was the way it dissolved the feeling of solitude: I wasn't alone, others had suffered and made something of their suffering. They had reordered the seemingly random cruelty of the illness into some kind of sense.

Poetry absorbed and revitalised me. Its condensed nature and sophisticated vocabulary required a concentration that shocked me into the moment in an almost physical way, freeing me from worries past and future.

My mother and I began with short poems, many of which are dotted through the text of *Black Rainbow*, a memoir I wrote about this time in my life. One favourite was *New Every Morning* by Susan Coolidge. Her advice particularly helped at the painful start of the day:

Every day is a fresh beginning,
Listen my soul to the glad refrain.
And, spite of old sorrows
And older sinning,
Troubles forecasted and possible pain,
Take heart with the day and begin again.

Another favourite was the lyrics to Oscar Hammerstein's song 'You'll Never Walk Alone', which my mother would repeat as she held my hand. Later, as my concentration improved, I turned to the seventeenth-century poet George Herbert for advice and comfort. When I read the first verse of 'Love (III)', I felt a bolt of electricity pierce through me. All the hairs on my arm stood on end.

Love bade me welcome; yet my soul drew back,
Guilty of dust and sin.

The idea that my soul was 'guilty of dust and sin' seemed the most perfect description of depressive illness. The poem pinpointed a sense of guilt that I should be depressed, even though I was blessed with a loving home, husband and children, feelings of shame that I had not previously acknowledged. I would also repeat phrases from 'The Flower', another Herbert poem. One of my favourites was *'Grief melts away/like snow in May'*; I wrote it on a Post-it note and stuck it on the bathroom mirror.

In those moments of the day when I held hands with Herbert, the depression couldn't find me and hope could instead. It felt as though the poet was embracing me from across the centuries, wrapping me in a cocoon of stillness and calm. Here was a new welcome voice in my head, preaching the virtues of acceptance and hope rather than struggle and despair.

And then a poem which exemplifies the need for hope: Emily Dickinson's poem with its startling opening lines comparing hope to a small bird.

Hope is the thing with feathers
That perches in the soul

I love the idea that hope is always within us; we have but to find it.

I find the requirement to concentrate on a poem roots me in the moment. I stop worrying about the future or regretting the past. Learning someone else's words by heart can stop me feeling anxious and help me nod off. I have to think about something else.

I'm not alone in finding poetry helpful. The concept of using words to alleviate stresses or sadness is not a new one: 'bibliotherapy' has sprung from a long, rich history of literary healing, dating back to primitive societies who made use of chants.

As the years have passed, I've adopted other strategies alongside poetry that have given me hope. I have found it healing to eat with care, prioritising good mood food, in particular dark green leafy vegetables, oily fish and dark chocolate. I found changing my diet so helpful I collaborated with a wonderful nutritionist Alice Mackintosh and wrote a cookbook of the recipes that help me. I've become much kinder to myself too. I treat myself rather like a nervous pet, who needs careful handling: early bedtimes, not doing too much, and developing a gentler inner voice.

If there is one theme that underpins all my toolbox of strategies to stay calm and well, that is a belief in my own agency. I think this is the one piece of advice I would give to my younger self and anyone who is struggling. You can make a difference. You can help your own recovery.

Ultimately it's impossible to disentangle all the different elements in my own recovery, from my love of poetry to the crucial role of doctors, family and friends. But what I do know is that feeling passive, and powerless to do anything about my condition, was part of being depressed. The more I discovered my own ability to take action, the better I felt.

This insight is the basis for my current approach to managing my own mental health. Every day I remind myself that I can make a difference. This begins as soon as I wake.

The first thing I do is to make my bed, the white duvet perfectly aligned and my pillows plumped. A small gesture, but one that reminds me that if I take control of small decisions in this way I will feel my own power to affect larger decisions. I also take care with the language I use to myself and to others. Instead of saying 'I'm at the mercy of my depression' I might say 'I can choose how to respond to my low mood'.

I don't regret what happened to me. My experience of depression is part of me, and has made me who I am. My strength has indeed been made more perfect in weakness. There is always hope, even in our darkest hour.

Rachel Kelly is a writer, and mental health campaigner. Her latest book *Singing in the Rain: 52 Practical Steps to Happiness* is published by Short Books.

Leon McKenzie
Fight It, Get Help, Talk

I believe just five words can change your life: FIGHT IT, GET HELP, TALK! These words changed everything for me many years ago when I wanted to give up on life. Now I truly believe that talking is the start of healing.

I would tell my younger self not to try and fix the things we can't control in life. Sometimes plans just don't go our way. It's only when we can really accept that, that we're able to see the world from a different angle. It was only when I decided to fight back in my life that things finally started making sense.

I've carried a lot of guilt over the years over some of the things that have happened. My beautiful babies have been wonderful and instead of seeing the negative, they find me inspiring. I have shown them how to fight back in life, and that still brings tears to my eyes. My mum and dad are great and always have been. My fiancée is a fighter and although I'm still not the easiest person to be with she rides life, good or bad, with me. I have a very close circle of friends and a few family members. Sometimes people pretend to care, which is why I keep just a few people close.

The turning point for me was knowing I had to start fighting back properly and giving back in a way that would make a difference to the lives of other people who are lost and vulnerable. When I tried to end it all I never really spoke about it; then when I lost my whole identity again at thirty-five, facing things that weren't part of my plan, I nearly gave up a second time. But this time, in my darkest hour, I held on and said, 'Not today, depression, I'm making a choice to be greater than I ever was.'

So, you may look at me today with my two elite sporting careers, boxing and coaching, and ask why I consider spreading awareness about mental health, speaking all over the UK, is my biggest achievement. It's because for me, speaking and listening can save lives and that is a greater legacy than any goal or belt I could ever win. I don't always have all the answers but if you take anything away from reading this, let it be my five words: FIGHT IT, GET HELP, TALK.

Leon McKenzie is a former premiership striker who played in all English leagues, scoring 115 career goals.

At the end of his eighteen-year football career, Leon suffered major depression and attempted to take his own life, before a breakthrough helped him to start fighting back.

He started professional boxing at age thirty-five and became a champion before retiring in 2017. Since then Leon has been speaking across the UK, raising awareness of mental health. He has also set up his own brand, FIGHT IT, and worked on *Tencount*, a documentary which features athletes looking at mental health from a fresh perspective.

May Gabriel

This isn't a story of a great moment that changed my life, or even really a story of a great kindness that I witnessed. This is a story of a sentence, a sentence that seemed so insignificant, a passing comment in a language that I don't even understand. Yet, this is my story of hope.

I was fourteen years old and in St Mary's Hospital, Paddington, London having just attempted to kill myself. I was in the children's ward and there were screaming babies everywhere. There were children there who were really ill, and I mean really, really ill, children with the most horrible diseases you could imagine and there was I, physically completely fine (bar a few cuts and bruises).

I had a one-to-one nurse who sat next to me, within arm's reach, at all times. She would come with me to the toilet, she would sit next to my bed, and she would preach to me about God. I'm sure that there are many stories about finding hope in God and religion, but this is not one of them. This one-to-one nurse would talk about how I needed to find God, how I needed to find religion, for if I was religious and believed in God none of this would happen. Can you believe? I'm fourteen, in hospital having just attempted suicide, and a nurse is telling me that I need to be religious?

The general nurses on the ward could see my discomfort, so after the first few days they started sending my one-to-one nurse away on long 'lunch' breaks, telling her that they would look after me. The sense of relief I felt when I was free from the preaching was indescribable. The nurses were called Roshni and Alana, and this act of kindness may very well have changed the course of my life. I began to spend my days helping Roshni and Alana out; I would sit at reception with them, I'd help them make the beds. It gave me something to keep me busy, to not let my dark thoughts fester. I would spend a few hours with them each day, and it really helped me get through. The rest of the time, I spent in my bed.

I had a window bed, overlooking the canal that runs behind the hospital. I spent my time painting with my mini watercolour set on the windowsill and studying for some upcoming tests that I had for school. See, I thought I would be going home soon. At the time I didn't think it was a big deal, you know, trying to kill myself. I thought, 'It didn't work so it's ok, life can go back to normal now.' Little did I know that this would be the start of a three-year journey in and out of hospitals.

Anyhow, one day I was studying for a French test. I hated French, I didn't know it then but I am super dyslexic and languages were really difficult for me to grasp. I was exasperated and stressed and it felt as though nothing I was learning was going into my brain. It was at this point that one of the nurses, Alana, came over to me.

Alana: 'Are you ok?'

May: 'I can't learn these words, they're not going in, I hate French.'

A: 'I studied French at school too, I can't remember anything from it aside from one sentence: "Quand fond la neige, où va le blanc?"'

M: 'What does it mean?'

A: 'Where does the white go when the snow melts?'

And that is it. That is my moment of hope, one of the most profound moments that has ever happened to me. I know it seems inconsequential, yet this moment has been my anchor, and for the past ten years I have thought back on it thousands of times. That sentence, 'Quand fond la neige, où va le blanc' has become my mantra. When I am going through difficult times, I repeat it over and over in my head. Weird, I know.

A quick Google search answered the question for me (spoiler: snow isn't really white), but the question has come to mean something so much more. To me, it symbolises the unknown in life, all of the unanswered questions. When I am in my darkest depression it reminds me that there is so much in this world that I do not know, and there is so much still to see. To me, it is a lifeline. Even when things are bad, I must continue to fight because there is a life out there for me to explore and to live.

So there it is, my story of hope. If you are in that dark place, try thinking about the snow and ask yourself: *Quand fond la neige, où va le blanc?*

May Gabriel is a mental health campaigner, media spokesperson and advocate specialising in mental health and wellbeing for those aged 13–25. May has platformed voices of young people with lived mental health experiences through her award-winning 'Its Ok Campaign', She lives between Brighton and London with her partner and cat.

Lucy Donoughue

Sat cross-legged in PJs on the floor in my family home, I ripped the Christmas wrapping paper from my gift. Underneath the garish paper was a book, with the words *OCD* emblazoned across its front. Although I don't remember the exact title, I do remember my cheeks burning with embarrassment as I looked up to eight pairs of unknowing and expectant eyes, waiting for me to share what I'd received.

I laughed it off – of course I did. I covered over the tight feeling in my chest and racing mind. My brother told me that I was welcome for the book and someone else started to unwrap their Christmas haul. The conversation moved on.

I was in my early twenties and the year was 2002. Friends Reunited was the major social media happening of the moment: Facebook, Instagram and Twitter simply didn't exist and neither, or so I believed at the time, did people like me.

I'd been having panic attacks throughout university but hadn't been able to understand or control the persistent, cruel and intrusive ideas that also plagued me. Every time, the same pattern – terrible thoughts about the horrific damage and hurt I could cause other people by my actions, followed by secretive (but maybe not so?), repetitive checking and reassuring to offset the evil I believed was lurking below the surface.

Receiving this book, as much as it hurt at the time, meant that I began to read about OCD in black and white. Although the language and theory felt medicalised and impenetrable, at least now I knew that it wasn't just me who experienced it.

While knowledge is power, knowing what to do next is the key. The shame I felt still stopped me from moving forwards. I convinced myself that I was exaggerating my symptoms, wasn't really experiencing OCD and, having picked up on language used around me at that time, was just being *a bit neurotic*.

Books, however, began to play a role in countering that sentiment. I would spend lunch breaks in a book store near work, perusing the shelves. Little by little, I began to piece together what OCD really was.

Although I didn't seek professional help until I reached thirty, two things happened in my twenties that made a huge impact on me, and stay with me even now.

The first was reading a book by Jeff Bell called *Rewind, Replay, Repeat: A Memoir of Obsessive Compulsive Disorder*. I consumed it greedily, only stopping occasionally when the similarities in experience felt too intense. I recognised the pain and anguish he was experiencing. His descriptions of obsessing and checking, getting no rest and having a brain that felt like it was on fire was so familiar that when I started to read about his hard-won freedom from the tendrils of OCD, and its chokehold on his life, I knew that there was hope for me.

The second – a notice in a bookshop for an OCD Help Group in Central London. After reading about people who had experienced something similar to me, I wanted to meet other people who were living with OCD at that moment.

So I went. The group was as diverse in age and experience as you can imagine. They'd gathered together to help themselves and each other, to share what they were struggling with, what they had learned and the stumbling blocks they encountered every day.

I don't remember what I said but I remember listening, heart pounding, a massive lump in my throat. Finally I was seeing, up close, other people who were hurting, healing, and for some, moving on with their OCD in check. I wanted that too – but it was also terrifying to see the ways in which this mental illness – this disorder – was real. While it wasn't all of me, at that point it was a huge part of my life and very few people knew. The secrecy I'd built up around it was beginning to feel as toxic as the condition.

However, in that room that evening, everyone knew, understood and cared, even though I'd never met them before. In the tea break, a woman who had spoken about recovering from severe maternal OCD, came across to me and placed her hand on my shoulder. 'Please get help,' she said gently. 'You don't have to live alone with this.'

I never went back to the group but I often think about it and that woman's words of kindness. I think about the books, and the gift from my actually very loving brother, who has since admitted that it was 'part trying to help, part taking the piss'. Whatever it was, it opened my eyes and started a journey to a better understanding.

I'm thankful that now information about mental health is easier to access, with social media, advocates, podcasts and immense awareness initiatives. I'm also deeply grateful to work for Happiful, a company whose mission is to help people find the help they need, and to share stories of mental illness and community support. I know first-hand the difference that can make.

My own OCD is much quieter now. I have coping mechanisms, I take medication and I know where to go for help and when. My cheeks will never burn with embarrassment when I talk about the condition again.

And, if I were asked to give advice to anyone reading this, who is struggling silently with mental illness now? I think I'd humbly borrow the words of a wise, wonderful woman I once met:

Please get help. You don't have to live alone with this.

Lucy Donoughue is the host of Happiful's podcast *I Am. I Have* and a contributing writer. She is the Head of Partnerships for the Happiful family, which includes Counselling Directory, Life Coach Directory, Therapy Directory and *Happiful* Magazine.

Lucy is training to be a counsellor, is a mental health advocate and an unapologetic lover of dogs.

River Hawkins
Don't Let Your Head Steal Your Day

'One of the greatest discoveries a man makes, one of his great surprises, is to find he can do what he was afraid he couldn't do.' Henry Ford

I quote others only in order to better express myself . . . That's also a quote from someone else – the genius Michel de Montaigne – but it's true, they do help me better express myself, although I'll continue in my own words. I heard someone complaining about hope once, saying that it leaves you in a state of wanting but never getting, or something along those lines. I disagree; hope is what kept me going through my darkest times, hope is what saved my life. Without hope, what else is there?

During that dark time most days felt like an exercise in survival. I did a pretty good job of beating myself up but also did a great job of pretending life was fine; even good.

After resisting for so long, when I eventually asked for help, I was put on a long waitlist where I deteriorated even more. I eventually received six 50-minute sessions. After the final session I said, 'What happens now? Because I need to continue, it feels like we've just scratched the surface.' I was told we could only continue if I was suicidal. Receiving this news as I sat in the small white room, my 50 minutes up, I felt defeated. But somehow I gained a determination to get better; hope was still flickering somewhere.

I decided that I had to create something that would help people before they reached their lowest point. Something that was accessible and appealing, not somewhere you're going to because you feel you're broken. I feel we have a responsibility to adopt a prevention approach as urgently as a crisis response. Rather than continue down the road of crisis response as the only option, I created

HUMEN on that founding principle: that prevention is better than a cure. There is no cure when someone ends their life.

From as young as age six, boys trade innate empathy and compassion for manufactured toughness. As the years pass, our emotions and social vocabulary dwindle at an increasing rate. Men are taught to suppress their feelings and to have no regard for emotional honesty. Rather, these wholly human reactions substitute themselves for a faux machismo which unfortunately stays with many men for the duration of their lives.

When I was at my lowest, my hope had diminished so much that it was only flickering, fighting to stay alight. But that flicker fought on through, it is what has brought me to where I am today. And that flicker was reignited . . . by the stranger discreetly handing me their new cotton handkerchief when they noticed me sobbing on the tube; by receiving my first well-paid gig after that point; even by the fleeting connection of a stranger smiling at me as we passed each other in the street. These seemingly regular actions told me that I was enough. They didn't need to be all bells-ringing, angels-singing 'signs' of hope – the little, seemingly ordinary, everyday acts of human beings were what brought me back to life.

To me, hope is one of the most powerful four-letter words in the English language. But hope, like most things, must be paired with action.

Whilst it may not feel like it during the low points, there will be brighter days, better times, and much more joy to come. But there will still be heartache, sadness and disappointment along the way. The key is to keep the knowledge that positive change is coming in mind, and not to let the bad times steal your day. Sometimes quickly, sometimes slowly, brighter days will always come back around.

Carl Jung once said that 'The word happiness would lose its meaning if it were not balanced by the word sadness.' I could not agree with him more. That one cannot exist without the other is factual, but we, whether we believe it or not, are able to choose to which we dedicate more of our time and energy. It reminds me of the story of the fight of the Two Wolves within us – one is evil, one is good, which one wins? It really does come down to the one we choose to feed.

At my lowest point, I no longer wanted to live, but at the same time I did not want to die. Deep down, I knew that ending my life was not the answer. As dark and as low as I felt, I knew that it wasn't the way out.

Hope is around us every day in little pieces. You can find a piece that could be the key to changing everything for you.

Another little piece of hope came when someone cared enough to make me call him every day before 11am, to force me into some form of routine. One day he said something which I don't think he realised would change everything for me: 'River, don't let your head steal your day. When it's getting at you, go to the bathroom, look in the mirror and say, "Thank you for the negative input, now fuck off!"'

Stay here for the hope that I promise is still there. Stay here for the person you will become. I hope there is a little piece of hope in you from reading this, and if there isn't, you will soon find one. The bad times feel longer because we want to be rid of them so bad. But the warmer days, even though they feel so distant, are coming.

Our heads can do a very good job at selling us lies; mine did for a long time. This has not completely stopped but the difference is that now I don't buy into them as much. They are not good value for money.

If your hope is flickering and yet to be reignited, remember that where you are right now is not your final destination.

I quote others not only to better express myself, but also as other people are what we need. Every piece of hope I have received has been intrinsically connected to someone else. Whilst there is still another human being in the world, there will still be hope.

River Hawkins is an actor and the founder of the mental health charity HUMEN. He directed and produced the five-part documentary *The HUMEN Series*, featuring Bill Nighy, Andrew Scott and Danny Cipriani.

Katie Thistleton
The Books That Changed My Life

I hope this book is providing people with hope. I am confident that it could be life changing, because books were life changing for me when I was in a dark place and feeling entirely hopeless.

I have always been a really anxious person. I didn't know that children could suffer with anxiety but now I realise that I probably came out of the womb worrying. My mum talks of how I had clammy hands as a baby, and as a child complained about feeling like I couldn't breathe, despite having nothing physically wrong with me.

I was a deep child, always thinking about the point of life. I remember being young and thinking, 'Why humans? Why the earth? Why getting up and going to work and watching TV and liking football and putting on make-up and going out dancing and getting married and having children and dying, and someone else doing that after you and this going on and on and on forever? What created us? Was it God? Are there other planets like us? Aliens? Is heaven real? What's the point?'

These thoughts, and my anxiety, followed me into adult life. I tried to settle them and find the 'point' in life in the ways we all do, by going through the motions and markers – we pass exams, we move on to the next bit of education, we pick a career, we start having relationships, we have hobbies and friends, we are obsessed with our weight and appearance, we compare ourselves to others. I made bucket lists and set myself career goals. I worked and studied and did as many exams and hours of work and hours of socialising as I could, trying to find the answer. I was diagnosed with anxiety finally when I was seventeen, and experiencing again those breathing problems I'd complained about as a child. Because I was an adult

I was allowed to be 'stressed' and I felt I had an answer for all of those physical symptoms I'd felt for so long.

I don't know what the cause of my depression was in the end. It happened around the time I ended a nine-year relationship, a year after I'd become a TV presenter and been thrust into a strange, vulnerable world of camera angles and unexpected criticism. It could have been these things, although a part of me thinks that the deep child would always have ended up suffering with anxiety and depression. Perhaps it was the years of questioning why, of trying to find the answers and the things we all feel we are missing, of trying to fix myself by being a workaholic and a general 'do-aholic' and neglecting my mental health.

I have spoken a lot about how antidepressants have helped my mental health, and breaking down the pill-shaming and stigma is something I feel very strongly about, but there were two other moments that were pivotal turning points for me. Both of them came from reading books.

One day I sat in a coffee shop in Manchester reading Matt Haig's *Reasons to Stay Alive* when I came across the section where he writes a list of things that make him better, and things that make him worse.

It was so simple, and so obvious, but something just clicked.

I discarded my bucket lists and career goals' lists and made two very simple lists instead. I felt instantly better. I realised that I wasn't even interested in doing half of the stuff on my career goals' list, I just thought success on those terms would bring me happiness. I also didn't want to do most of the stuff on my bucket list, I just thought learning to play an instrument, riding a horse or completing ten marathons in my lifetime would make me a better person, and my life more meaningful.

Instead I made a simple list of things that make me feel better – naps, dogs, certain people, etc.

And a list of things that make me worse – too much social media, too much alcohol, certain people, etc.

These lists have got bigger and developed over the years and when I'm having a bad day I refer back to them. They make me feel better, they make me feel in control, they give me hope.

The second book that changed my thought process was Cheryl Strayed's *Tiny Beautiful Things*. It's a brilliant book full of agony aunt questions and responses which inspired me and my publisher to do our own version for young teens.

Cheryl uses the magic of acceptance to help people to feel better. It was the first time I realised that accepting a situation you can't control, no matter how bad it may be, is the only way to be truly freed from it. After all, what's the alternative, wasting your one life being miserable? People who wrote to her had been in awful situations, but by encouraging them to be accepting she gave them hope that despite their despair they could still have fulfilling lives and feel joy.

Again, it was simple, but I felt an almost physical shift in my brain.

So I hope this book, too, gives you hope. I'm a stronger, happier person now than I was when I was in the depths of depression because of medication, family, lifestyle changes – and books. I remember lying in bed wishing my life would be naturally cut short because I hated how I felt every day and I couldn't bear living like that. Now I can't believe I wished away the happy times I'm having now. Now I want to live forever.

Thank goodness for hope and for the books that give us that.

Katie Thistleton is a TV and radio presenter, DJ, NCTJ-qualified journalist, agony aunt and published author. She is best known for her work on BBC Radio 1 and CBBC, being the longest-running presenter of CBBC's live continuity. Katie joined BBC Radio 1 in 2016 to host advice show *The Surgery* and now hosts BBC Radio 1's *Life Hacks* and *The Official Chart: First Look*, as well as a weekly podcast for the network. Katie's debut book *Dear Katie: Real Problems, Real Advice* was released in February 2018.

Jo Irwin

The best piece of advice I've been given in recent times came from somewhere unexpected, on a walk to a train station on a sunny day when the world was feeling a bit on the squiff.

A time not long after a particularly rough bout with my mind, which had left me feeling all at odds with myself. Bad news seemed to be following low moods and it felt like everything around me was in a funk.

In the myriad of things that go on in my head, a fear of not doing or being good enough has always been at the forefront of my panic.

I live in constant dread that I'm running out of time . . .

So I must write that book; my social feeds are awash with well-to-do twenty somethings, who don't have to worry about mortgages and gas bills so are spending their time writing meaningful things for fun. I must too.

I'm not good enough at my job; I must do better to achieve the dream of being the CEO I don't want to be, to fulfil the idea of being a #girlboss.

I'm not running that 10k everyone else seems to, because every time I go for a run round the block my mind tells me I can't run properly (who runs 'properly'?), so how would I ever train?

I must have kids and a wedding and a kitchen island. I must do all those things now because THE CLOCK IS TICKING.

I'm not good enough to be at fancy parties, I'm wasting my life by doing what makes me happy, going home and watching TV with a carbonara. I should be out, drinking and dancing and having meaningful conversations about politics with people I've no real desire to see again.

I'm not good enough at looking after myself and should make

the time between a working week, a relationship, family, friends and sleep to do dawn yoga whilst eating chia seeds because if I don't start now it'll be too late.

What am I doing with my life?

It's these racing thoughts of the future that fuel my panic. My panic fuels the undercurrent of anxiety that courses through me day in and day out, leaving me exhausted and feeling the dark days will be impossible to overcome.

But on this funny, sunny day, after more bad news and low moods, someone I know well turned to me and unknowingly imparted a bit of advice I'll carry forward always:

'Who knows what happens tomorrow. Just do your best today.'

Today. The one thing we have got. What does my best look like for today? Not how can today pave the way for tomorrow, and next Tuesday and the day I turn thirty-seven.

Because that's when the panic sets in. When you lie there at 23.57pm worrying that you've not done or been good enough. When the witch in your head comes out to play to tell you you've underachieved, been lazy, are shit.

So today I will go to sleep having done my best. And if my best today is not having a panic attack and managing to send three emails, then go me.

If my best today is having three panic attacks and sending one email, it's progress.

If my best today is bossing a meeting at work and taking a small amount of pride from it rather than beating myself up, then bravo.

But if my best today is sitting at work fuelled with dread that everyone thinks I'm a fraud, you still got to the office.

Some days my best was running a marathon, or speaking up for mental health, or really being a good friend. They were great todays.

But.

If my best today is just showering, when nothing else seems achievable, bloody well done all the same. Tomorrow, when it comes, is a time for new PBs, new mini victories and new steps forward.

And I'll worry about those then.

Jo Irwin started out as a blogger and her ramblings have taken her on a journey of mental health campaigns with the Royal Family, speaking at the WHO and becoming a volunteer and advocate for the 24/7 crisis text line Shout.

She continues to write on mental health.

INSPIRATION

Frank Turner

I was raised in a typically middle-class British family – 'small c conservative', as they say. We didn't talk much about our feelings, and there was a strong sense that you sucked up your problems, kept your upper lip stiff, and got on with life in the face of adversity. There's some mileage to that, some strength in resilience, but let's just say I wasn't brought up to openly discuss my issues.

Other aspects of my upbringing – not least being shipped off to an all-male boarding school (on a scholarship) at a very young age – fostered that sense of aggressive self-reliance. I didn't have anyone else to depend on, so I depended on myself. On top of that, as I came blinking into adolescent consciousness of the world, I found myself at odds with many of the values espoused by my parents and my school. My escape from that was into the world of punk rock.

The punk scene will always be dear to me because it was a safe space for me, probably the first time in my life I felt welcome some-where. I threw everything I had into that social milieu. And while I formed a lot of friendships, I also imbibed the ideas of hardcore bands like Black Flag, and got involved in the Straight Edge move-ment for a time. Again and again, resilience and self-reliance were the orders of the day.

When my music career started, I set out on the road. Living in vans, sleeping on the floor, surviving with no comfort or privacy, felt surprisingly familiar after my education, and I felt like my skin was already pretty thick. As my music career became successful, that came in handy. There's something quite odd about the way our culture encourages artists to commit their deepest thoughts and emotions to record, and then happily screams criticisms and insults at those artists for doing so. That's amplified a thousand-fold by social media, which came into its own as I reached real mainstream success. I knuckled down, sucked it up, pushed it away, kept punching my way forward.

In retrospect, something had to give. The model that I'd built for a life for myself, something between Hunter S Thompson and Henry Rollins, was a romantic one, but not a sustainable one. By 2013 I was living the high life – quite literally, as my drug use was starting to spiral out of control, especially on the rare moments I had off the road. I was into uppers – drugs that keep you awake, make you feel energetic, make you feel like you can pack more into life. It's a con, of course, and it's disastrous for your mental and physical health, as I soon found out.

In the end I came up against two stark, immoveable facts. The first is that there's a physical limit, no matter who you are. Sooner or later your body and mind has to rest. And secondly, affection isn't cumulative. No matter how many cheering audiences and one night stands I tried to stack up, I couldn't make them add up to genuine care and affection. My drive to live a manic, independent life was clashing with the bare facts of my physiology.

It all came to a head when I met Jess, with whom I immediately knew I wanted to spend the rest of my life. She highlighted to me how lonely and loveless my existence had been to date, and cast a sceptical eye over my social and chemical habits. Things reached crisis point, I was asked to choose, and foolishly chose wrong. I chose the road, drugs, independence. Almost immediately, I knew I'd messed up, and that was, at last, the push I needed to take a long hard look at my life and start making some changes.

With Jess's support, I started investigating CBT as a way of getting out of the bad habits I was in. I was fortunate enough to find a wonderful, wise therapist who talked me through how my childhood and formative experiences had built me into the person I am today, and where the problems were. For the first time in my life I was able to talk openly about some of my insecurities, anxieties and frustrations. And most wonderfully of all, I realised that I didn't have to give up everything I'd built, the good and the bad. I didn't have to throw the baby out with the bath water. I was able to see a way forward to being busy and creative, touring, writing and releasing music, but in a fashion that was sustainable in the long run and wasn't going to kill me before I turned forty.

So what advice would I give? A good friend once pointed out to me that I tend to be very generous with the shortcomings of my friends, very understanding, but I seemed incapable of treating myself in the same way. So there's my first piece of advice: be gentle and forgiving with yourself, as if you were talking to someone you loved. It's ok to be weak and fallible, or at least just human, to have limits. It's ok to stop and take a moment for yourself.

Secondly, and it pains me to say this on some levels, I learned that music is necessary but not sufficient for mental health. I couldn't survive without music in my life; I wouldn't be here. But in the final analysis I reached a place where just putting on another record and losing myself to the sound wasn't going to heal my wounds.

Mental health shouldn't be a scary thing for us to discuss, we're all just people trying to get by. It's ok to say, from time to time, 'I could use a little help.' It's taken me most of my adult life to be able to say that sentence out loud.

Frank Turner is an English punk and folk singer-songwriter from Meonstoke, Hampshire. He started out in post-hardcore band Million Dead, then embarked upon a primarily acoustic-based solo career following the band's split in 2005.

To date, he has released eight solo albums, four rarities compilation albums, one retrospective 'best of' album, one split album and five EPs. His eighth studio album, *No Man's Land*, was released in 2019.

Hussain Manawer
Dream

Once upon a time there lived a boy called Dream
He wanted to bring the night to life, and that is all that it
    seemed
When he started school he met a young girl, her name was
    Believe,
Who told him if you work hard one day you'll meet my
    cousin Achieve

Dream had a friend called Passion,
Whose brother's name was Ambition,
Whilst others studied Maths and English they both studied
    their mission.
They had cold nights and long days
And they hated this girl called Storm
Because she made them stay indoors during wet play and
    tried her best for them to meet her friend Conform
Their genuine aura kept peer pressure away with a simple
    word called nope,
During one lesson Dream was chilling when he met the
    new girl – her name was Hope
She said, 'Why don't you be like me, but don't hang yourself
    on that rope
Because if you do they'll sit there and laugh just like what
    they did to the boy who left,
Don't you remember Jonathan Joke'
As time went on they came to realise that they both slept on
    the same page
They both loved the same teachers and one of them was Mr. Stage

Mr. Stage was flawless, he allowed anyone to come as long
    as they entertained
One day they met Stage's old pupil, an old-fashioned
    woman called Complain
Then came along Ms. Talent, who said there is nothing she
    would forbid,
And as seasons passed and time went on Mr. Stage and Ms.
    Talent had a few kids
First there came Microphone who was the loudest in the
    family,
She created a lot of feedback with her brother Speaker but
    they got along happily
Then came along young Spotlight who always shone on
    others, she was always shining bright and was reflecting
    the best of her brothers
Dream was getting along great,
But somehow felt uncertain
As someone stood in the way
And that someone was Mr. Curtain
Hope came and said don't let Mr. Curtain put you on a
    pedestal,
And when he's not looking grab your monologue and break
    out of his fourth wall
If you don't they'll take you to the graveyard who's owned
    by Mr. and Mrs. Shelf
But if you go beyond the curtains you'll meet Mr. and Mrs.
    Wealth
We can't go with you, Dream
You have to go by yourself
But when they tell you to break your leg
Just remember, you'll be in the best of health

Hussain Manawer is an English poet, writer and activist who has
performed worldwide on stages including Global Citizen, One
Young World and Glastonbury.

In 2018, in partnership with King's College London and Hackney Empire, Hussain co-ordinated and set the Guinness World Record for the World's Largest Mental Health lesson, designed to help underprivileged young people better their personal psychological development.

In 2018 Prime Minister Theresa May awarded Hussain the country's prestigious Point of Light Award for his outstanding efforts in helping challenge the stigma of mental health.

Tom Ryder

There are a great many factors and people that have been sources of hope in my life. But if I had to select a single word to convey what hope means to me, to really sum it up and distil it down, I would choose 'creativity'. Creativity has been a phenomenal force for me, a means of processing emotions and making sense of situations. Harnessing it has been vital, shining light on some very dark times and, crucially, making my brain work with me rather than against me.

In my career as a journalist and musician, I spend a lot of time creating. I work with words, sometimes crafting them into songs, sometimes leaving them to speak from the page. But there are also occasions when words won't do the trick, and there is a need to express myself wordlessly. This is where the creative arts come in: we might paint, draw, play an instrument, dance, sing or cook our way to a healthier mindset. Music, combining intuitive creativity with lyrical expression, leads the way for me.

I was diagnosed with bipolar disorder in my early twenties, a condition that studies have aligned closely with the arts. Being bipolar is both a tremendous asset to my creativity and my loudest nay-sayer. Two per cent of the population have been diagnosed, and many with the disorder are artistically-minded. Singer Demi Levato, painter Vincent Van Gogh, writer Virginia Woolf, actress Catherine Zeta-Jones and musician Kurt Cobain are among those believed to have been affected by the disorder. Not everyone who has been diagnosed goes on to huge success, and those who do succeed often face mental conflict.

Long before it became my living or part of a diagnosis however, creativity was embedded in me. My imagination was a huge part of my school life. When I was eight, we were asked to write a short story: I went home and authored a 43-page epic. A girl I fancied got thrown out of assembly because I was singing the classic hymn 'He's Got The Whole World In His Hands' in an exuberant, mickey-take falsetto, and the teachers thought it was her. Aged ten, I enthusiastically belted out 'Who Let the Dogs Out?' at an all-inclusive resort in Greece. I was gripped by being the centre of attention.

At secondary school I got into drama, encouraged by Physics teacher Mr Hows, who had an unbelievable eye for theatre and put on some astonishing productions. Before he inspired me, he put a young Greg James on the school stage, allowing him to realise his talents and setting him on the path to his incredible career. I was very fortunate to be at a school that nurtured extra-curricular flair as well as academic ability.

At around thirteen I discovered music and wanted to play it, so Mum and Dad bought me a Spanish-style guitar from Argos for Christmas. There was a well-known Acoustic Club in our hometown of Bishop's Stortford. Plucking up some courage, accompanied by my friend Joe who was developing into an exceptional guitarist, I headed down to the club. Though we were barely into adolescence, they let us in and the night proved a fantastic platform and safe space to share songs. We started off playing covers, Oasis B-sides and so on, and over a few months started sharing our own original material. The compositions may not have been great, but what an outlet! To share something you've come up with in your bedroom with a welcoming audience is magical. We were hooked, and soon formed a four-piece band with schoolmates Cass and George. The band is still going to this day and we've shared some brilliant times together, musical and non-musical. Not only can we combine our collective creative ideas with each other and develop as players, but we are part of a loyal team, our own little community, which I've found to be an essential component in maintaining wellbeing.

I did well at school, despite some major exam-related stress and developing severe insomnia as I tried to live up to my own high expectations. An extremely supportive circle of family, friends and teachers got me through. Instead of heading straight off to university, I opted to take a gap year. We wanted to make a go of it with the band, and I also wanted to see whether a career in journalism was really for me. In March 2009 I headed off to Cape Town for my first taste of that other creative passion of mine, writing, and had an extraordinary month putting together my first stories and interviews for regional tabloid *The Daily Voice*.

I was on a consistent high by now, holding the firm belief that life was going to get incrementally better and travel on a consistent upward trajectory. Although I didn't make it into Oxford University after an interview there, I was beyond excited to be accepted to read English at Durham.

For the first seven or eight weeks at uni, the experience was total bliss. I worked at the college bar, played football, wrote for the student newspaper and gallivanted around the various open mics. Truth be told, I did everything except study, the whole reason I was there in the first place. In a furious rush to submit my essays at the end of the first term, the insomnia and anxiety that had plagued me before took on a whole new magnitude, morphing first into hypomania and then a full manic episode with psychotic symptoms. Put in plainer English, I didn't sleep at all for at least a week, decided to deface the walls and ceiling of my student accommodation by scribbling words all over them, was rushed to the GP and then waited for the crisis team for six hours. Eventually the police were called, I was cuffed, put in a van and taken to a cell for my own safety. By this point I was beside myself, trying to convert whoever would listen to a bizarre new religion I had just created. Thinking myself invincible and immune to pain, I attempted to grab a lit lightbulb out of its socket.

I was left in the police cell until I calmed down and then informed that I was being sectioned. I was taken to another secure facility, a psychiatric ward, and broke down crying as I had to strip naked in front of strangers while my clothes were reallocated to me. In a matter of hours I had gone from elated hyper-reality to a vivid nightmare. I had gone from playing music on stages to featuring in a hellish horror film of my own making: the deluded star. How could my mind, my friend for so long, trick me in such a dastardly fashion?

During the following weeks, I was medicated heavily back towards my right mind. I got some rest, but was furiously angry at my predicament, locked away from friends and family, many of whom were hundreds of miles away. The pills meant I was constantly hungry and thirsty, and in no time I put on a hearty three-and-a-half stone.

Over time, something struck me. As I looked around at my fellow patients on the ward, who were all very unwell, like me, I noticed a pattern in how they were coping with their predicament. Some were drawing or painting, others were writing poetry or scrapbooking, while others were dancing and singing. With little else to do on the ward other than eat, sleep and smoke, my colleagues – encouraged by hospital staff – were being creative.

I started writing. I was allowed access to my guitar, and it became my closest ally and confidante. Some of the songs I put together in hospital have remained with me to this day.

I had to drop out of my studies for that year but returned to visit my Durham friends after the exam season. I sang 'Feels Like Home', a song that I'd written on the ward, to the entire college. Emotions were running high and a lot of tears were shed, but the rush I felt, the togetherness in the room, the joy of music, the triumph in overcoming a horrible period and releasing all those pent-up feelings was incredible. Creating something that moves people, makes them laugh or causes them to sing the lyrics back at you is a magnificent feeling. Some songs can be very personal, yet resonate with others in surprising ways.

After four years of back and forth, steadiness and illness, I eventually abandoned my studies altogether. This was an exceptionally difficult decision to make; it felt like a failure, a character blemish. When I returned home I was no longer allowed to drive, and this compounded the crushing realisation that the path I was on was at an end, the dream was over.

In 2013 I was given the opportunity to work part-time as a teaching assistant at a primary school close to my mum's house. One of the teachers there asked me what I was thinking of doing for a career. I said I wanted to be a journalist, but at that time believed that this was a pipe dream; I didn't expect to move forward at all, everything had ground to a permanent halt. I confided in a close friend, telling him I couldn't finish my degree. He said of course I could, calling me the most talented person he knew. It was such a kind and motivational thing to say, but the words didn't register at the time.

A year after abandoning my studies, my driving licence reinstated, I got a steady journalism job in town. Fast forward another year, and I managed to secure a regular gig singing in a pub/restaurant. A number of flash Essex types used to frequent this pub and boast about how they knew Rod Stewart. I didn't believe a word of it until Sir Rod himself walked in one night while I was playing! I lingered around after my set, taking even longer than usual to pack up, when Rod walked up to me, shook my hand, and asked how my career was going. He asked, 'Do you love it?' and of course I said yes. I won't forget what he said next, as it has influenced all my artistic pursuits since: 'If you love it, and you want it, stick at it.'

In the time between these moments and today, despite the deep depths I sunk to, I have managed to establish a career as a writer and musician and fulfil my creative ambitions by working and performing all over the world. This by no means signifies that I'm out of the woods and my mental health journey isn't over; being bipolar is something I have to keep a constant eye on. I take lithium, a severe but effective medication, and expect to be on it for the rest of my life. Getting enough sleep and rest is essential, and I often have to make sacrifices and call it an early night or resist that extra pint. But wellness is worth it.

Countless individuals have supported me along this journey by showing unwavering love, and I'd like to single out one community psychiatric nurse in particular called Brian, who was an outstanding listener and an impartial friend come what may. And if I'm ever getting carried away, I can go and visit my nan for a dose of simplicity and refreshing normality. In addition to monitoring sleep and diet, exercising and maintaining positive relationships, music has been there for me always. Being on stage is still home.

In March 2018 I founded a non-profit community organisation

called Retune (@RetuneUK) that inspires young people to make positive adjustments to their mental health through creative outlets. We put on live shows, run workshops in schools and universities and host online resources including a YouTube channel and podcast. I'm so passionate about music, theatre, writing and all the other creative mediums, that I feel a strong duty to pass on that passion and its psychological benefits to the younger generation. Our wonderful NHS is struggling and the education system has enough on its plate. Finding a creative outlet is a simple method of self-care that we can all get on board with.

The impact of all this extends beyond schools and the NHS. With Retune I recently visited a prison in the south west of the UK. The inmates are permitted an hour or so a week in the music room. When I arrived they were jamming together, with bass, drums, keyboard and guitar on the go. Once the house band had found a groove, some of the other lads would take it in turns to ad lib vocals or deliver a rap over the top of the music. It was an astounding evening that reaffirmed the shared ability we have to exercise the imagination and handle trying times.

The theory often goes that some people are artistic and creative, while others are not. But it is actually quite easy to unlock your inner artist. You don't have to compose symphonies or paint a fresco, it might be as simple as jotting down your thoughts in a journal or singing very loudly (and badly) in a shower. Creativity is about expressing your thoughts and bringing what's inside to the outside. It's a way of making sense of things. A creative activity is anything we can lose ourselves in, and we are all more creative than we realise. By captioning a photo, putting together a funny gif or cooking something from scratch, we are unlocking that childlike imagination and playfulness that is often suppressed during adulthood, enabling it to roam free and experiment for a while.

Science backs this up. Listening to music has been shown to raise levels of our natural antidepressant chemical dopamine by up to 9 per cent. Playing lullabies to newborn babies relaxes their bodies by slowing down their heartbeat. Playing a musical instrument unites the left and right sides of the brain, improving cognitive function. And art and music therapy have reduced agitation and the need for medication in many dementia sufferers. You don't have to be good at it, and you don't have to take part for a long time. Even a single session has benefits.

I believe it's important for us all to allow ourselves time to reflect and reset our minds, in the face of a society that expects us to be 'on it' 24/7. It is helpful to periodically gather our 60,000 daily thoughts, to 'defragment' as those Windows PCs used to do. Mindful creative pursuits are a way to achieve this. One of the best pieces of advice I ever received was to take my foot off the gas and let things happen. You don't always have to take control and force things to work for you. Be patient and let it come of its own accord. And in the mean-time, try doing something creative; you might surprise yourself.

I will leave the final words to the late, great Bob Marley: 'One good thing about music – when it hits you, you feel no pain.'

Musician and journalist Tom Ryder has performed worldwide, as a solo artist, with transatlantic duo LOZT and with four-piece band The Kazans. In 2015, his debut record 'Silence Breaking through Sound' raised more than £10,000 for Macmillan Cancer Support. As a journalist, Tom has written for international titles across print and digital formats. In 2018 he founded Retune, a non-profit community project that inspires young people to improve their mental health through creative outlets.

Emma Wilson

During times of pain and despair, hope and recovery, writing has been my outlet. When it's hard to explain how I feel, words sometimes cascade out from pen to paper. I want to share with you my words of hope, starting with my own story. If you aren't in a good place and can relate to my words, please know you're not alone. And please continue to read. By writing about the bad times and the good, I hope you can hold on to hope that things can change in time.

When I was a child, I grew up with a severely disabled brother and home life was hard. I felt different from my peers, isolated and often alone, but too ashamed to talk about my problems. I bottled things up inside and it affected my health throughout my teenage years and twenties.

My brother will never speak, and we will never be able to share the milestone events that other siblings do. It breaks my heart every day, but talking about my feelings unlocks the guilt and pain I kept hidden within me for so many years. If you are someone with a disabled sibling and find things hard, just know it's ok to feel angry and upset at times. You're going through a difficult time and friends don't always understand. But I do. Please don't keep it to yourself. Talk to someone. Things will be ok.

I have also experienced several episodes of depression and struggling with an invisible illness can feel like a lonely and confusing place. After graduating from a Law degree, I was off full-time work for more than eighteen months because of health problems, and at times I didn't think I'd get better. But I did, over time. I know not everyone can become symptom-free, but know that things won't always be at their worst.

Alongside knowing your self-worth and talking about your problems, I try to see the beauty in the world, beyond all the fighting and hatred we see in the news. To break free of negativity I try to take a leap of faith into life. I want to feel happiness. I want to experience joy and find the strength to strive ahead rather than getting crushed in the stampede and battered by tragic world events.

Now I am in a good place. Something I thought was impossible for many years. I still struggle on some days but I live in a happy home with a partner and people who love and care for me. I hold on to my self-worth and work through the dark times by talking to other people. Please know that you're not alone and no matter how bad things feel, there is someone else feeling the same way. That person was once me – and things **can** and **do** get better.

Emma Wilson is a mental health campaigner and early career researcher in the field of mental health, with experience of depression, anxiety and eating disorders as both a teenager and adult. She is also a Mental Health First Aid instructor.

George Taktak

The Reason
I believed in a bigger force at play.
A great wind that would clear my way
Through pain and strife of a family life
That no-one I knew could relate to . . .
My father abused us.
Me, my mother and three younger brothers.
With scathing words,
Limits on food,
Beating hands
And ever-changing moods;
His presence turned our house into a prison.
I put my faith in the universe. Told myself that 'everything
    happens for a reason' and waited patiently for the day I
    could go my own way . . .
But it came twenty years too late.
Finally, with my parents divorced
I stopped speaking to my father, of course;
Adulthood was the freedom I craved.
My childhood was forgotten.
Remembering didn't serve the life I wanted.
I decided to start the business of my dreams.
Left family and friends and head for the sea;
Became captain of my own destiny.
Yet life was not what I expected it to be . . .
I thought I'd be free from tyranny.
I thought I'd become the person I wanted to be.

Where once I believed my father chopped the seas, I
      learned life itself was anything but a breeze.
~

One day the waves came crashing down.
All my work was about to drown.
And I too with it, without a sound.
Nobody knew where I had disappeared to . . .
Lost in emptiness
And disconnection
My inner-child broke through
The tension.
Tears flowing like never before,
Streaming toward the ocean floor.
Heart pounding to free itself
From its rib-caged treasure chest.
He liberated a love from deep within.
He reminded me I was
One
Of
Four
Children.
If I give in to suicide,
It wouldn't just be me that died.
My mother, my brothers, they too will fly
Upon the day I say goodbye.
So,
I let the tides of time subside.
Allowed my body and mind to rise
Until I reached the ocean's side;
A reef, a shore of life sublime.
My mother, walking along the sand,
Looked down and there she saw my hand.
My body, in pieces across the beach,
– Never before had she lost her speech.
She gathered my brothers

To find my heart,
And soon they recovered my every part.
Then, she found the strength to speak,
Washing my hands and kissing my feet:
'I'll never again let you out of my reach.'
'Nor me mama.' I rest at peace.

George Taktak is a mental health activist and social entrepreneur. He is the founder of How Mental, a global movement making mental healthcare accessible to all. George uses his personal experience of suicidal tendencies, depression and anxiety to humanise mental health support.

David Anderson

In August of 2014 I told my wife I didn't want to be married anymore.

I'd spent twenty-two years in an abusive relationship. The abuse had ultimately turned violent. For the last five years I'd been desperate to leave but felt completely trapped.

In those five years my mental health deteriorated. I ended up taking a dangerous amount of prescription and non-prescription medication to block out the incessant abuse. I also made physical attempts on my life. It got so dark that I can remember accepting death was inevitable and that became a comfort to me; at least there was an end in sight.

My behaviour was clearly irrational to everybody else. One night my father came to the house, tears in his eyes, and expressed his fear of losing me. I dismissed my behaviour, claiming I was fine.

I'm a very shy person. I have always found it very difficult sharing any details of what happened during my marriage. But I was desperate to talk to somebody and let it all out. I was referred to a group called CCC, a counselling team specifically formed to help male survivors of domestic abuse and violence. I'd never put much value in the idea of talking therapy, but I found the experience incredibly cathartic. From the very first of my sessions I felt lightened by sharing my experiences. During this therapy someone suggested that I was suffering from PTSD. This made me feel a bit of a fraud. PTSD is something that's suffered by soldiers and service personnel, people who have experienced the extremes of trauma. Surely that wasn't me?

After a few sessions I realised I was making some progress when I played a gig and someone mentioned a photograph that had been taken of me during the show. I'd used it as my Facebook profile and an old friend had commented during a rehearsal. He said, 'It's a great photo. You've got your smile back.'

I didn't think much about this until I recounted it during the counselling session. When I quoted what he had said to me, I broke down in tears. It had never occurred to me that the abuse had affected me so much that even my appearance had changed.

The tears were a mixture of realising how ill I had been and that I was starting to be happy again. Just having people believe what had happened to me, that I was actually an abused party gave me a lot of confidence. It still amazes me how important this talking was. Having someone give an external perspective on my life really helped me understand and accept my behaviour and actions.

It was a recurring topic in counselling that I wasn't pursuing any of the things that used to give me pleasure. I wasn't playing my basses, I wasn't listening to music, I wasn't riding my bike. I hadn't realised how during the abusive marriage I had removed everything that I enjoyed from my life. It took a conscious effort to reintroduce these things but they all gradually made their way back into my daily routines. Cycling, in particular, tires me out physically, which helps my erratic sleep patterns and the natural endorphins released after exercise help reduce my anxieties.

It's now nearly four years since I fled the home. I am not totally well; I still have bad days and nights. The experiences I had have changed me utterly. I am a different person now. I no longer take prescription or non-prescription medication. I have no suicidal thoughts. Each day that passes is another day away from all the events that caused my problems and that is how I am able to cope.

I no longer work as a lecturer since my breakdown, I just don't want the stress. Now I try to prioritise the things that make me happy. My lifestyle has changed dramatically. I was married with a home, holding down a good job, with all the material trappings. Life is simpler now, with a much lower income, but with that simplicity comes happiness and peace, a realisation of the importance of happiness over material items. I have my mind back. I walk my dog, I play my bass, and I listen to music and gain great pleasure and happiness from it all.

David Anderson has been a music professional for over twenty-five years, engaging in session and touring work as a bass guitarist.

Over the past twenty years, David has also built a lecturing and teaching career in music and production. He is currently writing a proposal for potential PhD study and still engages in music performance and recording.

Angela Samata

For You My Friend
Know that I love you
Know that I wish you hope
Know that love and hope stand by your side, defiant against
  everything the world throws
Know that it will pass
Know that you will feel hope's loss quicker than you feel its
  return
But, return it will when you least expect it
Know that love and hope bring the air that starts to cleanse,
  to repair, to heal
To create a new, thinner skin, sensitive to the pain of others,
  scars still visible
But there, healing day by day
Know that even on your darkest days you are not alone
Love and hope are there, quietly by your side, waiting

BAFTA nominee Angela Samata presented the award-winning BBC documentary *Life After Suicide*. She has worked in Suicide Prevention and the Arts for almost two decades, speaking internationally on both subjects.

Co-author of the NHS Award winning #SeeSaySignpost training, accessed by over 1 million people, Angela acts as a spokesperson and content advisor for broadcast media including the BBC, Channel 5 and Channel 4's *Hollyoaks*.

RESILIENCE

Alastair Campbell
Resilience

When I was admitted to hospital with psychosis in 1986 while accompanying Neil Kinnock on a visit to Scotland, a psychiatrist finally made me realise that I'd been drinking too much. There was something about Dr Ernest Bennie – I don't even know what that 'something' was – but he gave me the strength to stop drinking. I gave up for thirteen years there and then.

Another key moment was when Richard Stott, my former boss at the *Mirror*, offered me my old job back. This really boosted my confidence: I had to start again at the bottom, had to do night shifts etc, but it helped me feel that I wasn't defined by my illness or my breakdown. Initially I had doubts about returning to work, but most of my colleagues were very understanding. There was a real sense of camaraderie and friendship and some, like Syd Young, who sadly passed away recently, really looked after me.

It was then that I learned to take things one day at a time.

Working in politics, the depressions were mainly fairly mild. It was when I left they got really bad again. In 2005, a friend convinced me to get treatment. I saw a psychiatrist, David Sturgeon, and I have seen him many times since. In fact, my first novel is dedicated to him, and to Dr Bennie.

Before my breakdown I wasn't looking after myself properly, but I have since learned the importance of sleep, diet and exercise. I also love to play and listen to music, especially bagpipes. My dad taught me to play at the age of six. Both my dad and my brother Donald, who died after a lifelong struggle with schizophrenia, were very good players and my brother left me his bagpipes. I feel a great sense of connection with him when I play them. I like both the slow stuff and the fast – it all depends on my mood. I get very emotional when playing music, which is a good thing. One of the tunes that will always stick in my mind is the Gaelic lament that was played at Charles Kennedy's funeral. It was so moving. The best music either makes you think, or makes you happy, or makes you cry.

Staying curious is also important to me, as is walking the dog. During lockdown I was walking my dog at 6am, not a single plane in the sky. That's when you can simply live in the moment. I think that since the pandemic has hit, people have a better sense of who and what is really important: people who were all too often barely noticed before, such as the street cleaners and hospital workers, are rightly being recognised. I believe this can be a genuine moment of change in the world. You have to stay hopeful that something good will come out of difficult times.

These days I get out of a slump much more easily; in the past I would just go very quiet. Now I spot it when it's coming on, so I'm more conscious of it – if I'm tired, I will sleep, if I want to play music, that's what I will do. I have a thick skin, and that has helped me be resilient. Real resilience comes from something that you've had to endure, but it's also something that can be taught.

In many ways, my breakdown was the worst thing that happened to me, but it was also the best. That is where my resilience comes from.

Alastair Campbell is a writer, communicator and strategist, best known for his role as former British Prime Minister Tony Blair's spokesman, press secretary and director of communications and strategy. A former 'Mind Champion of the Year', he is an ambassador for several mental health charities. In November 2017 he was awarded an honorary fellowship of the Royal College of Psychiatrists for his role in breaking down the stigma surrounding mental illness.

He recently published *Living Better: How I Learned to Survive Depresssion.*

Tess Ward
Stilling The Noisy Mind

I grew up in a household where feelings were considered powerful and understanding them as valuable as all the money in the world. I know that I am lucky, my mother profoundly loves and almost smothered my brother and me, perhaps to equip us for sadness, of which we saw a lot during her years of depression. She taught us that we were imperfectly perfect in every way, that our moods and pain were part of the process on this weird and wonderful journey of life. Her teachings and her disposition towards melancholy didn't mean I had it sorted, though. It just made me harder. I was the strong one, I didn't cry much, just pushed my problems like fuel into a steam train, charging my way into the world to escape and enrich my body, mind and soul with all the new sensations I could find. But at twenty-eight it caught up with me, and I wasn't ready.

A year ago I was listening to Jim Carrey talk about his depression and how he related it to a breaking of character, that it was like shedding the avatar and allowing the body to transition through a period of deep rest. Deep rest, a restoration, sounds a lot like depression. A time when the body needs to heal and move slowly. A mental break, like a bone break, needs time, patience and care, it's a healing that's invisible to the world.

When depression hits, it's slow and leaky, like an oil spill snaking across the ground, viscous, dark and dangerously slippery. It can take a while for the tank to empty, replacing apathy with old feelings of capability. It's complex and heavy and feels exhausting. A lethargy that no nap can help revive. For me it was a process, with much mental physio. Moving through it felt impossible for months; it took me a year to feel like I could float again.

One thing I realised and I hope this is of some help, is that the fear of my feelings was so much worse than the reality. As soon as I sat with myself and unpeeled the onion (with a therapist) the fear and shame began to dissolve and it was then that the healing began. Sometimes when we sink into a feeling it's frightening and all-consuming, but there is a fearlessness in going right in there, because it cannot get worse than at the bottom of that black hole of darkness.

For me the ray of hope came out of stillness, in meditation and quiet. I filled my mind with the words of great authors and poets, I started writing to chart my progress. Stopped watching vapid TV and cleaned out my brain from the restless static. I stopped going to events that didn't serve me and culled friends that weren't supportive, I chose kindness over coolness and spent time being in nature. I got a dog, because ultimately there is no unconditional love like that of a sweet-hearted creature!! She loves me more than she loves herself and every day, even the worst one, is a reminder that I am lovable. Alba is magic and as I write this she sleeps draped over one leg, stirring to lick a toe or yawn out her very pointed tongue.

When I think back to the time before my first breakthrough (I think of it as such instead of a breakdown, because it was a life lesson, not a failure) I wish I had been more gentle with myself, more thoughtful with my lifestyle and dating choices, in less of a hurry to get somewhere professionally. It turns out we are only ever running on the spot. I have a good gut instinct and could have engaged it more with past agents and projects. It's remarkable how much we intuitively know if we listen more and still our noisy minds.

London-based food blogger Tess Ward is a Cordon Bleu-trained chef and has worked in the kitchens of River Cottage and The Ritz. She develops recipes for the *Grazia* restaurant column and for brands such as Le Creuset.

Louisa Rose
You Are Enough

Someone once told me that when I am in the midst of a depressive episode, unable to sift through the fog, the only question I should ask myself is whether I'd like tea or coffee (I don't drink coffee so that made the decision easier!). The idea is that we tend to fight the fog as opposed to sitting in it. We expect ourselves to be able to perform our basic functions but the fog sits above us, making everything nearly impossible and when we fight it, it becomes heavier. Focusing on such a basic question and removing the pressure of anything else allowed me to 'be' with the fog and wait for it to pass. It's not a cure, and it doesn't take away the pain, but it makes it a little more bearable at that moment in time.

I was an anxious kid, I worried about everything. And it manifested first in my stomach. From the age of six I spent hours in the school toilets. At six you have no idea what an 'anxious tummy' is. At the age of sixteen you get it, but it's not something you want to shout from the rooftops. I went from gastroenterologist to gastroenterologist until I was finally diagnosed with IBS (Irritable Bowel Syndrome). For me, IBS is triggered single-handedly by stress and anxiety and my stress levels got worse when my parents separated when I was thirteen. They told my sisters and I that they were 'unhappy'. Unfortunately, I found out the full details later and they shattered me completely. My relationship with my dad suffered dramatically. He would pick us up every day to take us to school but would have to wait for me whilst I was in the loo with horrendous stomach cramps. Shortly after, I stopped speaking to him and my mental health deteriorated (though twenty years on, happily, we have a great relationship).

This was at a time when antidepressants were handed out like sweets. My mum was my backbone; she picked me up every time I was down (or stuck in a public loo!). She took me from therapist to therapist but because no one really talked about mental health back then, it was hard to find the right one. My adolescent years were marred by anxiety and depression and without any successful treatment school was a nightmare. I didn't fit in. I thought I wasn't good enough. I wasn't pretty enough. I wasn't clever enough. I wasn't sporty enough. Add to that running off to the loo mid-class and crying in a corner about my parents' divorce, it made finding friends tough. School kids are mean. It was only when I went to university and could be anonymous that I discovered who Louisa really was. I met a bunch of amazing people, who are some of my best friends to this day. They accepted me – supported me (as I did them because, apparently, that's what real friends do!). And you know what? Turns out I was pretty cool. ☺

My life has always been clouded by the heaviness of depression and anxiety, but it all came to a head after my divorce when I was twenty-eight. I was admitted to hospital and prescribed a course of therapy that delved into my past intensively and included art and dance therapy. My mental state improved marginally but then I experienced another dip into darker states and during a 24-hour return to my mum's home I danced with death.

Depression is a monster that creeps into your mind and removes all belief in yourself and your potential. It adds a cloud of gloom to even your positive memories and destroys all hope of returning to those positive states. When that monster is there, there is no light. I believed that my only escape was death. If I succeeded, I wouldn't know the pain anymore and if I didn't, then maybe I would finally find the right help. I truly thought in those dark moments that this decision would be best for my friends and loved ones. It would release the burden of this depression that didn't just affect me, but them too. I won't tell you how, because I don't want to give you any ideas, but I did try to take my own life. Because of the love of those same people and their crumpled, devastated faces (and the quick response of two of my dearest friends, one of whom is a nurse) I am here to tell the tale.

It's this dance that has made me believe in the power of the mind because the same mind that made me believe death was the only way out has in turn made me believe that if death is that easy, we may as well fight a little longer. That's a notion I choose to remember because it moves me further away from the darkness and closer to the light.

As I moved along the road to my mental health maintenance (I don't like the word recovery because for me it isn't realistic to expect I'll never be affected by my depression and anxiety again) I met my now husband. On our second date, I offloaded my baggage to him. I was divorced. I suffered from depression and anxiety. My mum had cancer (thankfully she is healthy and free of it now). Instead of running 10,000 miles, he looked at me and said, 'Why would any of this affect how I see you? Life is tough and tough things happen.' In that moment I knew he was the one for me and that together we would be able to handle anything life threw at us.

So here's my note to young Louisa: You are enough. Life is tough and kids are mean, but the dark times are temporary and I promise you will find your way through. Oh, and if your IBS is stress-related, go to a therapist, not a gastroenterologist!

Louisa Rose is a freelance social media consultant and mental health advocate.

She now hosts mental health events called #UOKHUN, speaking about her own personal battle and topics including maternal mental health and the impact of social media on mental health. In 2021 Louisa hosted the first mental health festival for schools and colleges together with Jonny Benjamin's charity, Beyond. It reached over half a million people in 1200 schools and colleges around the world and they are planning future festivals.

Benjamin Janaway

Describing depression, without maudlin Sylvia Plath-esque poetry, can be a difficult task. The textbooks told me a list of symptoms, which as a medical student I was quick to map to my feelings, but the reality could only be captured in small parts. The feeling itself was one of distance, a bit like being away from the world you once knew, with the friends you valued passing like ships in the night, the old hobbies washed away, and the light itself dulled as if behind thick blinds.

I have had a few episodes over the years, and they always begin the same. At first I can't sleep, waking up very early with my mind already racing, but a feeling of confusion and blurriness as to why. Next comes the loss of appetite, for food and everything else. Then the feeling creeps in, not a profound sadness (although that does speak up in the darker hours), but one of loss, lack of energy and direction. In the end I become almost motionless, a shadow whilst the clock spins.

These are hard times, and I worry that they will return, but in the midst of my most serious episodes I find time to think, to appraise and analyse, to reconsider and recommit.

Depression gave me time and a microscope, and although the lens was often negative, it allowed me to see things about myself and my life that could be changed. I realised what would feed the beast in the darker hours, and what treats I would leave it behind me so it could always follow.

I realised that these periods of darkness, whether they were due to a paucity in neurotransmitters, or some personal loss, called not for isolation (which I would often translate them to) but rather to show me what I really needed: personal connection, purpose, warmth, authenticity, the consilience of meaning and all the other things depression tries to take. I found myself telling fantastic stories of how I would write some great fiction, or make some great change, to lift me out of depression and show the world that I was not just ok, but that the rest of the world could be.

Being a medical student (then doctor) meant I had access to information and direction that others did not, and I felt compelled to use this privilege (and that's what it is) to not just make something good from my despair, but to share the lessons onward. I realise now that martyrdom in the cause of greater things is not worth it, but in those early days it seemed to give reason to misery. As time wore on and I got better, thanks to medication and therapy, I realised that this kindness I wished to bestow outwards was also warranted on myself.

As such, I learned to be more assertive, to be more attentive to my inner voice, to be aware that parts of me liked the darker paths and would, even with a supposed curious eye, become swallowed by them. I learned that authentic connection to others, embracing emotions (good or bad) and valuing moments (spectacular or sullen) were the very twine that tied the fabric of my safety net. That although the world can be a cruel place, it is up to us as people to stretch that net over it and keep each other suspended above the woes and troubles that could befall us all.

Over the years I broadened my interests, found solace in science, found perspective in the immortal and wise words of Carl Sagan, found unity with others in the writings of Richard Dawkins, and some semblance of universal understanding in the musings of Kant, Nietzsche, Harris and others. I will not pretend to have understood it all, but within the darkness provided by depression I found light in the pages and words of wiser men and women.

I discovered new music, and that the greatest tales of the human condition could be shared through lyrics. I travelled across Europe, Asia, the Americas and further, looking to understand better the nature of us as people, devoid of the bizarre barriers that hold us apart. In doing so I became part of other stories, narratives spun by others who wore their pain and bravery on a collage of faces. I became calmer, more pragmatic, understanding (and, I hope, wiser) due to these trips.

Life showed me that depression, for all its faults, is an opportunity. In the darkest moments it can seem an insurmountable chaos, but the paths it attempts to hide in its morose apathy lead to something much greater. These are well-worn paths, with innumerable footprints indented eternally, where mine became lost walking alongside the others who had gone before. Depression showed me that there was something unspoken in my heart that needed to be heard, and that the silence of the night was an acoustic hall for its voice.

Now, as a psychiatrist, my role, as well as keeping myself well, is to help people find that light. To help them examine the history of their lives, to show them that fear is nothing compared to warmth, that isolation is a signal for greater connection, that they can climb my net whilst the frayed edges of their own sway in the wind. This is no martyrdom, it is something else, a unification in humanity and purpose, a great future hewn from the ashes of burned memories, formed in the kiln of years to become something real, authentic, human.

If I could take away my depressive episodes, I have often wondered if I would. Yes, there is pain, but each recovery shows me more of who I am, teaches me to look not just inwards, but outwards, to bring the world's opportunities together, to become a fuller human being, and to pass that on.

Dr Janaway is a trainee psychiatrist with an interest in evolutionary explanations of mental disorder and potential treatment applications. In his spare time he enjoys sleep, existential crisis and *Brooklyn 99*.

Charlie Wright

I recently complained to my therapist that I wasn't a very resilient person. After more than two years of therapy and a multitude of changes in my life, I still felt I was coming up against the same core issues that stopped me from succeeding when things got difficult. I was convinced that because of something innate inside me, I felt hardships more acutely than the average person. I was ashamed of this.

'Well, do you want to be a resilient person?' he asked.

'Yes.'

'How can you be a resilient person if your experience doesn't feel difficult?'

We went on to discuss two major struggles in my life and the different ways I have dealt with them. In one instance I discovered an ability to persevere regardless of difficulty. In the other, I found myself giving up, often before I'd started. This conversation helped me to understand what hinders me and what motivates me. I started the session by flagellating myself for my supposed lack of resilience but ended up commending myself for the struggles I had endured.

We are constantly exposed to stories of individual resilience. Whilst I also celebrate these stories, internally I feel spoilt, lazy and weak. I'm a white, cis man, born into an incredibly supportive family, and I've only ever been attracted to members of the opposite sex. The world is constructed to give people like me numerous advantages. Yet often I struggle to get out of my double bed in my pleasant neighbourhood, to go to work where I am privileged enough to run my own social enterprise. This has been an issue for years. I've often felt debilitated by the task of making my brand, Hopeful Traders, what I would deem 'a success'.

Alongside the extreme pressure I have put on myself to succeed in business, I have another stress. My son is now six months old, lives a plane journey away, and legal proceedings to ensure I can build a relationship with him are throwing the financial stability of both of our futures into disarray. There are details that make this situation far more strenuous but I won't share them here out of respect for my son. There is also no simple conclusion in sight.

I believed that I was being incapacitated by both situations. Most days I had anxiety about leaving the house and lacked motivation to even get in the shower. Although I have experienced periods of this for years, I felt that this newer situation with my son was making it even more difficult to get on with a productive day.

However, this conversation with my therapist highlighted that while I had often struggled to get out of bed for work, metaphorically I was 'getting out of bed' for my son. I was in often painful back-and-forth communications, trying to sort out how I could be present in his life. Every other week I was travelling, and still am, to a foreign and isolating place, sometimes just to spend a couple of hours with him while 'supervised' in a cafe. Every day it causes me stress and pain.

Resilience, by its definition, is to overcome, or recover from, hardship. If I was able to persevere in this difficult situation then I must have the capacity for resilience. So why did I struggle to motivate myself with work? On the surface, it looked like I just cared more about my son. But I also realised that I had a paralysing fear.

I hadn't been fully conscious of this until I started having psychodynamic therapy. All my life I had hidden behind 'not trying' as an excuse for any shortcomings. It was a way of never truly discovering that I was bad at anything. In business, especially the culture of unicorns and sexy startups, you must put up this perfect vision of everything you are and do. The pressure to be the obsessive startup bro, touting his innovative, ground-breaking brand was just too much. I would tell myself I would be more successful if I just cared more, worked more hours and gave up my personal life. The truth is that I care deeply about what I do but I care more about not failing. Specifically, failing when I have given it my all. My subconscious had developed an idea that there was nothing worse than doing your absolute best and still coming up short.

So what was different when it came to my son? In short, I care disproportionately about what I think society expects of me. We do scrutinise parents but we also have a much wider view of what it is to be a successful parent. The job is so varied and difficult that a genuine effort alone is seen as a great success. My situation, in particular, seemed so insurmountable that even tackling it seemed honourable.

In the startup world, the privileged millennial male, born into money, has, in my mind, no excuse to fail. The vision of a successful business is in some ways a much narrower concept than that of a successful parent. Money and widespread recognition are central to most people's assessment. As someone whose mind runs a constant narrative of what everyone else is thinking, these attitudes can be a huge factor in the way I motivate myself. The expectations feel high and the goalposts very close together.

In addition, the benefits of investing in my son can be brought easily into focus. The reward of my hard work literally looks back at me with my own eyes, even if only a couple of times a month. When away from him I look every day at the folder of pictures of him on my phone. I am reminded how worthwhile the struggles are for a few moments with him and more importantly, for the wealth of moments to come. But with a business it's hard to see the rewards I value when I'm organising a month of poor sales figures, or slaving through the company tax return. I have plenty of incredibly rewarding moments in my work but they are never quite as infinite and open-ended as the life I am trying to build for my son.

I am still in a position of quite extreme struggle with both these situations. Like many people who get depressed, I have good days and bad days, good weeks and bad weeks. I am still in therapy and certainly haven't found all the answers.

But I do see how facing my problems and feeling the pains attached to them is something positive. I am living through the pains when they come, rather than hoping they will be magically cured. I try to remind myself as often as possible why I am doing it. As trite as it sounds, it does help when I tell myself, 'This is hard. You are getting through it. You are resilient and this proves it.'

I broke into tears when I recognised how much I had struggled through for my son. For the first time, I mentally rewarded myself for how hard that had been. I had been so despondent about not managing to somehow 'fix' the situation that I hadn't appreciated how resilient I had been in enduring it.

I can't really tell you how you can help yourself, but I can share with you what helps me: I now embrace hardships. I wear them with pride. I take them as an opportunity to learn more about myself and sometimes I even give myself a rare moment's praise.

In 2015 Charlie Wright founded Hopeful Traders, an ethical clothing brand that raises money for charity through collaboration with people affected by homelessness and mental illness. Charlie wanted to share the opportunities he'd enjoyed, due to his background, with more marginalised people.

Geoff McDonald

I will never forget midnight of 25 January 2008, the day before my daughter, Jennifer's, thirteenth birthday. I awoke with a panic attack – I had never experienced anything like it before. I lay in bed with my heart racing, finding it difficult to breathe. I shook Debbie, my wife, and said, 'I think I am about to have a heart attack.' Startled, she asked me what was wrong. I repeated, 'I think I am about to have a heart attack, I can't breathe and my heart is racing.' She told me to try and get up, take some deep breaths and walk slowly around the bedroom. 'Have you got any pains in your chest?' 'No.' I got out of bed and did what she suggested. Some very deep breaths and walking slowly around the room seemed to calm my state, and after about ten minutes the feelings of panic slowly subsided.

I returned to bed and fell asleep for about thirty minutes, only to wake again, unable to go back to sleep for the rest of what was a very long morning. I lay there ruminating and worrying about all sorts of things, unable to get any of the thoughts out of my mind. This pattern of being able to fall asleep, only to wake at about 3am every morning, was to be with me for months to come.

As the sun eventually rose on that cold January morning, I felt terrible. Today was my daughter's thirteenth birthday and I couldn't even get out of bed, let alone share her happy day with her, and go ten-pin bowling with her and her friends as we'd planned.

I lay in bed thinking, 'What is wrong with me?' I was a guy who had run close to forty marathons, had competed in triathlons, ridden from Land's End to John O'Groats and across the Pyrenees. I'd done three ultra-marathons and ridden ultra-endurance mountain bike events in South Africa. I had an amazing global role in

Unilever, a happy family. And yet I could not get myself out of bed. I was almost paralysed with anxiety and sadness.

I watched the clock until it was time to go to the doctor. I hoped he would be able to diagnose what was wrong with me, because I had no idea! I got dressed and looked in the mirror. My eyes looked dead. I looked awful!

The doctor asked me what was wrong and I said, 'I have no idea, but let me tell you what happened to me at midnight last night.' As I explained, he leant back in his chair and then asked me a series of questions:

'What is your appetite like?'

'I have no appetite and I think I've lost about 6kg over the last three to four months.'

'What are your energy levels like?'

'I have no energy. I can't do the things I normally like doing, like riding a bike, or going for a swim.'

'How do you deal with bad news?'

'I cannot bear to receive bad news; I catastrophise over it. I cannot even watch the news on TV or read a newspaper, as there is so much bad news.'

I told him how worried I got over leaving the house, particularly if the girls were there on their own, thinking something might happen to them.

He asked me if I had had suicidal thoughts. I said yes. He asked me if I had planned anything and I said no.

I told him I had lost all confidence in myself and had become more and more isolated, was easily irritated, felt a sense of hopelessness, self-loathing, guilt, and many other feelings.

Now that I look back on it, there were other symptoms too: waking in the middle of the night with a very dry mouth; tingling feet and fingers. All these were physical manifestations of my illness. Behaviours included being reclusive, not wanting to socialise, needing feedback at work all the time, as I had lost so much confidence; being easily irritated; etc etc . . .

The doctor told me I was sick. 'Sick???' I exclaimed. 'Sick with what?' He said that if zero was general anxiety disorder and ten was manic depression, I was probably a four on the scale. Anxious/ depressed.

Me, depressed? I could not believe it. I was the most positive, energetic person people knew!

'Would you like some medication to address your illness, Geoff?' the doctor asked.

'Yes, please.' What a stupid question, I thought to myself. Had this been any other illness he wouldn't have asked me if I wanted to be medicated, so why so with depression or anxiety?

As I left the doctor's surgery that morning, feeling sad and anxious, I made a decision that, with hindsight, was probably life-saving. I decided I was not going to take on the stigma associated with this illness. I knew I was not a weak person, I was just ill and I had to get better as I would with any other illness. But I was also scared. This was territory I had never covered before and the doctor had warned me not to expect any quick fixes as the medication would take time to take effect. Yes, I was scared, but I was also determined to beat this.

I got home that morning and climbed straight back into bed. Pulling the duvet over my body I thought 'Why me? Will I ever get better, and if so, when?' Those duvet days were the worst.

Slowly, my recovery began. That night I forced myself out of bed and joined Jen and her friends at a bowling alley. Although I tried hard to enjoy the evening, I felt terrible and could not wait to go back to bed. Since then I have learnt not to fight these feelings and be more accepting of them. As someone said to me, 'Welcome the feeling as you would welcome a guest into your living room.' Fighting the feelings just makes us even more anxious and frustrated. I'm saying this to men, in particular. Don't believe the stereotype that men can't share their feelings. This stereotype is a burden that we carry and one of the reasons why so many men turn to suicide when depressed or anxious. Help is out there and people want to help you!

Initially I was nervous about telling my family, friends and work colleagues. 'What will they think of me? How will they react? Will they understand? What impact will it have on my career?' But maybe I am lucky – I have the type of personality where I wear my heart on my sleeve, which means I find it difficult to hide my feelings.

The most surprising reaction I had when I opened up about my illness was people commenting, 'Geoff, you're so brave to talk about this!' Brave! I'd thought they were going to think I was weak, but my experience was the complete opposite. Although they were shocked that I was suffering from depression, they knew that I was genuinely ill and with their help, support, compassion and empathy I would get better. During some of my darkest moments, knowing how much I was loved by so many people, including family, friends and colleagues, is what kept me alive.

Depression often strikes personality A type individuals. Psychiatrist Tim Cantopher describes depression as the curse of the strong, using a great metaphor: the oak tree falls over in the violent wind and storm, whereas the reeds in the river, no matter how violent the flood, will just go with the current. They will be damaged, but their flexibility saves them. Yes, I was like that oak tree. I thought I was a machine; I could just keep going and push myself harder and faster. Well, guess what – the machine broke down!

My recovery was certainly a journey, and one that had its moments of uncertainty, fear and hopelessness. This is an illness and like any illness it takes time to recover. There is no quick fix. It took almost eight weeks before the drugs I was prescribed began to take effect. Fortunately they did eventually work for me, but some individuals get side effects and may have to experiment with different forms of medication. But in most cases medication will eventually work; one has to learn to be patient.

I began my recovery with the mindset that taking medication for a mental health condition is not a sign of weakness. Had I had any other ailment and been prescribed drugs in order to get better, I would not have questioned it. So, why do so many people question the use of medication to address a medical health condition like depression or anxiety? It baffles me.

In addition to the medication I began a series of CBT (Cognitive

Behavioural Therapy) classes which taught me to think differently about myself, my identity and the things I used to feel so anxious about. One of the most significant lessons was learning about myself: who is Geoff McDonald and what makes him tick? For years my identity had been tied up in work and I had lost perspective. CBT helped me see that my identity was actually made up of a combination of factors, eg how I was as a father, how I was as a husband, how I was as a friend and a member of our community. To have over-emphasised the importance of work had been a real source of stress and anxiety. Today I realise I am more than just what I do at work, and this has had a very positive impact upon my mental health.

Seeing a good friend regularly was also key. This friend had something special; he had also been very ill with depression and had battled it for many years, sometimes even being hospitalised because of its severity. However, when I saw him he was well, and seeing someone so well, who had been so ill in the past, gave me so much hope. It gave me confidence that this illness can pass, it was a glimmer of light at the end of a very dark tunnel. In addition, he had so much empathy for my illness. Speaking to someone who could really empathise, someone who had been there before, was a great support.

Gradually I returned to work. This was very much part of my recovery. My employer, Unilever, was amazing – they understood what a gradual return to work meant and were fully supportive of me. Being able to go back into the same role, whilst knowing that I could get to grips with it over a period of time, was massively therapeutic. I would start work at about ten and leave at three and work some days from home. A careful and slow return, combined with a sympathetic employer, boss and team was a gift as I journeyed back to good health and I'm immensely grateful for that.

Love and a sense of hope were the most significant factors in my recovery. I would never have felt these from family and friends had I not been able to tell them what was wrong. The biggest lesson for me has been the importance of talking. This has now catalysed into my work today, where I have a real sense of purpose, helping create workplaces where people feel they genuinely have the choice to ask for help if they are suffering from mental ill health. As I know from personal experience, this may just save a life!

Previously the Global Vice President of Human Resources, Talent, Marketing, Communications, Sustainability & Water, Geoff McDonald recently left Unilever after twenty-five years.

He is now a global advocate, campaigner, consultant and Keynote Speaker, addressing the stigma of mental ill-health in the workplace. He co-founded the Minds@Work network, which helps break the stigma of mental health within organisations. Geoff is also a Patron of the International Stress Management Association and a Member of the Prince's Trust Youth Opportunity Taskforce.

Andrew Clarke

Just days before my depression hit, I had taken over as Chef Director at the Brunswick House restaurant in Vauxhall. This became a kind of anchor for me. If I hadn't had that, I'm not sure I would be here now. As long as I got myself out of bed and made my way to work each morning, the distraction of cooking and the energy of my team gave me purpose.

In the years since then I've had a lot of advice, but the standout for me was the importance of surrounding myself with positive quotes. The information we consume daily can be as good or bad for our mental health as the food we consume. Positivity was the one thing that was going to help me with the fight, so I needed to arm myself with as much of it as possible. Easier said than done, I know, but at least it was a goal.

In my darkest hours I didn't know where I wanted to be, I just knew I didn't want to be in that hell. I made notes to myself and left them around my flat. From the moment I opened my eyes there was positive language coming through from somewhere. I consumed positivity.

Winston Churchill's 'If you're going through hell, keep going' became the screensaver on my phone. It made me believe that time would pass and I wouldn't always be in pain.

Bruce Lee's 'Do not pray for an easy life, pray for the strength to endure a difficult one' made sense as I started to rebuild myself and found my inner strength coming back.

I also count myself very lucky to have friends and family who helped me through the darkest times. I was very open with them when I hit rock bottom. I had nothing else to lose, so what was the point in hiding anything anymore? Being open and honest about my problems was very liberating and another key to winning the fight. Being able to get something off my chest, or out of my head, eased some stress. And it certainly strengthened my personal relationships with everyone close to me.

My friends would check on me constantly, sometimes with phone calls at 3am, just to make sure I didn't harm myself. It was ridiculous and I started to see the funny side to it. But it really showed how much they cared, and I began to understand how much I meant to them.

When I spoke with my dad about how suicidal I felt, he was in tears. That's when I thought to myself, 'No matter what pain I'm going through, I don't want to pass this on to anyone else.' I was determined to get through it.

It's hard to pinpoint a specific moment when things changed for the better for me but one memory that sticks out is having a really great service on a busy Friday night in March 2015, several months after my lowest point.

We'd started to draw the attention of some high-profile restaurant critics. Fay Maschler, Jay Rayner and A.A. Gill all came through the doors in those first three months, giving us such positive reviews. I was cooking my best food and starting to find love in my cooking again.

That Friday night, the restaurant was firing on all cylinders. As a restaurant owner, this is how we hope all our evenings will be. The bar and dining rooms were lively, with convivial cheer. The front-of-house team danced through the restaurant with plates of food, drinks and joy.

In the kitchen, the larder team fired out plate after plate of perfect little starters, while my guys on the stoves sent me perfectly cooked meat and fish for me to plate. Nothing late. No mistakes.

And for a brief moment, while I was plating the main courses, everything stopped. An overwhelming emotion rose up from my gut and brought a tear to my eye. I love this place. I love this team. I love cooking. I love my life.

This is why I had to make my way out of the darkness.

Andrew Clarke is an award-winning chef and a prominent figure in the London and UK food scene. With twenty-three years of professional experience in hospitality, he is best known for his London restaurants, Brunswick House and St Leonards.

Andrew recently co-founded Pilot Light, a social good business which aims to raise awareness and tackle the stigma around mental health in hospitality.

In 2019, Andrew received the Innovation Award at the Craft Guild of Chef's Awards. In his spare time, he plays guitar in the metal band Kandadar Giant.

Steve Loft
Being PMS (Pale Male and Stale)

2017 was an amazing year for me. In February, I was invited to 10 Downing Street to be part of a roundtable discussion, which led to the recently published *Thriving in Work* report. In May, I left my job in Transport for London (TFL) after fifteen years' service and started a second career as a mental health trainer and speaker. Then in October, I was invited to Buckingham Palace for a Reception on World Mental Health Day, where I met the royals, celebrities and other amazing people doing great work around mental health, in recognition of the work I've done as a mental health campaigner. But my life looked very different five years earlier. The saying goes that all new beginnings are disguised as painful endings, and that has certainly been true for me.

2012 was an exciting year for London. The Olympic Games was coming to the city and there was a buzz about my workplace at TFL, as we prepared for transporting people across the capital during one of the highpoints in its history. However, one morning I found myself unable to get out of bed and off on my normal commute into London from Kent. Some people call it a breakdown, but I can only describe it as like hitting a brick wall and not having the energy to get up and brush myself off. Why was I feeling this way?

Alongside all the other hustle and bustle, I had just taken on a new role at work and my wife, Sharon, was quite unwell after a recent operation. I started to worry excessively. The signs of mental ill health were there but I missed them. I remember sitting at my computer staring at a simple e-mail for over an hour trying to understand it, or worse, finding myself standing at the end of the platform at Westminster tube station, looking down at the track and wondering for a fleeting moment what it would be like to be between the two rails. I then looked up and saw a child of about six, around my son's age, on the opposite platform; that little boy saved my life. He reminded me of what I loved and would leave behind if I jumped. So, thankfully, I decided to step onto the next train and went on with my business that day.

I thought a couple of days off work would help me but it didn't. The worry and rumination got worse. I rarely took time off work and felt I was letting other people down. Achieving and being successful at work had been very important to me since a young age. Now I realise this trait had become detrimental to my health.

I went to my GP and he prescribed antidepressants, which I took straight away. He also signed me off work for one month. The antidepressants helped me regain my energy, but not much else – I felt I was surviving but not really enjoying life. Later on my psychiatrist explained that these medicines are like clothes – they suit some people but not others. The ones I initially took must have been the wrong size and colour!

Up until this time I had had an exemplary attendance and performance record at TFL and was held in high regard by my workmates. So I tried to return to work after the month, despite the better judgement of others. When I broke down and cried at my desk on the very first day back, I knew I was clearly not ready.

After that, weeks off work turned into months – I was not improving. Yet throughout this time I was very lucky to have my supportive wife, a compassionate and caring line manager, Ian, and a patient and understanding HR (Personnel) Officer, Muriel. Their support and encouragement were essential at this difficult time for me. I remember one check-in meeting with Ian in a café near Victoria Station, where I opened up more than I ever had before to a workmate. I told him I had had enough of letting people down and just wanted to quit my job. Ian would not accept this and said he would stick by me until I got better. This faith in me – which was more than I had in myself – gave me my first glimmer of hope. I know sadly not all employers are like this, but I will be forever grateful for the support my work colleagues gave me.

After six months of 'surviving', I eventually got referred to a psychiatrist who diagnosed me with a condition called Generalised Anxiety Disorder (GAD). This anxiety had also caused me to have a depressive episode. This was the first time I had ever heard of GAD. My psychiatrist changed my medication immediately and referred me for psychotherapy sessions. From the moment I heard the words GAD, it was a turning point for me – I now knew what was wrong with me, and could research the condition and the medicines and therapy I had been prescribed – the internet is a wonderful thing in that sense! I was especially reassured by the fact that you can control and 'beat' the condition with the right support. The psychiatrist also explained that in my case it was likely that my condition was genetic – it had been passed on to me. So it was not necessarily just life events that caused my condition. I'd felt shame at not coping with these things and felt that it was some form of 'weakness' on my part – which I now know is common in men. I am fifty-six as I write this and from the generation brought up to show a 'stiff upper lip' and soldier on without showing or sharing our emotions; to be tough and resilient whatever the cost to themselves or others. I now say I had PMS at the time of my illness – I was Pale, Male and feeling very Stale!

Following my diagnosis, I worked hard to get better and return to work. A combination of the right medicine, along with twelve sessions with my psychiatrist and twenty with a psychologist, really did help me back to full recovery. A second ray of hope came from one of my early therapy sessions where I was presented with a plastic cup and a seed, along with written instructions on how to grow the seed. I was asked to bring this back to the therapist each week and I carefully tended to the seed in the plastic cup each day, watering the soil until it became a flower. I proudly presented the flower to my therapist one day. I remember the discussion at that session, how growing the seed was giving me hope that I, too, could flourish again like the flower. I also remember him telling me that some people took weeks just to read the instructions, let alone follow them like I had done; I realised then how well I was compared to other poor folk. This was such a simple exercise, yet it had a lasting impact on me about the importance of hope.

I returned to work a stronger and wiser person – much more self-aware and also armed with coping strategies for my anxiety, should it return. In the following six years at TFL, I was only off work sick for a couple of days and that was due to a damaged elbow – never again for my mental health condition; I worked hard to repay the faith they had had in me.

I am a firm believer that some good can come out of all bad things. When I returned to work, I started up a peer-to-peer support group to help anyone in TFL who was experiencing mental health conditions, to give them the support and hope that I had been given. Although I have now left, the group has grown to over 300 people and has won a national award for its work. It has created a lot of goodwill and kept many still in work because they feel supported and not alone. I am extremely proud of what has been achieved and the legacy I left there – it is an example of what can be done with the support of an employer. Energised by the peer support group, TFL also signed the Time to Change pledge in October 2016, with the support of all its top managers.

Eventually I needed a change and realised that my passion was now using my own story to educate workplaces. After leaving TFL I did some voluntary work for Time to Change and then set up my own business providing awareness training in workplaces. Life is good for me now. It will always have its ups and downs but I now feel able to cope with them.

Hindsight is a great thing but I'd like to leave you with some things I've learnt:

- If you are feeling down, anxious or behaving differently to your normal self, talk to someone who will listen to you without judgement. A problem shared is often halved and I wish I had done this much sooner.
- A man should never consider it 'weak' to talk to his family, friends, or work colleagues about what he is experiencing; in fact, it is the bravest thing you can do. You could be surprised who will listen and who has felt just the same.

- Please seek professional help if you don't feel any better after talking to others – your GP or charities like Mind can point you in the right direction for treatment or support.
- Mental health peer support groups in organisations are really effective in raising awareness, supporting and thereby keeping people in work. Organisations should consider setting them up if they don't already have them.
- Spend time keeping your mental health in as good a shape as your physical health; there are some simple and effective ways to maintain good mental health and I continue to keep my mind 'in trim'.

And finally . . . hope really does spring eternal!

Steve Loft was born in 1962 in Gravesend, Kent. He is married with a fifteen-year-old son. His interests include Charlton Athletic Football Club and punk rock, especially on vinyl. Steve has worked across a wide range of public services including accountancy, finance management and IT management and now has a second career as a workplace mental health awareness trainer and speaker.

Rikesh Chauhan
Veiled Surroundings

One thing I struggled with in my teens and early twenties was being on my own. Whether it was a small pocket of time or a few days at a stretch, the idea of it was just a little overwhelming. I didn't like hearing my thoughts and didn't enjoy sitting or being still. There wasn't really any reason for me to feel like this, I just did.

At times when I was alone in my flat, what I can only describe as a dark veil would descend upon me. Everything I was surrounded by would quickly turn grey, as if I could only see things in monochrome. I'd regress into a shadow of myself and switch off as if I'd given up caring. I wanted to go into a void and stay there indefinitely. I would break down occasionally, other times I'd have a panic attack, but more often than not it was a deeply intense numbness. A bit like an existential crisis. I couldn't bring myself to react to anything because what was the point? I slept a lot during these periods and it felt like the weight of Mount Everest was resting on my chest whenever I tried to get out of bed.

It took me years to overcome. Years of convincing myself that everything would be fine, telling myself that in order for me to help others I needed to be good to be around. Telling yourself that there's nothing wrong in being by yourself can, in fact, often be empowering. I began really slowly. I adapted physical actions and incorporated them into my everyday routine. Things like going on my commute without music or a book. It forced me to be aware of my surroundings and my thoughts. I would sit in for coffee without my laptop. I started going out to restaurants for dinner by myself. On the whole, I have definitely become more comfortable with myself but it's important to accept that I will have momentary lapses – and that it's perfectly ok to have them. We're not machines. We're emotional, passionate, pained, excitable, intense, aggressive, empathetic, conflicted beings. It's important to push ourselves, but it's important, also, to understand what our limits are. The harder we push ourselves, the harder it becomes to achieve our goals.

A few weeks ago, my partner was travelling for work and I had three days to myself. By this point I'd done this many times before but this was the first time in a while, so naturally the thought was a little daunting. I knew it would be ok but the pessimist in me was questioning things constantly. I ended up being fine, as expected, because I was at work, and for two of the three evenings I had plans. This evening I didn't, I decided to do it all – get some coffee, go to one of my favourite restaurants and go to the cinema. Something I had never previously done solo.

One of the things that troubles me is that I often feel conflicting feelings at the same time. I can be overwhelmingly happy, and in the same breath, incredibly sad. I'm terrible at making decisions because I can find an equal amount of pros and cons. People have tried to offer advice or opinions or to determine the cause of my angst (because we as human beings have to categorise absolutely everything under the sun). I get people telling me it's because I'm bipolar (for the record, I'm not), it's because I'm a Gemini, it's because I've had a bad week, it's because luck isn't on my side and I just have to 'keep my head up'. There simply has to be a reason. There has to be a reason someone is depressed (something I have actually been diagnosed with). But does there, really? What if someone is upset and feeling down without reason? What if someone is feeling at a loss when everything in their life is perfectly fine? One thing I still see often – usually when a celebrity or public figure passes away through suicide – is the idea that 'they had everything they ever wanted so how could they be depressed?'

This was one of the many things I started thinking about when I was walking from the restaurant to the cinema on my solo evening. I was looking at my surroundings and taking in every detail around me. I love this city. I love the sounds it makes. It's a beautiful place, where I live. The history behind the buildings, the people, the sense of belonging I have when I'm walking around. The family, the friends I've made. The places I find solace in. The wonderful coffee shops full to the brim with some of the world's most talented unknown creatives. The incredible food. The incredible vibrancy, buzz and cultural diversity. I love being here. I love where I'm at in life. I love my wife, my family, my friends. I love what I do for a living because it's enriching, creative, fun and enables me to grow every day. And yet, I've really struggled with depression. I still have days where it pains me to get out of the bed, even with all of those wonderful things in my life, and I don't know why. Twenty-nine years on this earth and I haven't even come close to figuring it out.

The feeling, as I described earlier, is like having a veil covering your physical body. It greys out everything you can see but, outside of the veil, everything's the same. Your life is exactly the same; the walls, the room, the roads, the buildings, the sounds, the friends, the family. Life is still wonderfully perfect, but you can't really . . . see it clearly anymore. It's there, and you know it's there, it's just a little out of reach, out of sound and eventually, typically, out of mind. It's replaced by thoughts that you wouldn't normally think. In fact, the only rational thing you can think is that you wish you had control over the veil. A little form of control. Anything.

So what is there for me to be hopeful for? Well, I'm lucky to be in a position where although I have this veil, I know that it eventually goes away. Sometimes it'll take a day and sometimes it can be a week or so. The real task is to keep it away for longer and longer periods of time. I believe this can be achieved by continuing to surround myself with the things I love and to ensure I'm doing things I find fulfilling. It may not be a permanent solution and may not work at all on the odd occasion, but it's a good enough start to help me get by.

When I'm really struggling, I try to speak to people. Whether it's to my wife in person, or to friends, or followers on Instagram. Any form to express myself and a way to exhale, almost. It's important to understand that you're not in it alone. There is always someone you can speak to – be it a family member, friend, colleague, someone on social media, even a helpline. My dad always says, 'You shouldn't feel sad about feeling sad', and it's that sentiment that has always stuck in my mind. I've learnt to give myself a break instead of fighting myself out of frustration for not feeling appreciative of all the good I have, as if being depressed negated the brilliant things and people I know. It doesn't. Of course it doesn't. I am living a wonderful life, with depression. It doesn't own me, but it does form a part of who I am. And if I didn't experience it who knows who, what or where I would be now.

I guess the ultimate thing we have to remind ourselves of is what we are grateful for – be it the little or the large things. Find some solace in some part of your world and let that be the light that helps guide you more and more as every day passes. And failing that, reach out to someone. You're only alone if you let yourself be that way. There's always a hand to hold, an ear to listen, a shoulder to rest on, and there's no shame in letting them know you need it.

Rikesh Chauhan, known as RKZ, is a Luton-born recording artist, menswear writer and photographer based in East London. Since 2011, he has been an ambassador for suicide prevention charity, Campaign Against Living Miserably.

Jo Love

In the darkest moments of mental ill health hope is in scarce supply. When staring into what feels like a vortex of emptiness, surrounded by the very darkest thoughts and loneliness, hope is chillingly absent. The illness locks out hope, it wants to keep you from hope, it grows by isolating you, like a bindweed slowly suffocating and strangling you, the plant, below. In order for mental illness to survive, to thrive, it knows it must keep hope away from you, at all costs.

It does this because hope holds you, hope hears you, hope sits with you, hope tells you things will get better, and you believe hope because hope is so confident, so sure of itself. And hope is right; hope does make things better, hope holds your hand and guides you gently out of the inky blackness into the light.

But letting hope in is scary and feels impossible under the suffocating crush of mental illness. And yet hope is determined, hope is always there, even if you can't see it or hear it. It's in the tiniest of moments, shining its dim light, hoping you notice it. And hope is potent stuff, you only need the smallest glimmer, the tiniest drop, to make a difference. Once it's caught your attention, hope is a fast worker, it grows faster and stronger than the weed, it shines brighter, it becomes bigger and ultimately helps you break free of the stranglehold of mental illness and walk into recovery.

Hope is lifesaving, hope is the answer.

Jo Love is an award-winning mental health advocate, speaker, writer and creator of the *What I Wish I Had Known* podcast. She uses her platform to break the silence on mental health issues, after spending a large portion of her life silently suffering with severe Depression, OCD (dermatillomania) and Generalised Anxiety Disorder. She was also diagnosed with postnatal depression after the birth of her first daughter, which led to PTSD.

Sarah Hughes
Life is a Mixed Bag, but You're Not Alone

Sometimes I wonder what I would tell my younger self, if I could go back in time. I imagine some extraordinary philosophy that I have accumulated into middle age, the meaning of life, a revelation so worthy it could have its own meme. As you can imagine, I have no such wisdom, I shall forever be memeless. Obviously there are some important life things like, wear more sun screen, wear a bra when you're asleep, don't worry about failing maths GCSE twice, and always take your make-up off before bed. Oh, and don't drink tequila and champagne at the same time (this will be a life-altering hangover that you can do without). This life laundry stuff is endless and relatively easy. The big stuff about love, grief, failure and sense of self demands so much more thought because it's the stuff that really counts in the long term. It's a cliché because it is true.

I was a serious child. My aunt said I was born an adult and my parents called me 'the girl in the bubble'. I didn't really play with other kids, I mostly read or played on my own. I loved being with adults, found them much more interesting than my peers. This seriousness has lingered throughout my life, my soft and friendly exterior hiding a very shy and often slightly weird and awkward woman. When I was a teenager this personality dissonance was the source of some unhelpful and difficult experiences. Attempting to fit in and a family trauma ultimately resulted in an overdose at sixteen. A charcoal stomach pump was a sobering experience, that's for sure. I was very unsettled, I gave myself a hard time. I would take any sort of failure deep into my central cortex, almost carrying it around as penance. I was one of the lucky ones though; I come from a loving family who were and continue to be right alongside me. I guess one of the things that motivates me in my work is that I know so many people don't have the same loving support, the consequences of which can be devastating.

I am one of those people that has dealt with lots of life stuff. Sometimes when I share my life experiences with people I can almost see in their eyes that they think some of what I'm telling them can't be true. I laugh with my mum about this; we imagine what my biography would be called, maybe 'you couldn't make this shit up' or 'life is like a box of chocolates and stink bombs'. People would read it like fantasy probably, but believe me the struggle continues to be very real. I describe my life as being one of fire, flood and fuckery, but in between I have experienced joy on an almost spiritual level. I guess this is my learning: life is a mixed bag and pain can fade and not invade your every waking moment. For sure, during the most frightening and isolating times it has been hard to believe this. The sense of doom and emotional pain, the feeling that it would never end, a belief that there was no way out, that I had been sentenced to a lifetime of feeling broken. Thankfully this hasn't been true.

There have been so many moments that have proved this to me. I will leave out most of the gory details but I do want to share a big one. My father died in 2012. He'd had a lifetime of health challenges and so we as a family half expected him to just recover like he always had. After two months of being in hospital he was diagnosed with a rare terminal cancer. I had just recovered from an episode of postnatal depression (which is a whole other story) and was starting to feel like life was going to be ok. Dad being so ill was a blow. More than a blow actually, it was like a nuclear attack on our lives. We looked after Dad at home, and he died in our arms. It was the most beautiful, yet the most despairing time. Grief is visceral and lasted for so much longer than I anticipated – it took me to the edge of the world. All I know for sure is that my family were all on the edge, staring out in shock and trauma. I believe now that we held on to each other in relay so we didn't all fall into the abyss. If you had asked me at the time if I thought I would survive those moments, that pain and sense of danger, I would have told you no. Those early days of grief are also complicated with a feeling that being closer to the pain is being closer to the person you have lost, and time passing by is not initially healing at all. People would say, 'Time is a healer' on a daily basis, and I think it's fair to say I imagined telling them to 'get lost' (or less nice language) pretty much every time.

Since Dad died I have had a precious second child, watched my daughter (first child) live with a life-threatening illness with the power of a lioness, got an epic new job, met some of my professional idols and now call them friends, laughed so hard it hurts, and had dinner with the extraordinary Stephen Hawking (I have photos to prove this). There is no doubt all of this would be better if Dad were alive, it's true, but it is also true that I can still live, love and laugh: these feelings are not binary. This is not 'moving on' (which I think is the worst of all the sayings), it is simply claiming all aspects of my life, embracing all my stories and what they have given me. It is this realisation that has allowed me to live with the sorrow without letting it consume. Sometimes it's so much harder than others, but guess what, I survive. Seven years later I can see that time has simply allowed me to regulate my grief, time is not a healer in itself, time just creates the space for you to learn how to live with a big loss. It becomes a way of life.

So, what am I saying? I guess I would tell sixteen-year-old Sarah that things will get better, but there will also be times when they get significantly worse. But you will get to middle age and know stuff, you will still be loved and love others, you will just about survive some things and in other ways you will thrive and flourish. I would tell her that she will learn to laugh at the most outrageous things, that she will develop a sense of compassion that will underpin everything in her life. Most of all, she will realise that being with the people she loves will literally save her life. Expect the unexpected, stay close to those who have your back, say yes to opportunities, don't worry so much about the small things, start Zumba earlier than at forty-three, turns out you love it, don't let your ego take over and finally, just remember you were never, ever alone.

Sarah Hughes has worked in mental health for over thirty years, qualifying as a social worker in 1994. She has worked across the spectrum of mental health services, overseen mental health and suicide prevention campaigns and is currently undertaking a professional doctorate studying women and leadership. Sarah is also married to her partner of twenty-five years, Lee, has two beautiful children and a very moody tortoise called Elvis.

Rose Cartwright

For people who experience enduring mental pain, it's not always easy to find hope. It took me ages to write this piece. Every time I tried to start, I found I wasn't feeling hopeful.

This year I began trauma therapy. For the first time, I stepped inside areas of my consciousness that I'd locked the doors to decades ago. In those places I experienced deep, inky waves of pain – pain which felt old and somehow at the core of me, both physically and emotionally.

As I processed these feelings, I started to realise that they were part of a continuum of experiences stretching from babyhood to womanhood. That the behaviours, ways of thinking and bodily sensations which upset me today had been ushered in by things which happened long ago, beyond my control. A valuable realisation, but where's the hope in it? What's done is done.

I'd always thought of mental health conditions as my enemy. That I was being attacked by my own psyche. That my brain had weaponised against me. But slowly, as I waded through therapy, I started to change my mind. What if things like compulsivity, self-harm and rumination were not in fact weapons, but tools that had once protected me – powerful mechanisms that had tried to control a pain that would have overwhelmed me if I'd felt it fully as a child?

What if all along it had been the control, and not the pain, that was the problem? This year I've been slowly teaching my body and mind that I don't need these controls any longer. That I'm not under threat anymore, that it's safe to down tools.

In the thick of hurt, things can feel hopeless. True – we can't avoid pain, but that doesn't mean it's immovable. It can soften and change, slowly, as we move through it with love.

Rose is a creative director, screenwriter and the author of *Pure*, as seen on Channel 4 and Netflix. She's also the co-founder of mental health non-profit, Made of Millions.

KINDNESS

Alexander Theo

My name is Alexander Theoharous, Theo for short. I was born into a Greek Cypriot family and grew up in North London. I'm an actor, writer and stand-up comedian or, as it's known in Greek, a failure. I'm twenty-four and was convinced that by now my anxiety would have lessened, my depression would have disappeared and my fingers would never have reached into my throat again. I was wrong.

Growing up, I always felt something wasn't right: I'd touch things more than once, preferably an even amount (as in lights etc), look at things for a certain time, twitch my face as if I was impersonating Jim Carrey in *Ace Ventura*. It became a slight addiction. People would look at me as if I was crazy. Maybe I was. Maybe I am.

I was constantly worrying as a child, about everything. I found it so hard to balance my emotions. I'd sit in my room in the pitch black, feeling so down, thinking, 'Is this what life is like?' Things just weren't right. I saw a psychologist. She told me I suffered from something called anxiety. It sounded like a little infection that would eventually go away. It didn't. It never has.

So here I am today, at twenty-four, trying to figure out on a daily basis what triggers these feelings. Although there are often no easy answers, trying to understand the trigger does help. It's bloody scary, because it sometimes takes you to the place you really don't want to go, but by going to that place you can help yourself come out of it. Sometimes when anxiety hits me bad, I find a tap. Wait – Hear me out! I run water and place my hands underneath it, feeling the cold; it helps me remember to be present.

Bulimia was a weird time. Growing up, I was overweight. In my opinion all Greek kids are. It's a thing. My parents were like Shallow Hal: the bigger I was. the skinnier I looked to them. As I grew up, I lost a lot of weight from attending the gym, not eating rubbish etc. So I was always nervous about going back to that old self, to being overweight. I also had a fear of being sick when young, when I was ill with the flu. I'd fear the puking. However, when I was mentally suffering, making myself sick was like finding a best friend, someone I could trust, who could listen to everything I was feeling without me having to talk. EVERY TIME I'd make myself sick, whether it was at a restaurant, at rehearsals or at home, it felt great. I became addicted, really addicted to the feeling. When I'd purge it was as if my emotions were coming out as well and all I had to do was flush the loo and goodbye emotions. It wasn't even just about weight anymore; it had become a release, an escape. It got to the point where one day I noticed blood. No, not beetroot; blood.

It seemed that society didn't consider a man suffering from an eating disorder to even be possible. But somehow I started to talk openly to my friends about it; it helped, so, so much. I'd even message a friend asking them to keep me occupied and tell me how Arsenal will win the league again one day whilst I tried to get over the fact that I really wanted to purge. Slowly, things helped. It took time. Things take time. Just keep breathing. Know you will get there. Take each moment at a time. Open up, talk. It really helped me get through it. It's bloody ok not to be ok. Keep going.

You'll find some people just won't understand what you're going through, or the term anxiety. That's ok; I don't understand why people will support a team that isn't Arsenal, and that's ok too, I guess. Don't ever let anyone tell you how you need to feel and when you need to feel. Just feel.

Therapy does help, though people are always quick to tell me it doesn't. It's taken me months to finally start opening up and talk comfortably with my therapist. Sometimes I have nothing to say. So I sit there and just, yeah, sit there, wondering what I'm going to say. Oh God, it's awkward. Say something, Alex, say something! 'Nice weather today!' I say, and in my head I'm thinking, 'Damn, we're in London, it's winter!' So I'll just stay silent and that's bloody OK!

So, what triggered everything?

Growing up, I had three people I looked up to, George Michael, my cousin Costandino and Jim Carrey. Jim Carrey was someone I could openly love. George and my cousin? Maybe not. They were doing what I thought I could never do: be Greek and openly gay. I'd be singing 'Freedom' daily with no one around; but as soon as I'd sense someone near me, I'd change the song.

Whenever I saw Costandino when I visited Cyprus it would be as if I had just seen a celebrity. This man was out and Greek, and that was so inspiring to me. He just did what he wanted to do. To me, he was bloody cool! I remember he secretly took me to a gay club out in Cyprus. Next day Mum asked where I'd been. 'Oh, just church.' Church!? What was I thinking? 'I mean church . . . club . . . Mum, it's a club called Church, like the church . . .' Stop talking, Alex! Just sashay away.

Last October we took a walk through the harbour and were taking life in when Costandino turned to me and asked, 'Do you mind the silence?' I said, 'No, it just shows how close we are.' That's what I loved, just the silent moments. It wasn't awkward and it summed us up.

My beautiful friend/cousin/partner-in-crime unfortunately lost his life to suicide recently. I'd love to thank him; I'd love to tell him how he inspired me. Maybe he knew? Maybe he's actually reading this from that place they call Heaven? No, not the gay club in London, the actual one upstairs . . . 'Hey cuz, if you're reading this, whenever I was in your presence, you always made me feel present. Oh, and you had bloody great trainers!'

All we really can do is care. Love each other. Sometimes just listen. Even when you don't know what to say, TRUST your inner being to just listen. That helps, I promise. So this is for anyone reading this who is suffering, worrying about a million things at once. Keep going.

Alexander Theo is a writer, actor and stand-up comedian. In 2015 he wrote and performed in a short film called *All Is Good*, raising awareness for suicide prevention. This led him to do a talk at world suicide prevention day and he has been working to raise awareness with mental health charities ever since.

Hope Virgo

I met my best friend Anorexia when I was just thirteen years old. She pulled me close, making me think she was who I needed. She tucked me up at night reassuringly, giving me the sense of purpose that I had been struggling to find. Little did I know that by listening to her, by letting her dictate my life, I was letting her slowly kill me. As the weight slipped off and my mind thought more about food, calories and exercise, it switched off from all the emotions, all the reality of life and I loved that. I loved the fact that I could get up in the morning and just focus on the anorexia and nothing else.

One of the problems with anorexia is that you get convinced that what she is saying is true. You go into full denial mode. I used to sit there opposite the clinicians whilst they told me the damage I was doing to my body and just not believe what anyone was saying. They would tell me my heart was failing, my hair would keep falling out, but I just didn't believe any of it. Or care. Even as I stood at the hospital entrance, I still didn't think I had anything wrong with me. And definitely not anorexia. Anorexics looked like skeletons and this definitely wasn't how I looked.

After three days in hospital, when I was completely fed up, one of the nurses came in to see how I was doing. I told her I hated being there and hated everyone in the hospital. After listening to me for a while, the nurse got me to draw myself on these pieces of paper, a life-size version of me. She then got me to lie down and she drew round me.

The outlines were shockingly different. Even then I thought she'd lied to me, somehow tricked me, but then there was this realisation that there actually was something really wrong in the way that I viewed myself. It wasn't easy though. I didn't have a wake-up, clicking-lightbulb moment. It was just an ongoing process, every day learning about the importance of gaining weight, learning to talk. Over time my guard began to drop. I began to let people in and that talking saved me. Many people with anorexia think that as soon as they are a healthy weight everyone will think they are fully fixed, but there is so much more to it than that. That's why we have to keep talking – so we don't feel the need to show we are struggling through not eating. It is hard and I am not saying recovery is easy (I wish it was) but when you get there and realise that anorexia is not your friend but a manipulative nasty piece of work, you will slowly but surely be able to find that strength to recover.

What I wish people had told me at the start, even before the start, is this: talking helps. It's going to be ok. It will feel at times emotionally and physically exhausting but you can do it. We have your back.

Hope Virgo is the author of *Stand Tall Little Girl*, and an international leading advocate for people with eating disorders. Hope helps young people and employers (including schools, hospitals and businesses) to deal with the rising tide of mental health issues, and has appeared on various media platforms as a spokesperson.

Amy Abrahams

As I grew up, grew older, and tried to make sense of my twenties and early thirties, my younger self played hide and seek in my shadow. While I studied and applied for jobs, fell in love, fell out of love, tried to be an *adult*, the person I felt I was when I was sixteen never quite stepped aside. She crept along beside me, she whispered her fears in the dark. It's not that my younger self was 'bad', but she was lost. She did not feel comfortable in her own skin, she doubted herself, she wanted to simultaneously be seen and yet fade away. It took me a long time to realise that I am no longer that girl. And it took even longer to give her the love she deserved.

*

Leah sat opposite me on a plush, salmon-pink sofa, smiling encouragingly, while I toed the carpet with my ankle boot, unsure where to begin. Spring sunshine thrust through the large window of my therapist's office, minutes from London's chaotic Oxford Circus. I crossed my legs tightly, preoccupying myself with my peeling red nail varnish. 'I don't think I need to be here. I'm in a good place,' I said, meaning it.

In fact, I'd recently written an article for a national magazine talking about how I'd tackled my disordered eating and just how great I felt. Because I did. I felt in control. Except an unexpected thing had then happened: a few days after publication, a psychotherapist who ran an eating disorders clinic messaged me on Instagram to say if I ever wanted to talk, to ask.

You can kick this for good, if you'd like, she wrote.

Something twisted in my stomach – like I'd been caught cheating on a test – but I batted away her suggestion.

Oh no, no, I'm fine, I typed back. *Though would love to interview you for another piece I'm writing if poss.*

When we finally sat down to talk, I never did ask her my interview questions. Instead, she gently challenged the food rules I was still bound by, and I found myself dabbing a tissue under my eyes, conceding that maybe I had some more work to do after all. I left the room with smeared mascara and a recommendation of someone from the clinic – Leah – who I could talk to as a private patient. And so a few weeks later I found myself in that room with the pink sofa, unintentionally in therapy for something I thought wasn't a problem anymore.

As a teenager, I'd once mumbled to my mother that maybe therapy would be helpful. 'What do you need that for?' she said. 'I've done nothing wrong.' I remember shooting an eye-roll in the direction of my older sister but said nothing more at the time. True, she hadn't done anything specifically wrong – I just felt there was something deeply wrong with *me*. So, instead, I became my own therapist over the next two decades, in an attempt to rid myself of insecurity and my complicated relationship with food: I poured my thoughts into journals; I found refuge in novels; I tried hypnotherapy and discovered self-help and wellness and marathon running and taught myself the language of introspection. I navigated my career towards becoming a health journalist – I spent my working hours interviewing psychologists and medical experts and writing pieces to help readers boost self-esteem and improve body image. I thought it was enough – and maybe it was more than enough – but receiving that message on Instagram revealed that someone had read between the lines and seen there was still more work to be done.

'When you're ready . . .' said Leah, patiently waiting for me to talk. Where to start?

'I feel guilty being here,' I said, guilt being my lifelong default setting. Why was I there when people felt far worse? When people more deserving couldn't get access to the services they so desperately needed? 'Plus,' I added, 'I feel like a fraud.' I was seeing an eating disorders specialist when I had never had a better relationship with food (mostly true). I was seeing an eating disorders specialist when I'd never had a clinical diagnosis (though another psychologist had said it very much sounded like I'd had one as a teenager). I wasn't ill. I was functioning. Why was I there when everything was *fine*?

'It's all historical,' I added, further trying to justify my presence. Leah nodded. But in truth I knew I was editing the story. While I believed my most difficult years were contained in the vortex of teendom, my past, like a volcano shooting steam with little warning, was very much still active in my mind, and it didn't take much to trigger an eruption. This meant unleashing the fears of my younger self, who'd felt ugly and undeserving of love. It was sixteen-year-old me instead of the grown-up version who baulked at asking my boss for a pay rise, or who struggled to end things with an emotionally abusive partner; it was my younger self who still used food – whether binging or restricting – as punishment or reward; it was my younger self who, in the deepest moments of despair or anger, considered a blade a possible release.

'You don't have to wait to be in a crisis to get help,' Leah said, thirteen soothing words that finally granted me permission to speak.

The words did not come easy though. I felt like I was staring into a murky lake, reaching in my hand to pull out memories wedged into the silt that had long grown weeds and algae, memories that were decaying and warped by time. I feared what would be unearthed. It's hard to describe eloquently what I felt was deep inside me. Something unlovable, something 'icky'. A strange creature.

I was fourteen years old when I decided that I was 'disgusting', my body loathsome, and that 'getting thin' was the only solution to fix this. It was as if I woke up one morning and a grey cloud hovered above me wherever I went. I have a distinct memory of sitting in a geography lesson and feeling disconnected from the rest of the class, isolated by this grey cloud, obscured by its drizzle. During these teenage years, I recorded my thoughts in diaries – pages and pages of terrible poetry and angst-ridden exclamations – 'I AM SO DEPRESSED!!! FUCK EVERYTHING!!' – but it was only as an adult that I realised I truly *was* experiencing bouts of depression. It makes sense to me now that in the chaos of growing up, food became one of the few things I could control.

I was obsessed with counting calories, getting by during school day on a powdered soup from the canteen, hiding food on my lap during mealtimes at home. When I did eat in front of people other than my family, I felt awkward and ashamed – my appetite a transgression. And yet I struggled to maintain this avoidance of food (a perceived failure on my part), so would sneak sweets and chocolate upstairs to my room and devour them in secret. Over the next two years, I alternated between months of feeling 'fine', then starving or binging or making myself sick. I even turned up for my GCSE exams having purged what little I'd eaten that morning.

No wonder I was irritable at school, no wonder I struggled to focus. One end-of-term report mentioned my 'insolence', another that I had become 'rude and apathetic'. I would fall asleep in lessons, started smoking during breaks. I once turned up to an English class having swigged whisky at lunchtime with some older girls in a disused garage they'd broken into. No one really questioned why I was acting out and I was never delinquent enough to get expelled – even in my rebellion, I was a mediocre bad girl. And I never got thin enough to cause concern. This was the mid-1990s and mental health wasn't part of the conversation back then. As a pupil at a high-pressure all-girls' grammar school, where eating disorders were seemingly on the curriculum, my behaviour wasn't even that note-worthy; it was my lack of Oxbridge potential and falling grades – rather than my weight – that marked me a lost cause.

I was also a master of concealment. I code-switched depending on my environment. At school, I was abrasive and facetious; at home, yes, I was undeniably grumpy, but I was also silly and gentle, the self-appointed peace-corps diplomat in my family home in a bland but safe London suburb. My parents were supportive, doting, loving, but were also careering towards divorce. I knew I was lucky and cosseted in so many ways. And so I felt guilty for feeling unhappy; back then, no one talked of 'privilege', but even at sixteen I was fully aware of mine.

Yet I also felt different. I was raised in an orthodox Jewish household, where we kept the Sabbath and wouldn't drive or carry or draw or turn on lights or the TV for 24 hours, from sunset on Friday night. I grew increasingly infuriated at being told what to do but felt locked into the tight-knit community – it was all I knew. I was also a youth leader in my local synagogue, I volunteered at the local care home, and had a Sunday job teaching Hebrew reading to six-year-olds.

'You feel comfortable in the "helper" role,' observed Leah. 'I guess,' I replied, wondering for the first time whether helping others was a convenient way to side-step my own needs.

Despite the dictates of religion, my parents were extraordinarily liberal. Yet I could not articulate my own emotions and I think, unconsciously, my parents were fearful to confront them. Perhaps to question my issues would have highlighted what they were not ready to talk about with theirs.

'She's a freak,' I remember a classmate saying about me – *in front of me* – when she'd spotted the neat row of cuts on my arm peeking out from my navy school jumper. Sat on a desk, swinging my Dr Martens, I did not say much. As painful as this accusation was, it was the only time anyone had acknowledged directly what I was doing. People wanted to believe the elaborate lies I spun to explain the marks on my forearm – I fell on a brush; I tripped and landed on a splintered drawer; I annoyed my friend's cat; whoops, I fell again . . . Endlessly clumsy. Another plaster. Always tugging down long sleeves with my thumbs. For the most part, though, I was very good at hiding what I didn't want people to know and when I wrote about it in my diary, the words were in tiny spidery scrawls, almost unreadable. It was my biggest secret.

'And what did the self-harm make you feel?' asked Leah. Something heavy lodged in my throat, drying up my words. I had never spoken about this before – and while it was something I no longer did, and had not done for maybe a decade, slight silvery scars on my arm remained everyday ghosts of my past. It was not called self-harm when I was at school – in the early days of search engines, before Google had even been invented, the term I had to type in to try to find like-minded people was 'self-mutilation'. The term felt barbaric, it scared me, it didn't reflect what was, for me, an attempt (if not a successful one) at release, and both a distraction and a focus. It was not an act of attention-seeking or a cry for help, or perhaps it was . . . (And, actually, what would have been wrong with that?) But in the end, no one helped, and I realised only I could fix myself. I pledged to stop once I left school, I mostly did. But I never liberated myself from the shame of this secret, and in the unspeaking of it over the years, the shame thrived in the dark.

What my parents did see, however, was my drinking. It was hard to avoid. Most Saturday nights when I was sixteen I was uncontrollably drunk, often crying, with my head over a toilet by the end of the evening. I enjoyed submitting to alcohol's toxic powers – even if, the day after, I felt saturated with regret and self-loathing.

But my mother stepped in and banned me from drinking; the first time such extreme boundaries had ever been laid down. And while I schemed up ways to get round these boundaries, this intervention marked the beginning of a change. I was taken out of the school that did not want me and sent for sixth form to a boarding school that saw people as more than just grades. Draconian as it may sound, this fresh start and the security of kind new friends kept me comforted when my parents finally separated. I left school with straight As and, at the very least, a B-plus in renewed optimism for life.

'What do you want to say to your younger self?' Leah asked. I had been asked this question during hypnotherapy a few years earlier, where I had hoped to Paul McKenna my way out of binge-eating. The answer I'd given then was to tell myself 'It's going to be ok,' and it had helped, but now I realised that was not enough. As I talked to Leah, I conjured my younger self into the room. It was as if she'd stepped out of the shadows and sat beside me so I could finally look her square in the face. I had feared a strange creature at my core, but now I recognised her for who she was – a kid. She was a kid with valid feelings. A kid who had felt unseen. I had been trouble, but not troubled enough. If only I had known then that everything is worth talking about. If only I could tell her that she was deserving of love too. 'I see you,' I told my younger self, and I meant it.

People often dismiss the feelings of teenagers – unpredictable, volatile, all hormones firing haphazardly like shiny pinballs trapped under glass. But I have never felt more strongly than I did back then, my memories and experiences are technicolour, visceral. No one had noticed me not eating, no one had noticed the hurt on my skin. By the time I got to adulthood, I feared invisibility. But beginning to discuss the past validated my experiences. The pain was real, even if no one saw me cry.

'You don't let yourself be held emotionally,' Leah had said earlier. I had nodded and 'hmmed', but in truth I had not processed what she meant. Was it time to hold myself? It was all getting a bit meta, but I acknowledged my younger self and held her until our session came to an end.

I closed the heavy wooden door behind me and stepped out into the street, tilting my head up and squinting into the sunshine. I was feeling vulnerable – emotionally bare – but also fortified by facing what I had spent so long trying to diminish. This was just the beginning of a longer conversation – and there was still more work to do – but as I picked up the pace, the sharp click of my heels softening as I fell into the crowds of Oxford Circus, I realised I did feel a little lighter already. My younger self was no longer weighing down my shadow, but willingly stepping aside for me to find a new path to thrive.

Amy Abrahams is a freelance journalist with a focus on health and wellbeing. She was the 2018 recipient of the Best Health Journalist award at the UK Wellness Awards. As a speaker and moderator, she has appeared on podcasts and at events and festivals including the Live Life Well Weekender, Fitfluence and Be You Talks. Amy is the co-founder of What The Health?, an events series focusing on health and wellbeing.

Nina Martynchyk

Following my mum's death, my reality irreversibly changed. I needed to go into foster care and spent a few years moving between placements. Unable to control what was going on around me, I started controlling what I ate instead and ended up becoming increasingly physically and mentally unwell. It wasn't long before I landed in hospital with severe anorexia and depression, which were my version of 'fuck you' and 'help me' to the world.

For just over a year, my eating disorder was totally in control, and my depression led me to suicide attempts. I didn't see how I could do more than simply survive in a state of suffering. However, just as there came a point when I was totally done with living, I also got totally fed-up of the fight I had waged against myself. I hadn't managed to die and as much as I tried to push it down, a sense of life was starting to grow in me.

Around this time, my new foster mum told me that she was going to go a Buddhist retreat in the South of France. The question of whether it might be possible for me to join her was mentioned. It would be in a remote field, in another country – and vegan. At the time of this conversation, I was sectioned and was being watched 24/7 by a member of staff, forced to eat by law. I am sure that many people would have deemed the idea of this retreat as a total impossibility. However, I could see that it would be the perfect test to see if I really did want to die or whether I could try to find happiness away from the confines of the unit.

Two months later, I was no longer sectioned and was seated on the Eurostar on my way to the South of France. The night I came back to England, I called the hospital and told them I wasn't coming back.

Six years after leaving that hospital, I feel so lucky to be recovered and able to live – really, truly live. My mum's death has inspired me to live twice as fully, once for me and once for her. As I feel closest to my mum on mountains, I have climbed Everest base camp and am writing this a few hours before I am due to fly to Tanzania to attempt to climb Kilimanjaro for the second time.

At my first attempt, a few hours before I was due to start my ascent to the top, I was sent back down due to altitude sickness. I had wanted to climb Kilimanjaro to feel closer to my mum, so not only did I feel like I had failed, but almost as if I was losing her for the second time. I had endured so many difficulties to get this far up the mountain and now my dream was being snatched out of my hands and I had no way to stop it happening.

We really can't control much of life, so a lot of my healing has come from following my heart, surrendering fully to new experiences and seeing where they will lead me. This has led me to booking a one-way ticket to Australia, where I will be flying out to shortly after I get back from Kilimanjaro.

Pain is hard to endure but working through the things that hurt you, and having a support system around you, can bring freedom. Even if a wave of pain hits you so hard that you need to escape to the shore with the water dripping off you, you have already got through one of the worst bits – the first hit. That is where the path to healing starts.

Nina Martynchyk is twenty-six years old and has worked as a mental health campaigner and a fundraising support officer at an NGO. At time of writing she is fulfilling her latest dream of travelling to Australia.

Angela Elliott

The earliest memory I have is of sitting in my highchair watching *Rag, Tag and Bobtail* on the black-and-white television. Not long after that, I was packed off to nursery school and the nightmare began.

I was born in 1957 in Derby in an ordinary two-up, two-down terraced house. My father worked in the county court and my mother was a housewife. The nursery school was a large Victorian building at the top of our road. There were around twenty children there. We were not allowed home for lunch and had to have an afternoon nap in cots with red blankets. I hated it. Everything about it terrified me. First off, I didn't understand why my mother didn't want me at home anymore. Secondly, the other children there were noisy and dirty, and I didn't like the food. The cook mashed it up and it looked like a plate of sick. This is an important thing for me because at three months old I had been fed some biscuit by my aunt and had choked on it. I was held upside-down and bashed on the back, went blue, stopped breathing and died. Of course, they did eventually bring me back to life. What this traumatic experience did psychologically is anyone's guess, but since then I have been terrified of choking and of vomiting – terrified to such an extent that I will do anything to avoid it.

For the entirety of my life I have been scared of food and what it might do to me. I do not view it as something to be relished and enjoyed, but as something that can kill. I will qualify that statement: I have never been anorexic; I know I have to eat. I have, however, controlled my intake of food to such an extent that I now have a real-life allergy to certain foods and am picky beyond belief. My mother, knowing this, used it as a way to control me. She told me absolutely everything would make me sick unless I did as I was told. If I stepped out of line like as not, I would be sick. Hence, the food at the nursery looked like a bowl of vomit and that for me was terrifying.

For years I will only eat Weetabix and my mother is beside herself with anger over it. When I'm seven we move halfway across the country and I'm bereft at having lost all my friends. I don't fit into my new school; my accent is strange and I've now got glasses and teeth that stick out. Everyone picks on me and no one wants to be my friend, so I keep to myself. I'm terrified and I'm bullied. I can remember holding on to the drainpipe in the playground while the other kids taunt me, my knuckles red raw from scraping on the wall behind. I disappear further inside myself. I am still terrified of throwing up – terrified of being ill. I spend every waking hour worrying if something I do might make me sick. I sleep very badly. Sometimes I cry all night.

Secondary school happens and a year into that my family moves again. My anxiety over food and sickness increases as I enter puberty. Every plate of food put in front of me is scrutinised carefully. I ask my mum if it's ok to eat. She tells me 'yes' every time, but I'm not convinced. Why should I believe her, when she has so successfully brainwashed me into believing that no food is safe? Age sixteen I go to art college and one Christmas get drunk and throw up. I vow never to get drunk again, and never have. I go away to university and hate it. I'm living in a stone-cold room and on Sundays the landlady serves cake that's going mouldy. I can only afford to eat beans and I don't eat beans, so I starve. I meet my soon-to-be husband, drop out of university and go to live with him. My father is beside himself with anger and my mother tells me my morals are shot and of course, it will make me vomit. The joke is, I've hardly ever thrown up – maybe a handful of times in my entire life. I can remember every single time.

I got married at twenty. It was a mistake right from the off, but I was young and foolish. My husband was an alcoholic, although in the early days that wasn't as evident as it was later on. The stress of everything caused me so much anxiety I lived every day on the edge of a breakdown. Nevertheless, I got a fabulous job as a process engineer and learned to drive. I was in charge of my own destiny at last and for a while it felt great, but as I rose in the world, so my husband fell. He lost his job. He went to work in a pub. I won't go into all the ins and outs, save to say that when my son was born in 1988 I started having five or six major panic attacks every single day. It got so bad that I couldn't even walk down the road without hanging on to the hedgerow. I would go shopping, get halfway round the supermarket, have a panic attack and have to leave. I'd go back the next day to finish the shopping and suffer the same thing all over again. I was breastfeeding, chronically undernourished, exhausted and terrified.

What first turned it around for me, albeit in a small way, was having shiatsu. That gave me the strength to get a divorce and move to London when my son was six. The other thing was writing. I'd started writing when my son was born and quickly won a BBC radio competition. I then submitted a piece to the BBC World Service and was picked up by a documentary producer, and spent many years scripting for TV and film. I managed to bring my son up as a single mother and struggled not to show him the true face of my anxiety. I had counselling and trained as a clinical hypnotherapist. I worked with victims of crime, supporting those affected by rape and sexual assault, domestic violence, gun crime and bereavement by homicide. Understanding the whys and wherefores and helping others with their problems helped me come to terms with some of my issues. Looking into my family's tangled mental health history has also helped me to understand why I am so badly affected by anxiety.

Take my dad, for instance. Having been in Singapore in 1945, he came back from the war with what we now call PTSD, but which was then called shell shock. He would have nightmares and scream and shout and my mother would tell him to turn over and go back to sleep. God alone knows what tortures he carried with him. We send our children to fight our wars for us. He was nineteen when he landed on the D-Day beaches, twenty when he was shipped out to Singapore to help rescue the Changi prisoners. Those experiences coloured his whole life. How do you recover from that?

My guess is that everyone can find someone in their family who has had mental health issues. I've never had a psychotic break, or hallucinated. I've never felt so bad that I wanted to kill myself, although I have stood on the edge of an underground station platform and wondered what it would be like to jump. I'm too scared to try it though. I'm terrified of heights so struggle with escalators, and elevators with glass walls. I can't imagine how anyone could have bulimia. Come on guys, it's my worst nightmare. I gag really easily at the dentist. I hate going anywhere by sea. I worry about throwing up on a train. I will fly, but only after a lot of travel sickness pills. I worry about bugs in water from a tap two streets away, on the basis that the 'local pathogens' might be different. I don't eat tuna because I once threw up after eating it. I don't sit with my back to any kind of heat because my mum told me it would make me sick. On and on it goes . . . it's a bloody nightmare. Sometimes I can rationalise it all away, but deep in my heart I know it will be with me to the end of my days.

I still wake up every single day and check in on myself. Do I feel well? Do I feel sick? It's like a curmudgeonly old friend whom I wave at as we pass on opposite sides of the street. I can distract myself for fairly long periods and if I have something really important to do then I will rise to the occasion, but afterwards I will be exhausted . . . and terrified. Always terrified.

One thing is for sure though, my anxiety is about how precious my life is – about how I don't want to die. I go back to that incident as a baby, when I quite literally choked to death. Everything since that time has been about keeping me alive. I guess my hyper-anxiety means I am really good at staying alive. I've got this life business cracked. I'm not giving up without a fight.

Angela Elliott is an author and scriptwriter who has worked on over thirty documentaries. Her novels include *Some Strange Scent of Death*, *The Finish*, *The Nine Lives of Antoine Montvoisin*, and *The Remaining Voice*, a novella.

James Downs

Everyone has a Pandora's Box story. We all have times when things seem to spiral, our chances of success seem to drop away and our boxes empty out. But somewhere at the bottom of our box, however bad things get, just like Pandora we find that there is always hope. Things will get better if we have the faith to carry on.

I've lived over half of my life with an eating disorder, and all the complex mental and physical health problems that come along with that. Gradually, as my health got worse and the support I needed was out of reach, the boxes that were once full of opportunity and promise – the relationship box, the health box, the work box, the hobbies box – started to empty out. Playing the violin and getting a place at music college. Keeping up with my friends. Taking up my offer to study at Cambridge. Keeping my place at medical school. One after another, these boxes emptied and I couldn't even look to see if there was any hope left inside them.

The worst times were when everything else was taken away, and the last thing I had left to hope for was that it was worth keeping going at all. That it was worth staying alive.

Losing hope that life could get better – losing that will to live which had been like a fire in my belly through thick and thin – was devastating. Thinking about ending my life became a preoccupation, even if I didn't really want to do it. For a lot of that time, it seemed nobody wanted to hear what was going on in my head. I was already in mental health services with anorexia, but when I told anyone about suicidal thoughts, I was given little space to talk about them. Doctors prescribed and prescribed, trying to minimise the risk of me actually attempting suicide rather than listening to what was driving the impulse. I didn't want to be drugged out of my pain and made safe enough until next time – I wanted to talk.

Powerful suicidal thoughts become more frightening when you can't talk about them. The fact that the professionals seemed uncomfortable with my suicidal talk gave me very little confidence that anyone else would be able to sit with the subject either.

So the thoughts grew, the plans elaborated, and my own death became a shadow ever closer at hand. A lot of the time I didn't really want to die – I just didn't want to live the way I was. There seemed little prospect that things would become easier. I was unable to access treatment for my eating disorder, was losing educational opportunities, and felt I was causing pain to those around me. Thinking about suicide wasn't a rejection of the value of life in general, I just felt I couldn't do life justice, and I wanted to protect those I loved. I thought they could live better without me.

During those times when I felt ambivalent about living, I attempted overdoses without the intent to actually die. Whilst I still feel ashamed about these times, I believe that if I'd received the help I needed before this stage, and had developed other ways to cope, then I wouldn't have needed to use an overdose to express my anguish. At one point a health professional actually told me, 'Some people think eating disorders are just attention-seeking.' What more could I do? It seemed I had exhausted all the options.

Just days later I took a large overdose. I wanted my life to end, I didn't want to wake up. But after some time, panic crept in. Was this what it felt like to die? Despite the terror that washed over me, I was still full of ambivalence about whether I wanted to carry on living. I didn't want an ambulance and medics – to be fixed and sent away without talking to a single person about my thoughts, as had happened before. I needed to talk, so I rang the last place I could think of – the Samaritans.

I can't remember much of what happened after that, or even how I got to hospital that night. But I do remember the power of someone finally listening to me without judgement, without rushing in to problem-solve and push the subject away. I remember the realisation that there were other options, that hope still existed outside of this dark place. Whilst the intervention of ambulance staff and medical care meant I could recover, it was talking that saved my life. It's a cliché to say, 'Where there's life, there is hope', but certainly for me, finding a grain of hope when I thought all was lost means that I am alive today.

People often say 'things get worse before they get better', but things shouldn't have to get worse. However, if they do get to this stage, establishing and strengthening hope will help to get you through. During my time in mental health services, I never heard that recovery was possible – I was told I would have to manage with an eating disorder for the rest of my life. I was never asked, 'What do you want your life to be like?', only told that things would get worse if I didn't comply. I was stopped from using ways of coping that, whilst they were damaging, also kept me safe. Why should I give up the shield of armour my eating disorder provides if I've got no hope that another way of being is possible? I was scared into trying to get better, rather than encouraged to have hope that a life worth living, on my terms, was within reach.

But there is another way, even if it's extremely hard work. There is more to life than eating problems, poor mental health, loneliness and isolation, shitty boyfriends, or lack of freedom and opportunity. For me this isn't 'recovery'. I don't even know what recovery means – surely that is all about getting back the things you've lost, or rewinding the clock to a time before things started to go wrong? But we aren't computers who can go back to a saved backup document to recover lost data. And besides, it has been so long that I've been living with mental health problems that I can barely remember what life was like without them. For me, the process of recovering is all about discovering – discovering a healthier and happier future, not harking back to a lost golden time.

In the end, talking saved me.

And I wouldn't want to go back anyway. This journey of mental health problems has taken me to places I would never have chosen, would never have wanted to go to, but also would not have had the chance to do so if none of it happened. I have met beautiful people, grown in empathy and awareness, experienced the richness of life in all its colours – all of which shine brighter for knowing what it is like to have all colour and light drain away. I've had opportunities to share my experience to change things for the better, and I've worked in jobs and studied subjects I would never have chosen in the first place, yet have brought me so much fulfilment.

Time moves on, and we have to accept what we have lost if we are able to have the emotional freedom to hope for better things. Accepting my own experiences has given me hope that my life can be rewarding, but also that whatever happens, and however hard it gets, I will survive. With the right help and the support of others, I can hope for even more than just surviving. Experiences can never 'unhappen', and bad things and hard times will always come around, but with compassionate acceptance that change is possible we can turn hurt into hope.

James Downs was born in Cardiff in 1989. At sixteen he developed a major eating disorder. Now well into recovery, he works as a volunteer for eating disorders services, campaigns for changes in policy and awareness, and studies psychology and education at the University of Cambridge.

Simon Blake
The Power of Hope

Hope is an extraordinary thing. We are all better for dreams, hope and imagination. It isn't always easy, but when we hold hope inside us, it can help us to keep putting one step in front of the other.

There have been times when I have wanted to pull the sheets up and ask the world to let me get off for a while. At those times I have needed to face feelings, do what I can to understand what is happening, and do all that is within my power at that time to bring about the change I seek.

So, a bit about me

I am a gay man. I was born in 1974 in Cornwall. I was the first in my family to go to university and to move away from home. My parents are beautiful people. They are ridiculously loving and kind. They taught my brother and I to work hard, play hard and be kind. I have a picture with '*work hard, play hard and be kind*' on the wall in my flat as a constant reminder. Underneath that they also taught us to use our imagination, to have dreams and try to make them happen.

As a child I loved reading, writing stories, drawing and animals. My peers at school seemed to know I was gay before I even knew what it meant. I was bullied a bit. At the time I didn't understand it to be bullying, however I did internalise shame about being gay. Despite being a vocal campaigner for LGBT rights, including being deputy chair of Stonewall, the LGBT charity, deep down I still carry some of that latent shame into adulthood. Ridding myself of it is an ongoing project.

I also acknowledge the enormous privileges that I have had. But saying that, none of us can say that our experiences are less or more difficult than other people's. They are just different and hard. I'm going to share two of my defining experiences in the hope that they may be useful. If they aren't for you, please feel free to just skip on past. Life is too short!

The two experiences I am going to draw on are when I came out as gay to my parents in 1996 and when my brother died in 2015.

Coming out to my parents was hard for me and hard for them.

It was 1996. Section 28 was still firmly in place, which prevented schools from teaching about gay sexuality. Gay men and HIV were synonymous in the public discourse. Gay men were considered by many to be a danger to children.

Against that backdrop, I had found the courage to come out to myself and some friends whilst at university. I had a graduate job that I enjoyed and I was open about my sexuality to my colleagues.

I had lived away from home for four years when I told my parents I was gay.

I wanted to come out to them because I felt like I was hiding an important part of myself. I wasn't being wholly truthful with them about where I was going, who with and what we were doing. And I also wasn't able to share the excitement, the joyfulness and liberation of discovering my sexuality and coming out with them.

I knew it was going to be a shock to them and in preparation I had spoken to lots of people about their experiences. Almost everybody I spoke to had experienced some rejection initially. Most said it took a bit of time but their parents, or at least one parent, had 'come round' eventually. For some it was weeks, for some it was months, and for others it was years.

I bought a book called *When Your Child Comes Out* by Anne Sheldon. I had read it at least fifty times by the time I handed it over to Mum and Dad. It taught me that I had had many years to get used to being gay, and my parents might need some time too.

Having read the book and talked endlessly to a couple of friends I scheduled the time and made a plan. When the time came, of course the rehearsed words didn't come out as planned. Despite my incoherence they eventually understood what I was saying. Just as Anne Sheldon had predicted they were upset, confused and given the climate of homophobia they were scared. Scared for my health, my safety, my employment prospects and my happiness.

Reading *When Your Child Comes Out* helped me understand what my folks were feeling and their point of view. That doesn't mean I liked it, or that I didn't feel down, but it did mean I hoped they too would be able to accept all of me. Which they did.

Understanding as much as I could about what Mum and Dad might be feeling helped me deal with their initial response. I wanted their validation and support. Through reading *When Your Child Comes Out* I had learned it was possible I wouldn't get that immediately, but I was lucky enough to trust they loved me. Ultimately I was hopeful that once they – like me – had time to process it they would support me. The book also suggested finding ways to manage my emotions, in order that I took responsibility for them and didn't direct them unhelpfully at my parents.

So as well as speaking to friends, I wrote letters to my parents, letters to my (fictional) children and letter after letter to myself. The letters set out my truths – the fears, anger, sadness, hopes and dreams. Some were about the fictional, future life I was going to lead and they included great things I was going to do with my parents. They helped me laugh, cry and dream.

It was at this time that I learnt that singing (loudly) and dancing (badly) to songs that took me to a place of freedom and happiness was a real boost. I still do that now if I need to shake out/off the day. My current favourite anthem is *Breakfast at Tiffany's (Club Mix) by Jackie O*. My dancing and singing isn't pretty to listen to or watch but it feels good, so who cares!

In July 2015 my brother died unexpectedly after ten days in hospital. We (my parents, niece, nephew, sister-in-law and I) were sat in the hospital with the curtains around us as the medical staff turned off the machines that were keeping him alive. It was awful.

I don't know how to express in words how I felt in that moment and in the hours, weeks and days afterwards. In truth, I don't remember much about the first six months after he died.

After the immediate shock and the funeral, I went into autopilot determined to 'look after' my parents which my partner, Jonny, and I did with care and diligence. I was overwhelmed by my own feelings at the same time. I went through the motions of getting up, going to work etc but none of it made sense. I cried a lot. I felt lost. I was confused. I had nightmares where I was responsible for his death. I berated myself for all the things I would have done differently if I had known his time was so short.

Again, I found reading about grief helpful. It felt so big and overwhelming and I couldn't imagine it getting any easier. I found the concept that grief doesn't diminish but you grow around it and bigger than it particularly useful. I could imagine that happening. It gave me hope.

I didn't want to see a therapist. I didn't want to rush the grief process and I didn't feel stuck. I wanted to feel the pain to honour his life as my older brother. I also knew there were a whole load of feelings that were making me feel heavy and like every day was extraordinarily hard work.

I read a book called *The Last Act of Love* by Cathy Rentzenbrink on holiday that year. I hadn't realised the content when I picked it up at the airport otherwise I don't think I would have bought it. Her brother had died after an accident. She wrote down and shared all the reasons she felt guilty. It was generous of Rentzenbrink to publish her list and it was a brilliant catalyst for me. I don't believe guilt is a particularly healthy emotion. And I certainly hadn't entertained the idea that I felt guilty about Andrew dying. Turns out I did.

As I wrote my guilt list, I discovered that I felt guilty for laughing and having fun, guilty for not being strong enough for my parents, guilty for crying, guilty for not crying, guilty for the Christmases I hadn't spent with them, guilty for staying away when I first came out. Ultimately, I felt guilty about being alive. Andrew has children and grandchildren and he lived close to our parents and so I thought it would have been kinder, better and easier if I had died rather than him.

Once I started writing down all the things I felt guilty about I realised just how much stuff was in my conscious and subconscious.

It was the start of a new phase of processing. Writing helped. With all those feelings and thoughts that I didn't even know I had, it was no wonder I felt so heavy and as if I wanted to stay in bed for a while.

Talking out loud also helped me reorganise and reframe my thoughts and feelings. I am lucky to have a great partner and friends who were always willing to talk. Sometimes, however, their desire to make things better was difficult to hear, or I didn't want to bore or trouble them.

That is where animals come in. Turns out they are pretty good at listening. I co-opted the help of my dog (Dolly) and horse (Ren). They were better for me than lots of humans because I didn't feel it mattered what I said, and they didn't need to make me feel better. They just listened even when I repeated myself or cried and rambled incoherently. And as a bonus they always smelt pretty good.

About six months after Andrew died a friend talked to me about practising gratitude. For me this meant thinking about three things I am grateful for as soon as I woke up. Noticing the good things – however small or big – was a game changer for me, especially as we went through the long winter and short days. I now use a Trigg Life Mapper which helps me with the practice of gratitude by helping me to plan, focus and reflect on a daily, weekly and monthly basis.

In summary the things that work for me, which may or may not work for you are:

- Reading, listening and understanding as much as I can intellectually
- Feeling the emotions: giving myself time and space to feel and express them
- Believing that things will change and practising gratitude to help to shift my mindset
- Writing down whatever comes to mind which helps me find out what I am thinking and reorganise or reframe my thoughts/get clear about what I want to be different
- Talking to whoever or whatever listens best and importantly doesn't try to make me feel better (for me that was often my animals!)

- Asking people for what I need – people who love you always want to make it better and sometimes that can get in the way of listening. If I know what I want I try to ask for it.
- Singing and dancing loudly and badly when no one can listen or see
- Laughing: sometimes we don't feel like laughing, but it is good for the mind, body and soul. I have started saving videos, gifs and jokes that make me smile for the days I need a boost. As Lord Byron said, '*Always laugh when you can. It is cheap medicine.*'

Simon Blake is CEO of MHFA England and deputy Chair of Stonewall. He is a trainer, writer, campaigner and activist. In 2012 he was awarded an OBE for services to the voluntary sector and young people.

Ellen Jones

Hope is an intrinsic part of my identity – in fact, it is my middle name. Despite this, I have not always been hopeful. In fact I spent a significant portion of my life regarding hope and the people who advocated for it with a huge amount of disdain.

Growing up, I thought hope was synonymous with the naive belief that everything would be ok in the end, an attitude I could never reconcile with my own personal mental crises or the situations of the wider world, which from where I am stood are – both literally and metaphorically – burning. In my mind, to hope was to ignore wider problems in the pursuit of an intangible, idealistic and almost mythical hope.

The irony, of course, was that hope was driving a lot of the work I was already doing. I started campaigning in LGBTQ+ rights at a young age (she says, at the grand old age of twenty), and as a result, I became hyper-aware of some of the injustices present in the world that some of my peers couldn't seem to grasp. When progress isn't being made, when the people you are trying to help are suffering despite your best efforts at changing things, it is hard to feel anything but hopeless.

Campaigning is mentally challenging because you are constantly engaging with information that is often distressing and emotionally charged, especially if, like me, you are tackling issues you are personally affected by. The onset of my mental health issues correlates exactly with my experience of coming out and the subsequent homophobia I faced. This included repeatedly being told to kill myself for being queer, that my parents would have been better off if I were dead and encouragement to self-harm. It was relentless. But as a young queer person, I thought this was normal and something I just had to accept as part of my life. When trusted adults failed to intervene or even check in on me and my mental wellbeing, I lost hope in them entirely. It was a dark time and I also felt ashamed for developing destructive coping mechanisms. I started self-harming to cope with the despair and anguish I was feeling and the overwhelming hatred I had for myself and for my queerness. Even now, six years after I came out aged fourteen, I still have not recovered entirely from what happened and am only just realising with my adult perspective quite how traumatic that experience was and how it continues to impact me to this day.

It was, and still is, hard to envisage a true recovery for myself whilst homophobia is present in the world, because not only did it traumatise me when I was younger, it can still trigger me today. Divorcing mental health issues from the context in which they happen is damaging because it ignores the external factors which influence wellbeing. When the message you get from society is that you are a lesser human being for being gay, it is very hard to counter your own self-hatred.

And if that wasn't enough, I also have bipolar disorder (type II – which basically means hypomania and heaps upon heaps of depression). I know what it is like to wake up in the morning and wish with every fibre of your being that the world would swallow you whole. I know what it is like going through the day thinking of nothing more than all the ways you could hurt yourself whilst you try and pay attention in class. I know what it is like to lose weeks or even months of your life to episodes of mental illness that you cannot even remember years later. I don't say that to frighten you – I say it because I want you to know that even at my worst, when I had nothing left to give, I have somehow been able to get through.

I started a newsletter called 'Reasons to Keep Going' in the autumn of 2018. It was a project that I started on a whim, in a particularly grotty pub, armed with my laptop, a diet Coke and a portion of chips. The title was self-explanatory: each week I would give people reasons to keep going. The newsletter came after the sudden death of a friend by suicide, during one of my darkest depressions. Everything about that time was hard, and a few weeks later I had a breakdown. Then I began medication and started therapy which has, I am glad to say, been very helpful.

What I realised was that the things that kept me alive were not the big things, but the minutiae of my existence; a meal with friends, finding a new hobby, a particularly good *Doctor Who* episode. These were my Reasons to Keep Going. It is hard to admit how hard I find life sometimes, and I often find myself swinging wildly between surviving and thriving, but my readers get it. The response was overwhelming, with people replying in their droves that I had helped either in my recommendations or in my honesty. The piece of feedback most commonly given was that I had given my readers hope.

Me? Give you hope? When I am such a depressed, self-loathing mess myself? I was incredulous. But what I realised was that my readers did not expect me to be perfect, or happy or even sane. What endeared me to them was that I was learning to navigate my world and my brain and keep going, in spite of not being in a good headspace. I think many of them saw themselves and whatever struggles they were going through in me. They also saw the possibility of recovery.

Many years ago, before I knew I had bipolar disorder but after I knew something really was not quite right with my brain, I started talking about recovery as a verb. Recovery as an end goal or a place you might reach never made sense to me but as an action, something you could do each day? Now that I could get on board with.

Recovery has looked like a lot of things and I cannot emphasise enough how much of a work-in-progress I still am. I have achieved an awful lot in the past few years and sometimes people misinterpret this as me being well. I hate to break it to you, but being sane and being successful do not always go hand in hand, whatever the media might tell you. I am brilliant, but I have bipolar – deal with it.

Recovery is hard, there is no two ways about it. Changing the world is also really hard. But now I am working with kids who are in the position I was all those years ago, and I'm even a role model as a proud queer, bipolar, autistic woman. And the value underpinning both my own recovery and my campaigning is hope that things will not always be this way.

Although my younger self would probably loathe what I am about to write, it takes extraordinary courage to look at the world and not just see how things are, but how they could be. I don't have all of the solutions and have never professed to, but I do know that hope is a catalyst for change – both personal and political – and it is also something I will never devalue again.

Ellen Jones is an award-winning campaigner who speaks and writes on LGBTQ+ rights, mental health, autism and gender.

In 2018, Ellen won the first-ever MTV EMA Generation Change award in recognition of her campaigning. In 2017, she was named Stonewall's Young Campaigner of the Year after running successful campaigns tackling LGBTQ+ inequality in schools and online.

CONNECTION

Martin Seager

I came from a family where we didn't connect much emotionally. Not an unusual story, especially in Southern England. I also went to boarding school between the ages of eight and eleven. Again, not that unusual, but all that time I was being shaped into someone whose emotional life was undernourished, secret and hidden. Being a boy also played into this emotional secrecy although I am not one of those who simplistically blame the whole male gender for not opening up. My two older sisters share some of these traits too. Everyone, male or female, can talk if the right people are listening. In truth, this opening up thing works the other way round. People need to open up their ears and eyes to boys who are already showing their feelings to those willing to look and listen. Boys just use a different language from girls.

For me, this turbulent emotional underworld came to a head when I went to university in 1977. The most common time globally for serious mental breakdowns to start is between the ages of seventeen and twenty-five years old. This is hardly surprising when you consider that this is the very time when people are trying to make the leap from childhood to adulthood. Growing up is hard and it cannot happen without some people around you who are grown up already. We need to be helped to form a secure identity through childhood and adolescence by those who've already been there. We need parenting, not just peers.

My parents only wanted the best for me and I am eternally grateful for all they did for me, and have no grudges. My dad's father was largely absent from his life and I can now see he wanted a son to fill this hole in himself, so my arrival was special for him. However this was his unfinished business and so it left an equal but opposite hole

355

in me. My mother was also from an emotionally distant family, although she was a constant and reliable presence in the home. These emotional patterns left me with strengths but also gaps and holes that have passed down through the generations, to me and probably to my children, though hopefully the holes are smaller now. Having holes in certain places is why we connect with certain people and not others and why we end up with the partners we 'choose'. It's to do with how our holes line up. Personal attraction is powerful and even magical, but certainly not random.

As a student I felt trapped, claustrophobic and overwhelmed and had to escape. I had what the psychiatric world called 'panic attacks with depression'. I wasn't exactly psychotic, but certainly felt alienated, paranoid at times and despairing. Though I never fully attempted suicide, I had constant suicidal thoughts over this period. I was lost to myself, somewhere between the world of the living and the dead. I had no compass inside me.

Forty years later I am much more at home and I'll attempt to describe in simple terms how I seem to have got here, what I think has helped me and how it connects with me helping others now, as a professional psychologist. It can be summed up as being mainly about filling those holes I mentioned, finding new attachments, parent figures and family networks. The major lesson I have learned is that gaining mental health is about developing a core sense of secure, embodied identity. This means healing damage, untangling twisted roots and meeting unmet needs. The term 'recovery' is probably wrong for the vast number of us who were never fully mentally healthy to begin with. This development takes re-parenting but there are many ways of getting re-parented and it does not have to be a therapist or even one person who does this for us. In fact, it usually takes several people and new families. The traditional African saying that 'it takes a village to raise a child' is probably close to the mark. We are ultimately social, tribal beings who need attachments, identity, love, connection and a sense of belonging.

So where was my village? Who were my second families?

As a student, being allowed to take a year out, do voluntary work (in a mental hospital, not surprisingly) and then switch from doing

Classics to Psychology gave me one new strand of identity that was my own choice. It gave me a purpose, a new tribe and a direction. I also reconnected with my teenage musical past and joined various student bands as a drummer. Suddenly I belonged to something social that was valued, a second tribe that created relationships focused around doing something, being something, expressing something, being heard.

I somehow managed to get a psychology degree despite these 'distractions' and after the almost inevitable break-up of the band I returned to psychology. Luckily I could still pursue music passionately as a serious sideline without it having to be my career. I wanted to help people but still didn't realise I was projecting my own pain, trying to help myself through helping others. In this spirit I had blindly trained as a Samaritan volunteer in my year off as an undergraduate. But even at the age of nineteen something unspoken must have told me I was not ready for this responsibility and so I did not take up the role. However, I still had not consciously learned this lesson because in the same spirit four years later I was again blindly training as a 'clinical' psychologist. Being a 'clinician' now meant becoming one of 'us' as opposed to one of 'them', the 'patients'. By 1987 I was now a hallowed expert with letters after my name. I was qualified to assess, observe, categorise, diagnose and classify the distress of others. It was now other people with the mental problems, not me. I had the cure, not the illness.

Fortunately, it didn't take me much longer to fully realise I needed to look at myself if I was to help other people look at themselves. How can you help someone else do something you are not prepared to do yourself? What kind of therapeutic figure does that make you? How can you connect with someone who needs to be reached inside if you are just looking outwards yourself?

Throughout my twenties (my training years) and even into my early thirties I was still largely unaware of the holes within me. In my late twenties I married. The attachment was intense, and so was the conflict and we had some good times. The breaking point came when we had a child. Both of us had hidden holes that we wanted the other to fill, so when there was a real child who needed both of us, we battled over whose job it was to take this on and we just couldn't share it. I guess we were both still feeling the need to be the special child ourselves. We divorced, but luckily this resulted ultimately in the sharing of care that we couldn't manage as a married couple. I have retained a good relationship with my daughter and I am very proud of the young woman she has become.

Throughout my thirties there continued several years of personal (psychoanalytic) psychotherapy which helped me to fill some of my holes or at least make them smaller. In this space I could speak more freely and let someone else try to help me make sense of it. The gag over my mouth was coming off because there were ears to hear. By 1997 I had trained as a psychotherapist myself.

In my late thirties I married again. This time, after ten more years of development, my holes were smaller and in a different place, so I met a different kind of person and we connected in a different way. I was now ready to have a soulmate rather than an infatuation. I became a father to two more children, another girl and a boy, who are now also both adults. Because of my development I had no need to put special pressure on my son. It has been a great joy for me to see all my children, albeit with their own inevitable issues and obstacles, negotiate their own transition to adulthood, especially as this was the very time in my own life when things fell apart.

Throughout my forties I took on senior roles in the NHS and my experiences meant I could be a better leader and a better manager of others. Being more secure in myself as a person I was also able to get closer to my clients and create a human connection with them that enabled me to innovate and improvise personalised forms of therapy, rather than follow impersonal treatment protocols. I did a bit of work with government and in 2007 created an advisory group that came up with five universal psychological needs of the human condition which have guided my work ever since:

1. To be loved
2. To be heard

3. To belong
4. To make a difference
5. To have belief and purpose

In truth, I believe mental health comes down mainly to these factors. I always now think not of treating mental conditions, but of meeting these needs of the human condition. Put another way, there is really only one mental condition and that is the human condition. I always get further with people by using this approach than if I think I am 'treating' them.

From my mid-fifties I took early retirement from the NHS and started working in the charity sector on the front line with homeless people, drug addicts, suicidal people and people who have been through the criminal justice system. The biggest thing I have learned is that we are all equally human. Everyone's feelings make sense once you get to know their story. There but for the grace of God go all of us.

Being a psychologist, I may have certain training and responsibilities but unless I make a connection with my clients as an equal human being I cannot truly help. Clients know instinctively when someone is trying to listen to them with their heart, not just their head. This is the hole in all of us that most needs filling. I have learned that the best way to help someone feel less suicidal is to truly listen to just how bad they feel. If someone truly listens, you feel a connection. If you feel a connection, then you feel an attachment to life. If you try to cheer people up or be falsely positive, the connection is broken and the result can be deadly. Being too positive with a suicidal person is usually more about trying to make ourselves feel useful and less anxious in the face of our own helplessness. Helping people is actually not about 'making' them better. It is arrogant and omnipotent to think you have that power.

If you come to see me as a professional psychologist, please be assured that the boy is still very much there inside the man and he knows he is human just like you. If he was not there and if I did not know him a little, how could I ever help you to become yourself?

Martin Seager is a consultant clinical psychologist and adult psychotherapist, most recently with the addictions charity, CGL. He is a clinician, lecturer, campaigner and author on mental health issues. He studied at Oxford University, Edinburgh University and the Tavistock Clinic and worked in the NHS for over thirty years, including heading up psychological services in two large mental health trusts.

He is now on the clinical advisory board of the Campaign Against Living Miserably (CALM) and is a specialist on male gender psychology and co-founder of both the Male Psychology Network and the Male Psychology Section of the BPS. He is co-editor of the *Palgrave Handbook of Male Psychology and Mental Health*.

Joe Sheerer

Seven years clean from drug addiction. No longer depressed. No longer thinking about not living anymore. Peace of mind. A life beyond my wildest dreams? Definitely. And it's not a dream – it's my reality.

From a young age I can remember feeling different to everybody else. Maybe that's normal and everyone else felt the same but if no one discusses these things it makes you feel isolated and alone. That's how I felt growing up: isolated, lonely and different – never talking about my feelings because it wasn't the 'manly' thing to do. I wanted to be a big strong man like my dad, I didn't want to be sensitive. I hated feeling so vulnerable. If someone made fun of me, I hated it. But then I learnt how to make the other kids laugh and that made me feel empowered and validated and part of a group.

At school I tried to blend in with the clever kids but didn't feel clever enough. I wanted to be part of the cool, trendy kids but didn't feel cool or fun enough. I grew up thinking I was ugly, unfunny and no one liked me. This despite the fact that I have amazing parents and sisters and our home was full of love and support. My home life was fun and happy. At school, however, I felt weak, sensitive and scared. I wasn't like the other boys (I thought) and tried to fit in by putting on a mask every day. I started acting like a pest, getting into trouble and trying to be the class clown, the joker! It worked for me for a while and made me feel good.

At nine years old I got signed by a premiership football club's academy and thought this was brilliant – it was my dream. However, the anxiety I had around school contaminated my feelings about football. 'What if they don't like me? What if I'm not good enough? What if I miss a shot? They will think it's my fault!' No one said these things but that's how I felt. At fourteen I was released from the football club because I'd stopped attending regularly and I hadn't progressed. My excuses, how I'd pretend I was ill so I didn't have to go, had won. I was released from the club I wanted to play for and now I was crushed. However, there was also relief . . . now I had escaped the pressure and the expectation on me to show how good I was. I was free!

By now I was getting a reputation in school as a troublemaker. I was intelligent and predicted A*s in all my GCSEs in year 7, but my behaviour meant I kept dropping down the sets. My mental health was starting to affect my future. Still I spoke to no one. I thought no one would understand, that I was the only one feeling this way. I thought I wasn't manly enough, that I was too sensitive.

By now some of my friends had started smoking and drinking. I was desperate to fit in and didn't like it when I heard stories of what people had done on the weekend and I wasn't there. So I joined them. I started to lie to my parents about where I was at the weekends and started to go out partying. I started to drink alcohol and all my feelings evaporated. Alcohol made me feel positive, confident, happy and that people loved me. I had the solution! 'Wow! It's this simple! All I need to do is drink every weekend and I'll be happy.'

I started to like myself. Before alcohol I was painfully shy and introverted, although no one could tell because I hid it with my flashy, cocky, arrogant act. However, now it wasn't an act. Alcohol made me a natural extrovert. Or so I thought.

Very soon I found drugs and by fifteen I was taking cocaine and other class A drugs. I felt like I was having a great time, going to nightclubs, taking excessive amounts of alcohol and drugs. What I know now is that as I was trying to change the way I felt, I can't have been feeling that good in the first place. But I didn't know that then. I thought drugs were the answer to all my problems.

There were some negative times, some bad hangovers. Which is sort of normal; everyone has some bad times drinking. But then the good times became fewer and the bad times more consistent. I started to take drugs every day – whatever I could find, painkillers, sleeping pills, anything. I thought I was too young to be addicted – I was only eighteen. My relationships with my family became strained and I was arguing with everyone. Girlfriends only lasted briefly – they soon saw what a liability I was. I started to cheat on girls even when they loved me – so I'd feel more attractive and secure. It's not an excuse, my behaviour was wrong. But it is a reason.

I used to do anything to change the way I felt, it could be drugs, drink, sex etc. Now I don't have social media as I believe this can be a fix for some people. They post pictures of themselves to get a lot of 'likes' and when they don't get enough, they feel ugly or inadequate and want to remove the photo! I worked out that social media was bad for me because I needed people to 'like' my photos. It was the same as taking alcohol/drugs: I needed something to fix me in order to feel better.

By nineteen my life was even worse. I started fantasising about falling in front of trains to take the pain away. I was crippled by fear and depression and no one knew. Still, I couldn't stop taking drugs.

I now know that although I was a drug addict, the drugs were never the problem. The problem was within me. I didn't know how to process and manage my emotions so I took substances to change the way I felt instead. Although this worked short-term, it was much worse in the long-term because of all the consequences of addiction: the lies, cheating, stealing, depression, the strained relationships.

How dark it is before the dawn!

One day a friend introduced me to a man at the pub who started telling me about his life. Apart from a few differences, he was basically telling my story, except this man was now three years clean from drugs and alcohol. He told me how he went to support groups to get clean and convinced me to start going with him.

That was a starting point but it took me three years of relapsing and pain to finally stop drugs. Aged twenty-two, I finally learned how to speak about my feelings and get the support I needed. I managed to work out some sort of 'programme', a bit like a gym plan for losing weight. This 'programme' helps me manage my wellbeing so I don't feel like fixing and changing the way I feel through harmful behaviours. I managed to turn my life around, one day at a time. I literally started to live one day at a time, sometimes one hour at a time, to make sure I didn't go and 'fix'.

Nothing changes if nothing changes! What that means is that nothing in our lives will change unless we change it. If I want things to change then I need to change my behaviour.

That was seven years ago. I'm twenty-nine now and an uncle to three beautiful nephews. I haven't touched alcohol or drugs for seven years. For the most part, I am happy and have good friends around me. I exercise a lot as it makes me feel positive. I meditate because it makes me feel calm. I am able to 'be' in most situations and feel happy. I have been to weddings and funerals, had positive and negative experiences since I have entered 'recovery' but I have not had to use substances to cope with them. I have watched my own sister get married and cried tears of joy without feeling less like a man – I love my family. I now only care about what I think of me and try to do good things for people as this helps contribute to my wellbeing.

Of course I still have fears, insecurities and anxieties. That's normal. Remember this: any feeling you have is normal. Sometimes we are meant to feel sad and unhappy. Don't hide that. These are normal human emotions. These days I express my feelings instead of internalising them and trying to push them away. I've learnt that that doesn't make them go away – it just suppresses them until they come back bigger and stronger.

I hope that when you read this you get something from this. I hope you feel hope and optimism and that you are not alone. The best advice I was given was to speak to someone about my feelings. If I can urge anyone to do anything in their life it would be that. Please reach out and talk.

You are not alone with your feelings and neither am I. The world is an amazing place to be in. Embrace it!

Now thirty, Joe Sheerer is nearly a decade clean from drug addiction, which started at fourteen. Uncle to three nephews and now living a happy and fulfilling life, he works for a charity helping young people with issues to speak about and manage their feelings.

Paulius Skruibis

I was fifteen when I got together with my first girlfriend but she was not sure about her feelings for me and this became very painful for me. Actually, I felt so much despair and hopelessness at the time that I'm not sure I have ever felt so bad since then. Now I'm thirty-nine, and of course I've had many difficult situations in my life – one could say much more difficult than the one with my first love. But I've never felt as much hopelessness as I did then. I guess afterwards I was much better equipped to deal with life challenges.

Back then, twenty-five years ago I would lie on my bed in my dark room late in the evening and try desperately to think of some solution. I don't know what I was trying to solve, but I was just thinking, and thinking, and thinking. I was glad I had the whole night ahead to think, but then I would wake up in the morning with the same pain and no solution.

One evening I decided to call Youth Line, a charity here in Lithuania which offers free emotional support. I remember saying to a volunteer that one reason I was feeling hopeless was that nobody believed that relationships at such a young age could have any future. Twenty-four years have passed since then, but I still remember very clearly her saying that nobody could be sure what would happen in the future. She also told me she knew examples when relationships at such a young age continued; people even got married. Not only these words, but also the fact that she listened to me and took me very seriously, were so important. I remember how relieved I felt after talking with her. I had some hope.

This relationship with the girlfriend was over soon. That was very painful. But I still felt very grateful for that late-night call. So much so that I became a Youth Line volunteer a year later. A couple of years after that I started to train new volunteers. Then I became a coordinator of volunteers, then a director of the organisation. Now I'm the chairman of the board of Youth Line. I chose psychology as my profession and I'm a practising psychotherapist.

The call that I had twenty-four years ago still reminds me in a very powerful way how much hope one sincere conversation can convey.

Paulius Skruibis lives in Vilnius, Lithuania. At sixteen he started to volunteer at the charity Youth Line before becoming a trainer and eventually director of the Vilnius branch and chairman of the board. He studied Clinical Psychology at Vilnius University where he now teaches and heads the Suicide Research Centre. He also teaches at the Institute of Humanistic and Existential Psychology and works with clients in his private practice.

Satveer Nijjar
A Different 'Better'

When I had my darkest days, people – friends, professionals, family – would always say that things would get better. I hoped they would. I didn't believe it though.

When I think about the word 'hope', I think of a word that attempts to keep us going, keep us in the 'game' that is life. Generally, people's hopes tend to be things like; 'I *hope* to win the lottery', 'I *hope* to have a big house', 'I *hope* to get married'. For me, growing up, it was more like; 'I *hope* to finish school', 'I *hope* that tomorrow will be a better day' and my biggest one, 'I *hope* I will leave this house alive.' At times hoping to win the lottery (that I didn't even play) seemed more realistic to me than living to see another birthday. I understand that this sounds very pessimistic, and not the way I should be writing, but to get to where I am now, I have to be honest. And for me 'hope' was an aspirational word that kept me clutching for a long time. But maybe clutching is just what I needed, because ultimately I was clutching on to life.

I grew up in a difficult home, witnessing and experiencing domestic abuse. It impacted on my education and the clown face that I put on so well at school started to drop in my teens. I turned to self-harm then, as a method of coping with the distress, but at seventeen, when I failed my exams, hopelessness set in. While on a biology trip in Aberystwyth, truly believing things would never get any better, I made an attempt on my own life.

I survived, and it did lead to me leaving that home at the age of eighteen, but things didn't get any easier. What followed includes honour-based abuse, domestic abuse, homelessness, teenage motherhood, poverty, isolation and ostracisation. All this on top of never having dealt with any of my childhood issues. My mental health further declined and any hopes for the future again seemed distant and hopeless. The self-harm continued, the trips to psychiatrists, psychologists and social workers continued, the suicidal thoughts and attempts continued.

What changed? Why am I able to write this now?

I changed.

When I look back for a pivotal moment or piece of advice that started me on the path of positive change – the only thing I can think of isn't specifically to do with hope. I can't remember who said this to me, or even if I read it somewhere, I could have made it up myself (wishful thinking!), but it was when I realised that although I can't change the actions of others, I can change my own actions and responses to them. For me, this thought was the final cog to click in an extremely complex wheel that allowed me to move forward. Prior to this, I spent therapy sessions being angry and, like a dog with a bone, obsessed with the notion that one day I would have deep meaningful conversations with those who had caused me pain and they would explain why they had treated me the way they had. I was convinced this was the only way I could move on. In my eyes, my only hope for having a future that was anything near normal was to get these answers.

I wish I could have told myself then that things would get better but it would be a bumpy journey. I can now admit that my idea of 'better' was unattainable – I wanted a life like the ones in *The Waltons / Brady Bunch* (yes, I am old!). Eventually I realised it was not about simply hoping things would get better, it was about actively making them better by engaging with the support around me and acknowledging that I needed to change my expectations of 'better'.

I needed a combination of medication and therapy – not everyone will need this. The medication stabilised my mood to help me endure (yes, endure) the therapeutic process. But the medication also helped me manage the therapy sessions, as at times they were extremely difficult. I wish someone had told me that. How difficult it would be to build up trust with a total stranger and then spend an hour a week talking about your darkest days to them. That would have really helped.

I was very fortunate, at the age of about twenty-four, to find an amazing counsellor through a local charity. Ros was kind, straight-forward, unafraid, persistent, calm, tough and funny, to name just a few things. I think therapy worked for me that time because I was *ready* to deal with my traumas and we connected. Previously there had been too many things confounding the sessions – I couldn't talk about my childhood because I was thinking about childcare, money, being a bad mother. Once these clouds had become lighter, I was able to focus upon the underlying causes of my distress. I started engaging with the therapy, not just turning up and ticking the box. I listened to the questions that I was being asked and bit by bit, unpicked the traumas of my life – past and current. It was then that I began seeing things could get better, not the 'better' I had imagined, but a different better. An attainable one.

Having people around me that believed in me, didn't dismiss me, who were brutally honest about what I should expect from life also helped me get through. My friends have always been my rock. Over the years some have drifted, others have remained, but without each and every one of them I wouldn't have managed. I learnt how to educate them about my depression and self-harm and how they could support me. This wasn't an easy conversation, but after we'd had it they seemed much more able to broach me when they felt I was struggling, and I them. Please, be honest with your friends – often people are afraid of mental ill health. They may avoid conversations, but it's not because they don't care. I now have friends whom I can just text and go and sit at their home and drink tea and say nothing more. They understand that sometimes that is all I need.

I now see hope as a positive. It is ok to hope. We all need hope to get us through the cloudiest, stormiest days. The dictionary tells me that hope is 'a feeling of expectation and desire for a particular thing to happen'. I now have that on a regular basis. I've also learnt that the hope needs to be attainable. I hoped to get a settled home, a degree, a relationship, raise my child well, see my family, have friends, be a good friend. I have achieved all these and now have raised the hope bar: I hope to travel, to get married, to buy a home.

All of these are realistically attainable (unless my girlfriend leaves me by the time this is published!). Remember that life isn't black and white. The dark days do pass, they may be painful, but they will pass.

Satveer Nijjar's experiences as a patient and then as a parent of a child with mental illness have helped shape her career. Her main focus is upon improving the understanding of, and response to, self-harm behaviours. Satveer delivers nationally to professionals, parents, carers and students.

Anne Tattersall

In 2000, when I was Mayor of Torrington in Devon, I was invited to a local secondary school to give a talk to a group of fifteen- and sixteen-year-old students at their 'Achiever's Day' assembly. As I stood on the school stage, scanning the faces of the young people staring expectantly at me, some of whom I knew were experiencing tough challenges, I realised that my meticulously planned talk was not going to be relevant to a lot of them. No matter how hard some of these kids worked at their studies, some of them would struggle to achieve academically. And I thought back to the moments in my life when I was going through tough times and how I never gave up hoping that tomorrow would be a better day.

As the Headmistress introduced me, I quietly scrunched up my well-prepared talk, took a deep breath and moved to the podium. Earlier the wooden structure had felt like a protective shield but now it felt like a barrier. I swallowed hard, smiled at my audience and went into free flow . . .

'When I was your age,' I said, 'I never thought that I would ever have the confidence to stand in front of such a large group and give a talk like this. I had planned this speech,' I continued, raising the ball of paper and tossing it across the stage, 'but sometimes it's better to speak from the heart. So today I'd like to share some of my own experiences with you.

'I grew up in Northern Ireland, the youngest of eight children. My parents never expressed their love for each other, or kissed or hugged in front of us. I never heard them tell us that they loved us. I was desperate for their love and would make up stories at school about how fantastic they were, the wonderful things we did at week- ends, the gifts they lavished on me. Unfortunately, my mother died when I was twenty and never did tell me she loved me. I was forty-seven when my father told me for the first time. He died a year later.'

Some of the youngsters smiled and nodded, giving me the courage to share a crushing experience I had had at eleven years old, that still causes me pain.

I told the assembly of the hopes I'd had of passing my Eleven Plus and going to Grammar School with my best friend, Angela Meenan. I choked a little as I described the morning I tentatively carried the brown manila envelope, the contents of which would define my future, up to Mammy and Daddy's room. I hovered expectantly at their bedside, waiting to hear the result. Mammy asked me to get them a cup of tea and then they'd tell me. Before going downstairs, I paused outside my parents' door and heard my father say, 'She's failed,' followed by my mother saying, 'Well, you didn't think she'd pass, did you?' I sank to my knees and sobbed – I'd tried so hard, yet I'd failed. All my dreams of going to a new school with my best friend had been crushed by that one simple word: 'failed'. From that moment on, I truly believed I was a failure.

A few years later, when I was sixteen, another devastating incident occurred. The British Army made a random raid on our home. My older sister and I were forced out of bed and made to stand naked in front of a patrol of young soldiers who sexually humiliated us. I remember the incident as though it happened yesterday. Although I've learned to live with it, the shame and humiliation still burns through me when I think of that day.

A few weeks after that I went to stay with my sister Deirdre in England. Although it was great to be away from home, I wasn't coping very well. Despite being quite thin, I started feeling fat and ugly and developed an irrational hatred of my body. I started to diet, and when the pounds dropped off me I felt a euphoric sense of being in control. My weight dropped dramatically that summer and when I returned home my mother took me to a doctor who diagnosed me with anorexia nervosa. Mammy, however, insisted that it wasn't anorexia. Instead, she maintained that I was just looking for attention. I didn't know why I wanted to be thin, so thought perhaps Mammy was right. I started college to train as a shorthand typist that year but instead of studying, I rebelled. I skipped classes, hung out in the bars and cafes. In the evenings I went to pubs, started smoking and drinking alcohol. At the end of the year I was expelled. I was just seventeen.

There was so much more I could have told my young audience that day – how my father communicated with me through his fists and beat me on a regular basis; how I ended up shoplifting, sleeping around, dabbling in drugs; how I switched from anorexia to bulimia nervosa and a near-suicide. I could have told them how I was abused in a confessional box at the age of eight, raped when I was twenty-three and brutally attacked in Israel when I was twenty-four.

But I glossed over those particular details and just said my life spiralled out of control as I listened to the internal dialogue telling me, 'I would never amount to anything' and 'I was a failure.'

At my lowest point I was almost twenty-five and by now living in London. I ached with hopelessness and it was a constant battle to get through each day. Thankfully, my oldest sister Eileen, who was always a strong, inspirational woman, had just bought a flat in London. One day, in desperation I rang Eileen and poured out my hopelessness to her. As she listened, I knew instinctively that I had reached a turning point. When Eileen turned up at my bedsit and together we packed my few belongings into her car, I felt hopeful for the first time in years.

Several things happened when I moved in with Eileen. She continually reminded me that I was a good person. She never judged me when I told her of my past misdemeanours. Instead, she told me I had my whole life ahead of me. I signed up again to a shorthand typing course and after three months, passed with flying colours. I secured a job at Charing Cross Hospital and was fortunate to have Robin Williams, a truly amazing man, as a boss. And I met my now husband, Chris. I was also still struggling with bulimia nervosa. By now, binging and vomiting had become a way of life for me and as hard as I tried, I still felt worthless. I lost five teeth and my weight changed daily.

I soon realised that my relationship with Chris was serious and, wanting to be honest, I gave him a copy of a short book about a young woman struggling with bulimia nervosa, explaining it was what I had. After reading it, Chris simply said, 'I love you, Anne, and will help you get through this.' There I was thinking he would be so disgusted that he would want to leave me, but instead it seemed to strengthen his love for me. After sharing my struggles with Chris, I decided to share my story with my boss. Like Chris, he was non-judgemental and supportive. He arranged for me to talk with a counsellor at the hospital, who in turn referred me to a psychiatrist. Shortly after, I began a cognitive behavioural therapy course.

Although I can't pinpoint any one thing in my healing process, I'm convinced it was hope and love that saved me. My sister Eileen gave me love and support and the sanctuary I needed so I could study and find a decent job. My boss at Charing Cross Hospital gave me every Wednesday morning off work so I could attend my cognitive behavioural therapy. Dr Chima, the psychiatrist, was kind and patient. Finally, my husband Chris showed me the true meaning of unconditional love. I sometimes pushed his love to the limit, but he never gave up on me and was always rock solid in his support for me.

Since then, I feel I've achieved so much – Chris is still central to my life, I have two wonderful sons, a loyal circle of friends, and a beautiful home. I've written two novels and am working on my third. Since moving to Devon, I've been involved in setting up and taking part in charity events which have given me great joy and a strong sense of worth. The pleasure I get from giving is way beyond that I get from receiving.

Earlier this year I was awarded a British Empire Medal in the Queen's Honours list in appreciation of all the charity work I've undertaken. I accepted it not only for myself, but for everyone who has contributed to my charity events. With a bit of self-belief and the support of others, we can achieve anything.

Although I didn't think it was appropriate to share my complete personal history with the school children, I felt optimistic that an abridged version might help them to develop a sense of hope and purpose about the future. I ended by saying:

'Despite going through some horrible experiences, I've managed to develop positive coping strategies and I believe that some of my past experiences have made me a better person. I try to be kind and empathetic and not a day passes without me being grateful for everything I have. Chris and I have been married for over thirty years now and our love feels unconditional. I've also learned to love myself and firmly believe that whatever start we have in life, we are all capable of changing. We don't need to carry around the baggage of our past. We should try to surround ourselves with good people, believe in ourselves and most importantly never give up hoping that tomorrow will be a brighter day.'

Anne Tattersall was born in Derry, Northern Ireland and grew up during the Troubles. After working at Charing Cross Hospital as a medical secretary she got married and travelled extensively. She has recently held various jobs in North Devon, including charity and writing work. Anne was Mayor of Great Torrington and has received a British Empire Medal for her charity work.

She is currently working on her third novel and helping her husband, Chris, produce cider at Honey Wood Orchard.

Michelle Morgan

January 2017: 'It's a bit awkward when you talk about your mental health to the business, Michelle.'

Crushing, embarrassing, silencing. And just like that, because of one careless and stigmatising remark, under a cloud of immense shame and even greater self-loathing, I stepped out of the business I had co-founded fifteen years previously, the youth-led creative network and agency Livity. I communicated my departure through a vague, vanilla, even slightly chipper message to my business colleagues, my dear Livity family. Just look at all those cheerful exclamation marks!

> *Hi Livity Fam,*
> *I hope you're all having a brilliant start to 2017!*
> *It's going to be a good one, we have a great plan, great people and a great purpose. Here's to a great year!*
> *I wanted to let you know that I will be out of the office for a short while addressing some health matters. I'll be staying connected to the biz remotely for the next few weeks and then will be offline for a bit concentrating on making a full and speedy recovery.*
> *I'll be really looking forward to catching up with you all soon!*
> *big love, Meesh x*

This is the mask of mental illness. It's amazing how long we can pretend to be 'just fine' when we're really not fine at all. What I was experiencing at that time was a violent physical and mental burnout which was fast developing into a terrifying, undiagnosed, severe depression and anxiety. *'I'll be really looking forward to catching up with you all soon!'* In fact, I never went back fully to the business.

2016 had simply been 'one of those years', we all have them. It was the year of referendums, new prime ministers and presidents. The business landscape was volatile and uncertain, the world in general even more so. I had led Livity through a significant social investment deal and was suffering from increasingly challenging physical health issues, which were unresolved. I developed a permanent headache that I fondly called my 'investment headache', putting it down to working even longer days than usual. I had also developed tinnitus and my periods had become so heavy and painful that I'd lose two whole days most months. I experienced an upsetting and frightening incident on a business flight, my daughter Lili had started secondary school (which was great, but she seemed to join every extra-curricular club and activity possible that year) and my husband's art career was also soaring. So we were finding the juggling of co-parenting and dual careers even more challenging than usual.

The rushing and running felt relentless and the fun that had been at the epicentre of Livity's success had all but disappeared. The emotional responsibility I felt for not just the young people coming through the business, but for all young people, was weighing me down. On reflection, there had been very few boundaries in my professional life for a long time and that was now not serving me well. I wasn't looking after myself and every night I would arrive home and find myself crying and crying, then the next day putting my leadership mask back on. I promised myself that once the investment deal closed in June, I would head to the doctors to sort out this permanent headache and buzzing in my ear. When the deal took longer to close, I promised myself, 'When we close the deal in July, then I will begin to look after myself.'

When we eventually closed the deal in August, all the promises to myself and my health went out the window, and I decided (unwisely) to be the brilliant and dedicated businesswoman role model I thought I should be and 'embrace' the first 100 days of the new role. Oh yes! We'd double down on working hard, to get off to the best of starts! I mean, it wasn't as if we weren't working really hard already, so really this was nonsense, but this is how I was wired. Approximately 110 days after the close of the deal, at the beginning of December, on the day the removal team were packing up my house as we moved out for a while to complete some major renovations (just another on the list of stressful life events), I sat at the bottom of my stairs and thought, 'I just can't go on.' I was utterly broken, and I knew I needed help. I called my GP and amazingly got an appointment that day. As I sat in the surgery I found I couldn't stop crying, I felt destroyed.

After a few more GP appointments which began to address all my different physical and mental challenges, it became clear that I needed to take some time out from the business. What was interesting was how much easier it was for me to talk to my board colleagues about my heavy periods, my rapidly growing fibroid, my now diagnosed anaemia, the fact that I had to have a hysterectomy to deal with all the above (and so, on top of everything else, had to come to terms with the loss of my fertility), than it was to talk about my mental health. Because let's face it, no one really wants to talk about heavy periods around the boardroom table. But that was definitely the easier topic. In fact, bringing my physical ailments into the conversation was a welcomed diversion from the slight tumbleweed moment the words 'I'm a bit worried for my mental health' had created. I must say, I was entirely complicit in this. I felt pretty embarrassed about my list of physical health challenges, but so much more ashamed about how I was feeling mentally.

Christmas that year was horrible. While it was a relief in some ways to be able to stop and rest, to my horror I realised that not only was I burnt out physically and mentally, but passion for Livity, the business I loved so much, had truly burnt out as well. This was a devastating moment for me and I was already feeling extremely vulnerable. My anxiety started rising rapidly and I entered a constant state of terror and insomnia. This was the moment I knew I needed to step out of the business for a while to get properly better, and the moment that unhelpful 'it's awkward' remark was thrown my way.

I call Depression and Anxiety 'The Evil Twins'. It's someone else's phrase, I read it in an article once and felt it described what I was feeling so accurately (I can't remember the article or the writer, so if it's you please let me know as I quote it ALL the time!). Poor mental health comes in many different forms. For me, the burnout happened, then the anxiety kicked in, and then the depression surfaced. I suspect the depression had been lingering for a good part of 2016 and in the lead-up to my burnout. Looking back now, with my Mental Health First Aid Instructor hat on, there were many signs, but gosh, it really reared its mean and ugly head once I had stopped working. Flip-flopping between these two states was exhausting and terrifying. For me, anxiety was characterised by feeling EVERYTHING, whilst depression was feeling NOTHING.

During this time of despair, as a way to help myself, I bought Ruby Wax's book *Frazzled*. During the worst days of my depression, when I could barely leave my bedroom, I read the book in my PJs and tried to practise being mindful. There is a point in *Frazzled* where Ruby describes falling into an episode of depression. With tears rolling down my cheeks, I said quietly to myself, 'Hold on a second, what she is describing is how I am feeling, but hang on a minute, she's calling it depression.' It was a 'that's me' moment and it got me back to my GP and into a very honest conversation that led to me being treated for clinical depression. The combination of reading Ruby's experience and getting a diagnosis was game-changing for me. Until then, I hadn't had the words, the language or maybe even the permission to describe how I was really feeling. A big part of my own personal mission now is to create more 'that's me' moments for others.

So many different things happened during this time, but I'd like to share with you some hope and some joy. You see, I spent an awful lot of time in my pyjamas during this period, because I couldn't face getting out of them. I'd stare for hours at a favourite piece of art to try to calm, or kickstart, my mind, and one day I must have reached the crossroads where brilliance meets madness (where all great ideas come from?), and the PJs that represented everything holding me back became my inspiration instead. I wondered if other people could see the duality of the PJ day, both good and not so good. I wondered . . . could we make the most kind and caring pyjamas, designed by brilliant artists and use them, their packaging, the platform from which we sell them and the people we put around them as a way to share stories of hope and help? Could they help make mental health an everyday conversation and banish this notion that talking about it is in any way awkward? And could we call them Pjoys? I then wondered if I had lost my mind. I said the idea out loud to my husband Remi, who didn't laugh and said he would love to design a pair. I shared it shyly with my best friend, global brand expert Susie Moore, who also didn't laugh and said that she loved the name and the purpose and would help me get it off the ground, as a way to create a positive legacy for her dear brother Dave who had taken his own life just a few years before.

And so Pjoys – PJs with purpose – was launched. (On International Women's Day 2019, after smashing a crowdfunding campaign launched on World Mental Health Day 2018.) Gently tapping into my entrepreneurial and creative skills, it helped me organise my recovery around a renewed purpose, with my husband and best friend by my side. Since then we've sold hundreds of pyjamas, raised money for and shone a spotlight on the good work of so many great mental health organisations and charities and, most importantly, we've started hundreds of conversations about mental health. And you know what? It's not been awkward. Apart perhaps from the three to seven seconds in our heads when either I'm going to tell you about my mental health or ask you about yours, because we are human, and we're feeling vulnerable, and we're not quite sure how the words are going to land. But if we can push through that tiny moment of awkward, with kindness in our hearts, we will make deeper, more meaningful connections with each other. Plus, the more quickly we can talk about our poor mental health, the more quickly we'll get help and into a place of recovery, because recovery (whatever that looks like for you) is the most likely outcome.

My story is not exceptional but it is real and honest and what I've found extraordinary, now I've shared it hundreds of times, is that it is the ordinariness and commonness that people connect to. When I share my story, someone will always share theirs back with me. It's working. Our PJs are conversation starters and we're talking more and more about mental health every day. And do you know what – it's not awkward. Did I say that already? Well, here we go again, on repeat, on FULL VOLUME! IT'S NOT AWKWARD!

Without a doubt this was a truly awful time, and now I work really hard on not working too hard (yes, I know, imagine being me). The Evil Twins regularly tap me on either shoulder, but I know them much better now. (What's the saying? Keep your enemies close!) I manage them with a daily discipline (which is also really hard, but worth trying), and yes sometimes they get more of a grip, but I now use techniques to keep them in check including: regular therapy with a Clinical Psychologist, hypnotherapy, EFT (Emotional Freedom Technique), daily meditation (mostly), regular exercise (I'm on a big journey with this one, but that's another story), drinking alcohol in moderation (mostly), talking to family, friends and colleagues about my mood and my fears much more (often), asking for help (getting better!).

In no way do I regret what I experienced, it is simply a part of me and I have learnt so much because of it. I am truly grateful for the experiences that have shaped me. Thank you life! Thank you Jonny for asking me to share my story. I hope it helps create a 'that's me' moment for someone else, as reading Ruby Wax's book did for me. The more we share our emotions, our moods, our experiences and how we are feeling, both good and bad, the more we are likely to make mental health an everyday conversation.

Michelle Morgan is co-founder of Livity, an industry award-winning youth-led creative network and agency. She is also winner of the Queen's Award for Enterprise, the Lloyds Business Awards and EY Entrepreneur of the Year.

On 10 October 2018, Michelle launched Pjoys – PJs with purpose. The brand has now sold hundreds of PJs and started hundreds more conversations about mental health. In September 2019 Michelle was announced as an ambassador for MHFA England.

Marsha McAdam
Finally a Sense of Belonging

In 2008 I took a near fatal overdose that left me in an induced coma. I actually died twice and had to be brought back to life – even now I have fleeting moments of wishing that they had just allowed me to slip away. But then I remember my son Zack and how he has been left with emotional scars, not only from the near-fatal overdose but from all my other self-harming before and after 2008. Borderline Personality Disorder (BPD) not only robbed me of my twenties and thirties but also robbed Zack of his childhood.

After receiving the diagnosis of BPD I was actually relieved. It meant that I wasn't evil after all, and could start to understand why I acted the way I did. However, at the time there was massive stigma associated with the label. I was treated without any respect by the hospital A&E staff and attitudes were not that different among mental health professionals. Admittedly, at times I really was disruptive. I spent most weekends in A&E after self-poisoning and many repeated attempts at suicide. I remember being taken there once in an ambulance by the police; I said to the police officer that there was no point in him staying with me until I was seen because I would just be sent back home. I was known to the police and there were a number of occasions when they had to search for me. The persistent disruption of my moods was terrifying. I lost years of my life through disassociation and living in a reckless manner.

After the overdose in 2008 I was finally referred for mentalisation based therapy (MBT), which turned out to be life changing. Not just life changing but life-saving. MBT is a type of long-term psychotherapy. It helps you to make sense of your thoughts, beliefs, wishes and feelings and link these to your actions and behaviours. It was the most difficult thing that I have ever done but I am really glad I did it because I am now able to pause the millions of thoughts that go through my mind and by pausing and dealing with the most intrusive and critical of them, I can live my life as best as I can.

Since having MBT, for the first time in my adult life I've been able to build trusting and stable relationships. I now have barriers in place to protect myself from hurt and pain. The best thing is that I can now be a grown-up to Zack instead of vice versa. He is no longer obliged to be the young carer he was from the age of ten until eighteen years old. If it wasn't for my mother being the second parent to Zack, he could have ended up going into care.

I remember once being asked what had changed for me. I said it was due to my best friend, who I always refer to as my 'guardian angel', being around for me throughout the MBT therapy. No matter how much I tried to push him away he kept saying he wasn't going anywhere, and nine years later he is still here for me, willing to listen to my fears and worries each day. It was him not leaving me which helped me cope with what is still almost always there: my fear of abandonment. Everyone always left me, so I used to push people away before they pushed me away. But with my Guardian Angel that hasn't happened. By showing me empathy he taught me how to empathise with others too.

In 2013, I recorded a Patient Voices story. 'Can you hear what I say?' This happened after Jo, a manager from my Crisis Team, encouraged me to use my voice to help shape mental health services in Manchester. It helped me start to believe that my voice did matter and it gave me courage to go out and start asking questions.

In 2017, I attended the Health and Care Innovation Expo in Manchester. Just as Jeremy Hunt (Secretary of Health at the time) finished his speech, I put my hand up. My voice quivered as I told him that I had BPD and that I had received MBT and it had turned my life around. I asked if there could be a pot of money for helping people with BPD. I still have the letter from his office saying how much they had allocated to mental health, and the last paragraph was written by hand. His attention encouraged me to get involved in regional engagement projects.

On the second day of the Expo I saw Ruby Wax (comedian,

actress and mental health campaigner) being interviewed. I put my hand up again, thanking her for all that she has done for mental health and then repeated what I had said the day before to Jeremy Hunt. Ruby extended her arm and said, 'Well you can thank him yourself.' At first I didn't know what she meant but then I realised that Peter Fonagy, who is the co-creator of MBT, was the person interviewing Ruby. I said something like, 'You are joking, you changed my life.' Every time I tell that story of meeting Peter I get goose pimples. At the end of the talk I waited to speak to Peter. We swapped email addresses and agreed to get in touch. I really could not believe it!

For the next few months I continued to be involved in various mental health projects, both regionally and nationally, while using Twitter as a support network – especially on a Sunday night at 9pm, the time of an established BPD Chat worldwide forum. On one of those nights I tweeted about service user engagement, which led to meetings with the Greater Manchester Health and Social Care Partnership. I really wanted people with BPD to be given the chance to get therapy, not just for them, but also for their family and friends, who often bear the brunt of bad episodes.

More meetings with a series of Executives led to me helping to create a Greater Manchester Personality Disorder Strategy. Since then I have been involved in several strategy meetings and as I sat next to these Executives, I know it sounds daft, but I actually felt equal to them. When I look back, this was a huge step for me: for so long I felt associated with the BPD label and the stigma that accompanies it, and believed that I was far from anyone's equal.

I am now co-chair of the Greater Manchester Personality Disorder Strategy. What makes it meaningful for me is that it really is about patients leading the way. For the last year, I and three other Experts by Experience have been working with Experts by Occupation to improve care and treatment.

This is so exciting because we are helping people who previously weren't mentioned in any NHS transformation programmes. Many of the experts I work with saw me when I was not too well, and busy throwing my toys out of my pram. This was at the beginning, when I struggled to trust anyone, so for me to be able to trust someone in authority is a big deal. In some ways, I personify what making a difference really means. Being given respect is not just a necessary part of a health service, it is the healing process itself.

I hope that by reading my story you will feel hope that your voice can and does matter. I want to encourage you to find it, whether you feel confident when respectfully challenging someone, or whether it is with a trembling hand and a shaky voice. I still sometimes get imposter syndrome and worry that I will wake up and be back where everything was just black all the time. But I quickly remind myself of how far I have come.

The overdoses over the years have impacted my body and I now struggle with a range of health problems including fibromyalgia, type 2 diabetes and other co-morbidities, including episodes of depression. My mobility is limited and I am forced to use a scooter to get around outside and have carers for personal care and meal preparation. Despite this, having the support of carers means that I have the energy to go out and be involved in society. They, along with friends and associates, help me to live a far more fulfilling life than I ever thought possible.

Marsha McAdam is a mental health influencer and ambassador for many organisations and social movements including the Centre for Mental Health and the Speakers Collective. Marsha has used her lived experience to help people and services over many years and has sat on some of the most transformative boards and panels, most recently as an active member of the Lived Experience Group for Equally Well and as Co-Chair of the Greater Manchester Personality Disorder Strategy. Marsha is also a national speaker on matters such as parity of esteem, personality disorder, stigma and discrimination. In 2018 Marsha was also a member of the government's Mental Health Act Review Team focusing on Service User Autonomy which developed the groundbreaking recommendations which have been adopted and are currently working their way into legislation.

Jonny Jacobs

Being entrepreneurial at a young age had its advantages.

At seven years old, I was the local marble king pin. Whether you were in need of small marbles or big marbles, I was the kid to see. Earning a few pounds a week from my school chums was never going to make me rich so, aged nine, I started running the neighbourhood car wash business, knocking door to door in my local Glasgow neighbourhood.

Beneath my youthful entrepreneurial ways there was a lot going on. Growing up in a working-class family where my father had two jobs meant I was always conscious of how and when we spent money and, more acutely, that we didn't have a lot of it. Growing up feeling inferior, living in a small flat in Glasgow, being driven to school in a car that had seen better days, I would see my classmates with their mansions and luxury cars. I felt different.

I never quite fitted in at primary school, although (or maybe because) I was slightly ahead of the other kids academically. Added to that, one evening I was playfully jumping on my bed when I landed headfirst into the corner of a wardrobe. Blood spurted from my forehead and after many stitches I was left with a lifelong scar just above my brow. Like Harry Potter, but sadly without the wizardly powers. Now I wasn't the same physically, either. Feeling different started to become my new normal.

My father had a gritty football memorabilia business in the glory years of Celtic and Rangers. From a young age, I roamed many parts of Glasgow selling the matchday programme, often in fear of being chased down a lane by the local gangs. The experience taught me a lot about physical resilience, with the Scottish winters especially cold and wet. Generally, though, I was fine until my parents' divorce. Suddenly I found myself at thirteen living with my father. Already low on confidence, I began to feel even more isolated. My dad was working incredibly hard on two jobs, and I had to fill the gap of running the household.

A standard day for me would be going to the supermarket on the way home from school, trying to put together an evening meal, doing the cleaning and learning to get by. I became obsessed with tidiness and cleanliness around the house and would spend disproportionate amounts of time in the evenings alone, ironing shirts for school, cooking and cleaning. I guess I was trying to hide my living situation to anyone on the outside. Whilst I never felt my need for cleaning and order was anything compulsive, it was probably verging on OCD. Whatever it was, there was rarely any time for me to be 'normal' and do things like go and play football after my homework. No one ever really asked me about my situation, or how I was. My formative years became solely task-focused, the goal just to get by each day. Some folk did tell me to have more fun, chill out. But I felt even more isolated and lost.

I took my need for order and safety into the academic world and focussed on getting good exam results. With nothing much to fall back on, I started to fear having nothing. One day I was doing my usual catastrophising when the thought of having to sleep under the Kingston Bridge, the main motorway joining one side of Glasgow to the other, began to haunt me. I decided that I needed to obtain the best possible grades at school, so I could get a proper job and make a life for myself.

Meanwhile, the fear of having no financial security became overpowering. I couldn't let it go. My thoughts became darker, like a storm cloud in my brain, like the storms that made my fingers freeze outside the football grounds. I started to wonder whether anyone really cared. Did the world actually need me? Who really cared about me? These thoughts were with me constantly. I started to write imaginary letters in my head that I intended to leave behind. I wasn't sure if anyone would be there to read them, but if they did, they would explain my inner thoughts. They would replace the conversations that somehow never took place.

Added to the constant cycle of tasks, going to school, home chores, my part-time jobs, I now had this new chore of reciting the last letter that I had written in my head.

Eventually, I got the grades to go to pretty much any university I wanted. I dreamt of heading to London or even trying for Oxford or Cambridge but I didn't know anyone else who had, so I opted to study Accounting & Finance at the University of Glasgow. I was sixteen. Being a year ahead of my school peer group meant I didn't know anyone when I got there and no one ever told me that there was more to university than getting good grades. I knew nothing about having fun. While the rest of my class was partying, I was out selling football programmes or working as a Pizza Chef at my local takeaway.

When it was time to get internships, I felt even more at sea. Everyone else seemed to have a plan, often getting positions through friends and family. I didn't even know where to start, or which firms to target. Rejection after rejection followed. Eventually, a fellow student and I decided to set up a faculty magazine giving insight into careers. This unintentionally led to us striking up relationships with some of the firms and luckily an internship followed. I was so grateful that I promised to myself if I ever had the opportunity, I'd try to help other young people get that vital experience.

I left university with a top degree and a job offer from a leading accounting firm, but sadly with little memory of much else. But the hardships I'd endured actually gave me many advantages. Having effectively lived alone for years, I had a real resilience and being sent around the UK to work on projects didn't phase me. My ability to multitask and juggle lots of different things were second nature to me as I had massively over-developed these skills from childhood. I'd also inherited my dad's work ethic. My approach to performing tasks was unrivalled, though I wasn't so great at relationship building.

I'd never really had a specific ambition, but was just conditioned to keep running as fast as I could to ensure I would have some security, and wouldn't find myself living under that bridge in Glasgow. In some respects it was as simple as that. I've always been running and suppose I didn't really know anything other than moving in fifth gear.

Nevertheless, fast forward many years and I'm now married with a wonderful, supportive, beautiful wife, who teaches me the power of being kind and focusing on the personal impact each one of us has in this world. And in my career, I've been fortunate enough to work with numerous multinational businesses.

When I landed at United Biscuits, the owner of the UK's favourite, McVitie's, a key item on the government's agenda was Internships. I volunteered to take one on, and was so proud when our first intern arrived for their first day at work. In my time at United Biscuits, over twenty young people have received work experience as a result of the intern programme we launched. I look back at my young self, satisfied I may have helped someone like me.

Then when pladis (formally United Biscuits) signed the Mind 'Time to Change' pledge, to end the stigma of mental health in the workspace, I became one of their Mental Health & Wellbeing Ambassadors. My own lived experience drew me to the cause, as well as knowing some of my closest friends and family have suffered from various forms of mental illness, including depression, OCD, anxiety and bipolar.

I was also incredibly humbled to be asked to become an ambassador for the Institute of Chartered Accountants of Scotland (ICAS). However, being thrust into the limelight filled me with fear! The thought of giving the keynote speech at the next Admission Ceremony made my heart pound, never mind flying off to Colombia to represent them at the One Young World Summit (a bit like Davos for younger people).

It's fair to say that attending One Young World changed my life. The summit assembles young leaders from around 195 countries to discuss how they can effect positive change across a whole range of issues, from climate change to health and wellbeing. It struck me that the folk I met there knew what their purpose was, and I left the summit with even more motivation to try and make a difference. I realised we had a huge opportunity to progress the mental health agenda at pladis and perhaps I could be the catalyst. Suddenly I felt my struggle become a wider struggle.

So I used the ICAS keynote speech to raise the issue of mental health in the workplace. A few hours later a young person came up to me and emotionally explained how my talk about mental health gave them hope about their own situation. That moment did something to me and I wanted to carry on.

As Director of Strategy & Transformation for the UK pladis business, I was convinced that business could play a wider role in breaking the stigma of mental health. With a plan in hand we went around the senior leaders trying to gather support. Our mission was to create an environment where we could support colleagues in tough times and promote positive mental fitness. Eventually we created a fully integrated plan that would start to shift the culture and create a much more open environment. The programme was called Positive Minds and it resulted in a commitment from the business to train every single line manager on mental health awareness training.

As we pieced it all together, we kept coming back to the power of talking. And where better to start a conversation than over a good old cup of tea. And here in the United Kingdom, there is one thing we are fanatical about and that is a biscuit with our tea. So that's when the idea was born: Tea, Talk and Biscuit. After months of hard work, McVitie's created a tie-up with the UK Mental Health Charity, Mind, launching the 'Let's Talk' initiative, a national campaign to raise awareness of mental health.

Within months, the campaign had reached millions across the UK. 'Let's Talk, by being kind to your mind with McVitie's and Mind' was a message seen across transport networks, billboards and on biscuit packs in people's homes. And more importantly, it raised money to fund new champions and face-to-face sessions.

Yes, I'm delighted for McVitie's and pladis for standing up for what's right. But for me, most critically, if this initiative has helped even one person to be brave and have a conversation then the difference is made.

Now, as a Finance Director at Starbucks, I'm part of an

organisation where our mission is 'to inspire and nurture the human spirit'; what else could you ask for? And I'm even more privileged to be a Trustee of the UK Mental Health Foundation and a Goalkeeper for the Bill & Melinda Gates Foundation.

None of this would have been possible without the support of the most incredible community I've now found myself part of. As I go through my own journey I've come across some remarkable people, and together we are breaking the stigma of mental health in the workplace and beyond. To those people, I'm forever grateful. Thank you.

I also sit here with memories of that thirteen-year-old boy, who in his own way represents millions of people going through similar experiences. Life could have gone in a very different direction for me. And I'd like to think that maybe now, someone might reach out to that thirteen-year-old boy and ask if he was ok, or even just say, 'Let's talk.'

Jonny Jacobs is an award-winning Finance professional. Prior to his current position as a Finance Director at Starbucks EMEA, Jonny was Strategy & Transformation Director at Pladis, the global snacking business whose brands include McVitie's and Godiva. As the Executive Board sponsor for Mental Health, he pioneered the Employee Mental Health & Wellbeing initiative, which led to the national 'Let's Talk' partnership between McVitie's and mental health charity, Mind.

Kamel Hothi

Story

Mine is a story of two halves.

One part maps the steps of an individual who worked her way up from cashier to senior executive in the banking industry. Who broke glass ceilings as the first Asian female bank manager. Who was architect of numerous programmes and strategies, including networks to help BAME and women in finance have a voice, for which I was honoured with an OBE for diversity in banking.

Who helped turn things around after the 2008 banking crisis by redesigning a new blueprint on charity partnerships and volunteering methods, in order to win back the trust of customers. Who has fundraised over £20m across six years. Who retired in 2017, after thirty-eight years, to become a Trustee on charities like the Alzheimer's Society, Teenage Cancer Trust, The Queen's Commonwealth Trust and NED on TLC Lions.

When people read my CV, I'm humbled by their feedback and use of such words as inspirational, confident, determined, ambitious.

These words are difficult for me to hear as I was just trying to do the best job I could with what was laid in front of me. However, more than my huge imposter syndrome, it was the secrets of what was going on in my personal life that kept me wanting to hide and not come out of the shadows to acknowledge any of my successes.

Hidden Life

The other half of my story is my personal life, where it feels like I am talking about my twin, someone who looks like me but doesn't talk like me, dress like me and definitely doesn't behave like me.

I was born in Punjab in north India, post the partition of India

392

and Pakistan. It was a difficult time and my parents lost everything. Father was a civil engineer who built one of the biggest dams in India and was recognised by Indian Prime Minister Nehru for his work. However, following a calling to come to Britain to help build the country at the time of the now infamous 'Windrush' generation, Dad decided to move to the UK.

Unfortunately, it wasn't open arms that welcomed us to the UK but racism and Enoch Powell's 'River of Blood' speech. All this resulted in extreme bullying at school for me and my brothers. As Sikhs, their turbans were often removed and the other school children made fun of my home-made clothes. So much so that our father decided to take my brothers and himself to the barbers and cut their hair in order to help us integrate better. This had a huge impact on my mother who was very religious, but as a woman her silent tears went unnoticed.

Dad refused to let me go on to further education and instead arranged a marriage for me within a couple of hours of meeting the family. I was nineteen.

On paper we looked compatible: we both came from big families, he was an accountant and I was in banking. However, he was fearful of a young girl who had been raised here in the UK, possibly with western views, and tried to control me with strict policing. The home environment was difficult and the only way I could keep the job I loved was to do everything, including all the chores. With no say over my children or my needs, the bullying went on behind closed doors for years, along with the 'pep talks' given to me by my mother to be obedient, never to complain to my husband, that my main purpose in life was to look after my elderly in-laws. That I should never come running to my brother for help as I should never divulge the personal issues of a family home. This huge burden of responsibility, honour and reputation was drilled in so hard, and my fear of breaking the code of conduct was real.

All this pressure became too much one day and I felt a great need to end it all. Without a second thought, I started self-harming – amazingly, I didn't feel the pain until my son came running in, his brown eyes filled with fear. In that moment, my darkest deepest shame became my turning point.

One of the things that gave me hope was my job. Although I was facing challenges and glass ceilings in the workplace because of my gender, the opportunity to work, to develop initiatives and improve processes gave me a sense of self-worth. This was more than just a job for me and when the exec approached me to roll out my ideas across the group, the realisation that someone had heard me and I had something valuable to add gave me a new sense of confidence that shaped my career and slowly filtered into my personal life.

If I could go back and talk to my tender nineteen-year-old self, I would say, 'Speak up! Find a wise counsel who is prepared to listen and guide you, even if it's the doctor.' I'm sure if I had, it would have saved years of heartache and emotional trauma for my children and me. Cultural and family pressures should not be seen as reasons to allow bullying or abuse to blindly continue.

As a mother-in-law myself now, I try to guide my sons to be more liberated husbands who are prepared to listen to their wives, to give them a choice of career and a voice. As for my daughters-in-law, I'm trying to rebuild a new style of 'mother-in-law' – one that supports, encourages and guides these young women to be empowered and to speak and live out their ambitions and dreams whilst building their families.

Family and friends are usually the first port of call in a crisis, and they have certainly played a part in my own journey. My brother helped influence my father to allow me to find a job in the bank, so I'm forever grateful to him. My father-in-law provided me with wisdom on how to navigate the females in the maternal home so that I was allowed to continue working. This was suitable advice in the beginning but it also meant me keeping my successes and achievements quiet, and soon I found myself struggling to balance the two worlds. Sometimes mentors can be out of sync with your needs as life moves on. It is wise to find fresh thinking to adapt to as you get older.

Life is challenging and curve balls will come when you least expect them. It's how we deal with these moments that helps us navigate our path through life. Having friends and tools to hold on tight to during these difficult times is one way of coping. However, for me it's knowing myself that helped me understand what was important to me and what made me tick.

Purpose gives us meaning, it inspires us to carry on and it helps build our self-worth. Once I had found my purpose both at work and home it helped me find a way to balance my two worlds so they weren't clashing so much.

Finally, I find it best not to focus on just one aspect of your life, ie career, and totally disrespect the personal side; this will only come and bite you a few years later in the guise of regrets, bitterness or loss. If you can find a way to give equal attention to both – maybe not at the same time, but in turn – over the years this balance will give you a more fruitful and fulfilling life that allows you to be your whole self.

Arriving in Britain as a migrant in the 60s, Dr Kamel K Hothi OBE worked her way up from cashier to first Asian Bank Manger to Director, Strategist and Architect of numerous groundbreaking programmes and initiatives. Experiencing first-hand the struggles of discrimination and gender imbalance in banking she was recognised as one of the 100 most influential Black, Asian and minority ethnic leaders in the UK and awarded an OBE for services to promoting diversity in banking.

Having retired in 2017, she now acts as Trustee & Advisor to Alzheimer's Society, Teenage Cancer Trust and the Queen's Commonwealth Trust.

I have worked in the field of mental health for over thirty years as a clinician (Consultant Clinical Psychologist) and a researcher (Professor of Evidence Based Research and Practice).

Since my work is all about using scientific findings to help make a practical difference to those with mental health difficulties, I thought the best way for me to contribute to this book was to share thoughts on how some of the research evidence (and even lack of it) might instil hope. These are not final truths – I am still learning new things every day.

Below are three 'evidence-based' insights from my area of research, which particularly focuses on disabling anxiety and depression in young people, that give me hope. I have included up to two academic references for each, for those who want to explore the science.

1. Being challenged by mental health problems is part of most people's lives.

Researchers who follow large mixed groups of people over many years (eg from childhood to adulthood) have found that the majority of people report thoughts, feelings and behaviours that put them in the category of having mental health problems at some point in their lives. This is true across different geographical regions and has been consistently found by different research groups. One study (Schaefer et al 2017) found 87 per cent of a general population of people in New Zealand who were assessed periodically between the ages of 11 and 38 had some sort of mental health 'disorder' as judged by an independent assessor. The researchers conclude that having mental health difficulties is the norm at some point for most of us before we reach middle age. The researchers suggest that the 13 per cent who had 'enduring (good) mental health' were the unusual group.

Reason for hope: It would appear it is neither strange nor unusual to have some sort of mental health difficulties. This runs counter to the common narrative that people with mental health problems are the minority (even if a large minority). You wouldn't expect to go through life with no physical health problems and you shouldn't expect this for mental health either.

Key References:

Schaefer, J. D., Caspi, A., Belsky, D. W., Harrington, H., Houts, R., Horwood, L. J., . . . & Moffitt, T. E. (2017). Enduring mental health: prevalence and prediction. *Journal of abnormal psychology*, 126(2), 212.

2. Experiencing anxiety and depression comes and goes

Some people have one time of challenge and then never experience another. For others the challenges are more extensive, but for the majority they come and go. How each person finds ways to manage the difficulties may differ. For some it may involve treatment, for others it may involve finding different solutions. For most people, whichever route they choose, things do not stay at an extreme level of challenge. Researchers who looked at how depressed people did without treatment across a range of studies found around half had no depression within one year (Whiteford et al 2013), whilst researchers in Finland who followed up on over 5000 adults with major depressive disorder found that 86 per cent no longer had any diagnosable disorder a decade later (Markkula et al 2016). But for many the problems come back and then go away again.

Reasons for hope: Having problems is generally not a life sentence. Most people find a way through. For some this will involve use of medication or talking therapies, others may additionally or alternatively use different approaches not currently categorised as 'treatments'.

Key References:

Markkula, Niina, Tommi Härkänen, Tarja Nieminen, Sebastian Pena, Aino K. Mattila, Seppo Koskinen, Samuli I. Saarni, and Jaana Suvisaari. 'Prognosis of depressive disorders in the general population–results from the longitudinal Finnish Health 2011 Study.' *Journal of affective disorders* 190 (2016): 687-696.

Whiteford, H. A. Harris, M. G. McKeon, G. et al (2013) Estimating remission from untreated major depression: a systematic review and meta-analysis. *Psychol Med* 43:1569–1585

3. There may be many routes through – you will find what is right for you

We have learnt a lot about the benefits of talking therapies and medication, but there is still much to learn about individual differences in what works for whom, in what context and why. For example, colleagues and I looked at published literature addressing anxiety and depression in young people other than those that involved the input of a specialist mental health professional. We found over 100 different ways suggested (ranging from swimming to sleep hygiene, from pets to peer support). Of these, only a handful had ever been researched (Wolpert et al 2018). When we consulted on this list of 100 ways with a range of young people in the UK we found that people reported finding different things helpful, although some things came out high for most people including listening to music and taking showers!

Reasons for hope: Whilst more research is needed to understand what most helps different people, it is clear that there are things that can help. What works for you may be different to what works for me. That there is no one answer about what may be the best help for you may feel frightening, but can also be liberating. There are people and resources available to support you find the right therapy or other approach that works for you. One UK-based resource for young people that I was involved in developing is: annafreud.org/on-my-mind/

Key References:

Wolpert, M., Dalzell, K., Ullman, R., Garland, L., Cortina, M., Hayes, D., . . . & Law, D. (2018). Strategies not accompanied by a mental health professional to address anxiety and depression in children and young people: a scoping review of range and a systematic review of effectiveness. *The Lancet Psychiatry.*

Professor Miranda Wolpert is Head of Mental Health Priority Area at the Wellcome Trust and Professor of Evidence Based Research and Practice at UCL. Miranda's focus is on bridging research and practice in youth mental health and helping create a world in which no one is held back by mental health problems.

EPILOGUE

Britt Pflüger
Be More Matilda

The first time I came across the word 'burnout' was in the late 80s. It was the tail end of 'yuppie' culture, when shoulder pads ruled and everyone was talking about the movie *Wall Street*. During my last year at university in London, teaching Business German in the City to support myself, I became all-too familiar with corporate lawyers and bankers bragging about working up to a hundred hours a week, reeking of booze during their early afternoon lessons and adamant that they'd retire at forty. Although I suspected a heart attack might take them out first, I always just nodded politely. These were the people who had brick-like mobile phones stuck to their ears, wore designer suits and talked about buying a boat, whereas I dreamed of landing a job in publishing, no matter how badly paid, and maybe, maybe, one day writing a half-decent novel.

So when, more than thirty years later, I was finally forced to admit that what I was experiencing was in fact burnout, it came as a massive shock. How could this be? I had finally had my first book published and enjoyed the great luxury of being able to work from home as a writer, translator and editor while looking after my friends' senior rescue Staffie Matilda, who loved nothing more than watching me from underneath her blanket while I slaved away at my laptop. Surely burnout was for high-flying executives?

True, the last few years hadn't been a picnic. There were two messy relationship break-ups, one from a partner whose schizo-affective disorder had had a huge impact on my own mental health, as I'd previously been diagnosed with severe depression myself. Then there were financial problems after my twenty-plus-year career in literary scouting came to an end, not to mention the long-term effects of Crohn's disease and a volatile childhood (personality disorders seem to run deep in our family). There were the years of self-harming, OCD and an eating disorder. Suicidal ideation upon which I very nearly acted twice in 2007. But now it all seemed to be coming together . . . didn't it?

As for most depressives, autumn and winter are always particularly challenging for me, falling leaves heralding cold days and even colder nights, anxiety increasing as the days become shorter and shorter and January looms. Nothing but darkness and emptiness to look forward to. At least Christmas – which I mostly enjoy for its colours and lights, and guilt-free days off work – was relatively carefree that year. Travelling back to London after a wonderful Christmas at my friends' house in Devon, I promised myself that the New Year would be better. Our book was going to be published in May and we were already getting plenty of publicity.

And yet, January and February proved just as difficult as all the previous ones. The fear of some unknown impending disaster became overwhelming again, threatening to drown me during the darkest hours of the night until I would finally fall back into a restless, nightmare-filled sleep, only to wake with my heart threatening to jump out of my chest.

My anxiety peaked with the arrival of the Beast from the East in February that year, the icy Siberian storm that swept through Europe before battering large parts of Britain, bringing snow and ice such as we hadn't seen for years. Living and working in a draughty Edwardian conversion suddenly lost its appeal, and Matilda the Staffie and I found ourselves huddling under mountains of duvets for several days. Already frozen, I was paralysed by fear when one morning both Matilda and I sat up in bed, wide-eyed with shock, after hearing an earth-shattering bang just as the sun came up. In hindsight I believe that it was the ice cracking in the gutters, but that day I convinced myself that my radiator pipes had burst and that with the inevitable thaw I would be responsible for flooding the entire house. Living on the top floor, and not being able to afford household insurance, floods have long been a major source of anxiety. (Years ago I made the mistake of watching the movie *Dark Water*, a remake of a Japanese horror film of the same name, in which a single mother and her young daughter move to Roosevelt Island outside New York City, only to find their apartment constantly being flooded by a mysterious and sinister leak from above. If you have OCD and worry about anything to do with water, floods or leaks, I strongly advise against watching this movie.)

Anyway, for me the Beast from the East coincided with the stark realisation that there was something wrong beyond my old 'faithful companions' depression and anxiety, and I was finally forced to admit that I hadn't been firing on all cylinders for quite a while. Brought up in an overtly agnostic, but culturally Calvinist family, I've always had a very strong work ethic. 'You want to enjoy yourself? Well, you'd better earn that privilege first!' 'No pain, no gain' was also a firm favourite. Unadulterated fun for its own sake was frowned upon, almost as though it were a sin. So when I was diagnosed with Crohn's disease at nineteen, and even more so in my early thirties when I finally received the diagnosis of severe depression I had avoided for so many years, work became my escape. Long before smart phones and widespread Wi-Fi, when I was hospitalised after major surgery and life-threatening sepsis, I had friends bring me work. During my darkest months of depression a few years later, when I became suicidal, the thing that saved me, in my mind at least, was working seven days a week. Anything to escape the pain. In hindsight I also suspect that I felt somewhat virtuous doing it. I was the good daughter, the good Calvinist.

And yet here I was, twenty years later, finding myself unable to work. Dreading it. Afraid of reading emails and tackling my freelance jobs. Even after our first book was published, I felt like a fraud. Why on earth would anyone entrust me with such a big project? I was useless, talentless, but nobody had the guts to tell me. The world had turned grey, and only Matilda gave me joy. What I was feeling wasn't the depths of despair, the screaming pain of depression, but rather numbness. Even my limbs felt heavy and I struggled to get out of bed in the morning. Unsurprisingly, I fell behind on every single assignment, most notably a full edit I had been commissioned to do by a lovely novelist in Spain. I was mortified, not least because he had paid me in advance and all the money had already been spent on basic living expenses. I'd become trapped in a vicious circle of crippling paralysis and shame. I was still making some progress (in between watching daytime television and sleeping) but eventually, once I realised that I had all the classic symptoms of burnout, I decided to open up to my client and tell him exactly what was going on. Certain that he would digitally 'shout' at me and demand a refund, it took me a couple of days to pluck up the courage to read his reply. When I did, it triggered a turning point. Far from 'shouting', he asked for my address because he wanted to send me a present.

There are many lessons I have learned from these painful but ultimately life-changing experiences, and a lot of them have to do not only with hope but with values. The latter were always hidden within me, I suspect, but it has taken the past eighteen months for me to be truly passionate and vocal about them. One is, always be kind. To yourself, as well as others. My client's single act of kindness jolted me out of my paralysis and made me believe in myself again. The other one is be kind to animals, and this takes me to another important part of my recovery: my love for Matilda.

There is a quote commonly attributed, albeit in varying forms, to the author Wayne Dyer: 'How others treat me is their path, how I react is mine.' It speaks to many of us, but especially the depressives, prone as we are to take even a minor slight or perceived insult to heart. Lying awake at night, reliving every shameful moment, blushing furiously in the dark. Even if deep down we know that we didn't deserve to be attacked like that, we cannot help wondering whether we did something wrong. Maybe the other person was right and we are a terrible person after all, not worthy of walking the earth?

This is where Matilda comes in. Long before I came across Dyer's quote, I noticed something interesting about her behaviour. A supremely confident dog despite being a rescue, she often finds herself barked at by other dogs in the street, but instead of retaliating, she just smiles that beautiful Staffie smile of hers and wags her tail. At no point does she think that their act of aggression has anything to do with her. It's the other dog's problem, and she reacts with nothing but kindness before going on her merry way. Water off a Staffie's back.

Matilda has also given me a reason to live. Even when I'm at my lowest (and I still am at times), I tell myself that I can't leave her behind. When I'm lethargic I pick up her lead and take her for a brisk walk, rain or shine. Because of her, I have met neighbours I never knew. Some will cross the road because their ignorance makes them fearful of her breed, but most love her. 'Is it not a Matilda day?' they ask when she's with her dad. They remember her name but not mine, and I'm fine with that. When her boyfriend, a gentle giant called Bertie, died, his dad and I cried together in the street, and Matilda went into mourning for two days. She knew. She always knows. A while ago I had a Crohn's flare-up when she was with me overnight and for the first time ever she didn't ask to go out first thing in the morning. Instead, she jumped onto my bed and lay behind me, soft belly pressed against my back and her paw grabbing my hair. Not moving a muscle until lunchtime, when I felt strong enough to let her out.

If Matilda can overcome her difficult start in life and still show others kindness and live every day to the full, then so can I.

Born in Germany, Britt Pflüger has lived in London since university. After a long career in literary scouting, she set up her own literary consultancy, Hardy & Knox. She has also written extensively about modern art and translated articles on art history from German into English for various publications.

Her first book with Jonny Benjamin, *The Stranger on the Bridge: My journey from suicidal despair to hope*, was published by Bluebird in 2018.

AARON AARON ABBIE ALASTAIR ALEXANDER THEO ANDREW CLARK
BALICK GILLIES MITCHELL CAMPBELL AMY ABRAHAMS ANGELA ELLIOTT
ANGELA SAMATA
ANNA WILLIAMSON AYLA LYN BEN DR BENJAMIN BENNA WAITES CHARLIE
ANNE TATTERSALL JONES WEST JANAWAY CARRIE GRANT MBE WRIGHT
CHARLOTTE CARL BURKITT DANNY SCULTHORPE DAVID ANDERSON DICK MOOR
ELEANOR
WALKER DAN SCHAWBEL DAVE CHAWNER DAVID WISEMAN SEGALL
ELIZABETH DAY DR ERIN FRANK GAIL PORTER GEORGE GEORGE
ELLEN EMMA TURNER TURNER
JONES WILSON ERICA CROMPTON GEOFF MCDONALD HODGSON TAKTAK
GIAN GLORIA HENRY JOHNSTONE JADA JAMES JAPHETH OBARE
HOPE HUSSAIN
POWER REUBEN VIRGO MANAWER SEZER DOWNS JAZZ THORNTON
JENNI JO IRWIN JOE SHEERER JOE WICKS MBE JULIETTE
REGAN JO LOVE JOE TRACINI JONNY JACOBS BURTON
KAMEL KATHRYN KATIE DAME KEVIN LARRY LAURIE DAHL
HOTHI OBE GRANT PIPER KELLY
KATIE THISTLETON HOLMES HINES MEYLER LEMN SISSAY MBE
LEON MCKENZIE LOUISA LUCY DONOUGHUE MARSHA MARTIN MATTHEW
LOTTE STRINGER ROSE LUCY NICHOL MCADAM SEAGER KYNASTON
MAY GABRIEL PROFESSOR NATASHA NICOLA NINA MARTYNCHYK
MICHELLE MIRANDA OLIVER PAULIUS
MORGAN WOLPERT MBE DEVON MBE THORP KENT SKRUIBIS
POORNA BELL REBECCA RICHARD RIKES RIVER HAWKINS SARAH
RACHEL DR RADHA ROSE CARTWRIGHT
KELLY MODGIL ELLIOTT COSGROVE CHAUHAN RYLAN CLARK-NEAL HUGHES
SATVEER SHOCKA STEVE TESS TOBY CAMPION VICTORIA VIDYAMALA YVETT
NIJJAR CASTEL
SEANEEN SIMON LOFT WARD TOM RYDER MAXWELL BURCH ZOE SUG
MOLLOY BLAKE OBE STEVE GILBERT OBE

AARON AARON ABBIE ALASTAIR ALEXANDER THEO ANDREW CLARK
BALICK GILLIES MITCHELL CAMPBELL AMY ABRAHAMS ANGELA ELLIOTT
ANGELA SAMATA
ANNA WILLIAMSON AYLA LYN BEN DR BENJAMIN BENNA WAITES CHARLIE
ANNE TATTERSALL JONES WEST JANAWAY CARRIE GRANT MBE WRIGHT
CHARLOTTE CARL BURKITT DANNY SCULTHORPE DAVID ANDERSON DICK MOOR
ELEANOR
WALKER DAN SCHAWBEL DAVE CHAWNER DAVID WISEMAN SEGALL
ELIZABETH DAY DR ERIN FRANK GAIL PORTER GEORGE GEORGE
ELLEN EMMA TURNER TURNER
JONES WILSON ERICA CROMPTON GEOFF MCDONALD HODGSON TAKTAK
GIAN GLORIA HENRY JOHNSTONE JADA JAMES JAPHETH OBARE
HOPE HUSSAIN
POWER REUBEN VIRGO MANAWER SEZER DOWNS JAZZ THORNTON
JENNI JO IRWIN JOE SHEERER JOE WICKS MBE JULIETTE
REGAN JO LOVE JOE TRACINI JONNY JACOBS BURTON